Lecture Notes in Economics and Mathematical Systems

93

Bernd Lucke

Price Stabilization on World Agricultural Markets

An Application to the World Market for Sugar

Springer-Verlag
Berlin Heidelberg New York
London Paris Tokyo
Hong Kong Barcelona
Budapest

INTRODUCTION

International commodity markets have traditionally attracted the attention of economists, econometricians, and policy makers especially in and following politically tumultuous times. For instance, the primary commodity price boom of 1973/74 and the subsequent period of highly volatile world market prices initiated increased research on commodity markets which quickly focused on possible price stabilization schemes, particularly on buffer stocks. Simultaneously, the issue clearly advanced in priority on the political agenda, such that the United Nations Conference on Trade and Development (UNCTAD) proposed an "Integrated Program for Commodities" (IPC) intended to stabilize the world market prices of ten so-called "core commodities"[1] (UNCTAD (1974, 1976a), Behrman (1979)).

Many developing nations welcomed the IPC almost enthusiastically, but it did not receive more than lukewarm support by major industrialized countries, apparently due to the experience with some thirty international commodity agreements past World War II[2]. Critical evaluations have, among others, been presented by McNicol (1978), Gordon-Ashworth (1984), and Macbean & Nguyen (1987). The most detailed of these studies is Gordon-Ashworth's, who concludes that "on balance ... the performance of international commodity agreements has been too unreliable and their distributive effects too uneven to secure the development goals that have been set" (1984, p. 284)[3]. Consequently, the IPC turned out to be quite controversial a topic on the UNCTAD's 1976 meeting in Nairobi and has not been able to gain any impetus since.

---

[1]These were cocoa, coffee, copper, cotton, jute, rubber, sisal, sugar, tea, and tin.

[2]Six of these agreements related to tin, the others aimed at the market control of agricultural products: Cocoa, coffee, olive oil, rubber, sugar, tea, and wheat.

[3]The quotation actually reads "... goals they have been set". I have corrected this presumably typographical error.

market interventions on domestic markets may not only be crucial for the desirability of price stabilization on the world market, but also may it cast doubts on the conventional equilibrium interpretation of observed prices.

This latter property has – to my knowledge – so far gone unnoticed in the literature. It is fairly obvious, however, for the more domestic market distortions insulate consumers and producers from the world market, the less price elastic becomes world excess production and the more price elastic must stock demand be in order to equilibrate the market. But stockholders (unlike consumers) do not simply buy when the price is low. Rather, they buy when the price is lower (by a certain margin) than their expectation of future prices. Since depressed prices today might signal depressed prices tomorrow, it is conceivable that under certain circumstances a market with positive excess production cannot be equilibrated by any price, however low. The same argument holds for negative excess production and rising prices.

In fact, some authors have clearly recognized that world primary commodity markets need not be in equilibrium. For instance, Hwa (1979, 1985) estimates partial disequilibrium models in his studies on seven of the ten UNCTAD core commodities. He unfortunately fails to provide a sound theoretical explanation of why precisely markets may not clear, and does in particular not make any reference to protected domestic markets. Consequently, subsequent studies with similar intent (Chu & Morrison (1984, 1986)) do not adopt his approach.

It may be tempting to take a possibly unequilibrated market as a justification for market regulation. But similar to the earlier argument concerning constrained Pareto–efficiency there is no a–priori–knowledge on whether there exist interventionary mechanisms which shift the market towards equilibrium. In fact, there is a simple reason for why a *theoretical* analysis of the effects of price stabilization or other market interventions might be of not more than limited use: Any form of market regulation may affect a model's parameters or functional forms in an unpredictable manner. (This is the general critique of policy modeling advanced by Lucas in his famous 1976–article and shortly thereafter articulated with reference to commodity markets by Adams (1978, p. 51)). So again, for the study of many interesting questions, it is empirical investigation which is called for.

Little work has been done so far to cope with the Lucas–Critique. Ghosh et al. (1987, p. 189) have suggested to model the interactions between a buffer stock authority and speculative agents in a game theoretic setup and Palm & Vogelwang (1988) in their empirical analysis of the world coffee market cautiously distinguish between two regimes. But most authors – even as prominent ones as Newbery &

---

results they obtain are disenchanting.

Stiglitz (1981) – simply assume the invariance of the model parameters. Whether this is an appropriate simplification for general primary commodity markets is doubtful; its legitimacy must, in any case, be checked in applications to selected markets.

The above discussion suggests that an empirical investigation is an almost indispensable component of primary commodity research. This is a widely accepted view and econometric studies of primary commodity markets exist in large numbers. Labys (1978) provides an extensive bibliography of commodity models listed by commodity and Labys (1980) reviews those which deal with stabilization issues. As a more recent reference, I cite Herrmann (1988), who presents investigations on cocoa and coffee and gives further references.

For the applied part of this study I have selected the world sugar market. The choice is motivated in detail in Part II below. Apart from the older sugar market studies listed in the above mentioned bibliographies, a number of more recent papers exist: Schmidt (1981) presents a simple time series model designed to forecast short–run estimates of world sugar demand and supply. Seasonal patterns are of prime concern to him, while the effects of the International Sugar Agreements[9] (ISA) receive but little attention. A quarterly econometric model for the formation of the world sugar price is presented by Frohn (1984), who estimates export and import functions for the top four sugar exporters and importers, respectively. He finds some significant dummy variables for subperiods in which price stabilization measures have been in force, but does not attempt to specify distinct regimes. Two studies by Gordon–Ashworth (1984, pp. 163–188) and FAO (1985) give a descriptive account of the performance of the ISAs and try to evaluate them heuristically. In a similar spirit is the more recent paper by Tewes (1988). Institutional aspects of the ISAs and the negotiation process are the focus of Jaenicke's (1985) book; a formal model is not presented. Hannah (1987) discusses possible structural changes in the world sugar economy other than those attributable to efforts of price stabilization. Sturgiss et al. (1987) are concerned with asymmetric supply response to price changes; they argue that government–designed market distortions make production respond less sensitively to low world market prices than to high. Zeller (1988) analyses the competitiveness of the world sugar market in a constant market share approach; export policies of the EEC are of key importance to him. Finally, the fine book by Abbot (1990) provides a useful survey on worldwide production and marketing of sugar; however, this author also pursues a non–formal approach.

[9]These are agreements negotiated under the auspices of the United Nations and aimed at stabilizing the world sugar price.

The above survey demonstrates that the world sugar market has received quite a bit of attention in recent years. Surprisingly, however, it seems that no author has ever tried to evaluate the effects of the International Sugar Agreements by means of quantitative methods. This is what I will attempt to do in Part II and III of this study. The questions to be posed are: Did the ISAs have a significant effect at all and if yes, have there possibly been ineffective subperiods? Have the effects of the ISAs been in accordance with their self–defined objectives or have they been counterproductive? How strong have the effects been? What kind of economic mechanisms caused success or failure of the ISAs? Has a subset of the participating countries benefited from the ISAs while others have done so only to a lesser extent or have not benefited at all? What policy conclusions regarding price stabilization can be drawn from the experiences with the International Sugar Agreements?

The scope of the study is as follows: In Part I, a partial equilibrium model for the domestic market of an agricultural product is introduced. Under the assumptions of risk neutral producers and protectionist government policies I establish the desirability of price stabilization[10] on the world market. Aggregating the country models gives a model for the world market in which, as I will show, no equilibrium in rational expectations exists. A linearized version of this model can then be used to analyse the cyclical pattern of world market prices.

Part II starts with a description of the institutional aspects of the world sugar economy. Production functions are estimated which make it possible to distinguish between a systematic and a stochastic component of production. The world market price is then tested for its influence on systematic excess production with the finding that the null of independence can only be rejected for lagged prices. This justifies the use of a time series model in the spirit of Part I. The estimates of its structural relationships are obtained under the implicit hypothesis that the International Sugar Agreements have been completely ineffective.

Part III gives a detailed account of the mechanisms of the International Sugar Agreements of 1968 and 1977. I then apply tests for structural change to the functional relationships estimated in Part II. Whenever the null is rejected, the functions are reestimated under the alternative hypothesis of two distinct regimes. These results may be used to evaluate the expected effects of the International Sugar Agreements by means of simulations. The Conclusions finally summarize the main results.

---

[10]In the proposed model, consumer prices are fixed due to protected domestic markets. Thus, strictly speaking, I demonstrate the desirability of *supply* price stabilization. Assuming fixed consumer prices is a limiting–case–assumption whose adequacy will be discussed below.

PART I

PRICE STABILIZATION ON WORLD MARKETS FOR AGRICULTURAL PRODUCTS

Chapter 1: On the Desirability of Price Stabilization

The introductory chapter has shown that price stabilization is often discussed with reference to primary commodity markets, i. e. to the markets of foods and minerals. It is commonplace in the literature to analyze both groups of primary commodities within one model. However, this represents an – in my eyes – unjustifiably high degree of aggregation. For note first that protected domestic markets do mainly prevail in the range of foodstuffs (and not so much among minerals). Further, agricultural production is typically subject to strong stochastic influences such as wheather conditions and pests, whereas this is not the case in, say, the mining of metals. On the other hand, demand for minerals is probably considerably more sensitive to macroeconomic shocks than is the demand for basic foodstuffs[11]. I will therefore deviate from the tradition of covering both types of primary commodities by one model and henceforth confine my attention solely to agricultural products[12].

1.1 The Domestic Market

Modeling agricultural product markets has quite a long history in economics and some of the models have become classical textbook examples, as is the case for the

[11]The latter may in fact be thought of as being predetermined.

[12]Strictly speaking, I will confine my attention to agricultural products produced for human consumption. Agricultural products of purely non–nutritional use like e. g. fibres are not intended to be covered by the analysis.

well–known cobweb model (Ezekiel (1938)) or Nerlove's adaptive expectations model (Nerlove (1958)). Most of the subsequent work has followed the footprints of these early studies by focusing on supply–price–dynamics. This approach seems basically correct, since demand for agricultural products is largely predetermined by the population's need for foodstuffs. However, many formal models do not incorporate government intervention or other institutional market distortions which actually shape the supply–price–dynamics. Some authors such as Adams & Behrman (1976) have justified this neglect by asserting that it does not significantly affect the behavioral properties of the market to be modeled. Yet as Adams (1979) admits "more disaggregated analysis, particularly one oriented towards questions of commodity market control and stabilization, must recognize the institutional and political constraints that apply".

Most countries in the world interfere quite strongly in their agricultural markets. This is true by definition for centrally planned economies, where government–administered prices prevail in all official markets[13]. Similarly, developing countries, even if market oriented in their overall economic conduct, often aspire a tight control of prices for basic goods such as food and clothing. Doing so, they apparently intend to prevent outbursts of political unrest in the case of supply shortages. Finally, many industrialised market economies have increasingly protected their agricultural markets from cheap foreign imports and have subsidized their domestic farmers by systems of guaranteed prices. See OECD (1988) for details.

In general, as Bale & Lutz (1981) have shown, industrialised countries tend to set domestic prices for agricultural products above the world market price level, whereas developing countries pursue the opposite strategy. In both cases, a system of export and import controls must be established in order to secure the sustainability of regulated prices. This task is considerably eased by the fact that agricultural commodities were excluded from the General Agreement on Trade and Tariffs (GATT) in 1947 and have also been omitted from linear tariff cuts agreed upon in both the Kennedy and the Tokyo Round. The problem is presently on the agenda of the GATT's Uruguay Round, but an intransigent position of the EEC makes the prospects for substantial progress appear rather slim.

There are basically two ways of regulating agricultural product prices in a market economy: Unlimited intervention or a quota systems. As to the former (prevalent for instance in the EEC's grain markets), the market regulating authority fixes an

---

[13]It remains to be seen whether the economic reforms in the formerly socialist Eastern European states truely aim at and succeed in creating unregulated markets for agricultural products.

intervention price and offers to acquire any quantity of the commodity in question at this price, provided certain quality conditions are met[14]. As to the latter, quotas may refer to either outputs (quantity of the crop) or inputs (e. g. acreages). In the case of production quotas, for instance, quotas are issued to the farmers together with the government pledge to pay a guaranteed price for production within the quota, while any quantity exceeding the quota is payed far less favorably. An example of such a regulatory scheme is the EEC's sugar market[15]. Acreage controls, on the other hand, are frequently encountered in US agricultural markets.

It is easily seen that unlimited intervention is just a limiting case of a quota system, namely the case when quotas become infinitely large. Thus in the following I will suppose that all domestic markets are governed by (production) quota systems. The few qualifications that arise in the limiting case will be discussed subsequently.

1.2 The Model

Imagine a government–regulated domestic market for an agricultural product. For reasons not under investigation in this study, the government has chosen to fix the product's domestic price at its once–and–for–all level p^d. This price will, merely for the sake of simplicity, be both the consumer and the farmgate price. I assume consumption to be non–stochastic, i. e. consumptive demand and consumers' expenditures are fixed and can thus be neglected throughout the analysis.

Turning to the supply side, the market operates as follows: Farmers will be allotted individual production quotas on the understanding that any quota–covered production will be transferred to the government at the price p^d, while for any production in excess of quotas farmers receive precisely the current world market price. It is important to note that farmers must neither offset individual surplus and deficit production intertemporally (i. e. on account of next year's quota), nor among

[14]In the EEC the intervention price is complemented by a so–called threshold price, which is slightly higher than the intervention price. The difference between the threshold price and the world market price defines the variable import levy an importer is obliged to pay. This mechanism essentially assures that the actual domestic price lies between the intervention and the threshold price. For simplicity, I will assume that the intervention price is equal to the threshold price and transportation costs are zero, thus the domestic price is fixed.

[15]In fact, this is just the basic structure of the EEC's sugar market policy. The actual sugar market scheme is much more complicated, cf. Manegold & Sommer (1986).

each other[16].

By imposition of a variable import levy the government sustains the domestic price at its level p^d: If domestic needs are larger than domestic production, importers are charged the difference between p^d and the world market price (i. e. they receive a subsidy if this difference is negative). Analogously, in case of excess supply within the country, exporters receive a subsidy to make up for the price differential (are taxed accordingly if the world market price is larger than p^d). For simplicity, let all international trade be channeled through government agencies or government controlled private traders. Then government and ex– and importers coincide, hence the variable import levy may be suppressed notationally. Assuming away transaction costs, this specification does not entail any loss of generality.

Now consider a farmer with total area x^{max}, who intends to produce quantity y of the crop in question[17]. Assume the technology to be such that area planted x, $0 \leq x \leq x^{max}$, may be viewed as the sole variable input, while all other factors of production (human labor, machine usage, fertilizers, herbicides, irrigation, etc.) are strictly proportional to x. Thus we may write the function of *planned* production y as $y = y(x)$, and I will assume $y(\cdot)$ to be nonnegative, twice continuously differentiable and increasing with decreasing returns, i. e. $y' > 0$, $y'' < 0$. Further, variable costs will be a linear function of x with slope $k > 0$, i. e. the cost function in terms of planned output y is strictly convex, since $y(\cdot)$ is strictly concave.

Let $\Theta\, y(x)$ be the actual harvest of the crop, where Θ is a random variable denoting multiplicative risk[18]. I assume $E[\Theta] = 1$ and $0 \leq \Theta \leq \Theta_0$ almost surely for some upper bound $\Theta_0 > 1$. Further, let the world market price be represented by the random variable p and suppose p and Θ to have a joint distribution[19] $F_{p,\theta}$ and a joint density function $f_{p,\theta}$. Assume that the second moments of this distribution exist and denote the marginal densities of p and Θ by f_p and f_θ, respectively. Finally, let q be

---

[16]What appears to be a simplifying assumption here, actually follows established quota systems in the first place, see e. g. the Common Market's regulations for products such as sugar and milk. Incidentally, this specification also facilitates the analysis.

[17]I will generally speak of "crop" and "acreage", although production of livestock is also a valid interpretation of the model. For instance, in the cases of cattle or poultry x^{max} would be pasturage or stable capacity, respectively.

[18]I do not introduce different symbols for a random variable and its realization. Which interpretation applies will be clear from the context.

[19]Modeling a joint distribution of p and Θ is often nicknamed the "large–country–assumption". This is misleading, since in fact this does not constitute an assumption at all. Merely postulating that p and Θ be independent is rightly termed the "small–country-assumption".

the farmer's production allowance (quota). Then his revenue R is given by:

$$R(x) := \begin{cases} p^d\, q + p\,(\Theta\, y(x) - q) & \text{if} \quad q < \Theta\, y(x) \\ p^d\, \Theta\, y(x) & \text{if} \quad q \geq \Theta\, y(x) \end{cases}$$

Under risk neutrality the farmer will maximize expected profits. Assuming away corner solutions[20], he may confine his attention to the open interval $(0, x^{max})$. Since $x \in (0, x^{max})$ assures $y(x) > 0$, we can safely define $\Theta_q := q/y(x)$, i. e. (ignoring fixed costs) the farmer's maximization problem can be written as

$$\max_{x \in (0, x^{max})} \quad E[R(x) - kx]$$

$$= \Big\{ p^d\, q + E[p\Theta \,|\, \Theta > \Theta_q]\; y(x) - E[p \,|\, \Theta > \Theta_q]\; q \Big\}\; P[\Theta > \Theta_q]$$

$$+\; p^d\; E[\Theta \,|\, \Theta \leq \Theta_q]\; y(x)\; P[\Theta \leq \Theta_q] - k\,x$$

$$= p^d\, q \int_{\Theta_q}^{\Theta_0} f_\theta(\Theta)\, d\Theta \;+\; y(x) \int_0^{\infty} \int_{\Theta_q}^{\Theta_0} p\, \Theta\, f_{p,\theta}(p, \Theta)\, d\Theta\, dp$$

$$-\, q \int_0^{\infty} \int_{\Theta_q}^{\Theta_0} p\, f_{p,\theta}(p, \Theta)\, d\Theta\, dp \;+\; p^d\, y(x) \int_0^{\Theta_q} \Theta\, f_\theta(\Theta)\, d\Theta \;-\; k\, x.$$

Using Leipniz' rule we obtain the first derivative with respect to x:

[20]Typically, production quotas are intended to restrict production, i. e. we may expect $q < y(x^{max})$. Had a farmer in the absence of production quotas aspired to produce $y(x^{max})$, the introduction of the quota might make him decide to produce less. Corner solutions in a quota system might thus be less likely than in an unregulated market.

$\frac{d}{dx}$ E[R(x) − k x]

$$= -\, p^d\, q\, f_\theta(\Theta_q)\, \frac{d\Theta_q}{dx} + y'(x) \int_0^\infty \int_{\Theta_q}^{\Theta_0} p\, \Theta\, f_{p,\theta}(p, \Theta)\, d\Theta\, dp$$

$$-\, y(x)\, \Theta_q \int_0^\infty p\, f_{p,\theta}(p, \Theta_q)\, dp\, \frac{d\Theta_q}{dx} + q \int_0^\infty p\, f_{p,\theta}(p, \Theta_q)\, dp\, \frac{d\Theta_q}{dx}$$

$$+\, p^d\, y'(x) \int_0^{\Theta_q} \Theta\, f_\theta(\Theta)\, d\Theta + p^d\, y(x)\, \Theta_q\, f_\theta(\Theta_q)\, \frac{d\Theta_q}{dx} - k$$

Four terms cancel such that the first order condition (FOC) is given by

$$y'(x) \int_0^\infty \int_{\Theta_q}^{\Theta_0} p\, \Theta\, f_{p,\theta}(p, \Theta)\, d\Theta\, dp \; + \; y'(x)\, p^d \int_0^{\Theta_q} \Theta\, f_\theta(\Theta)\, d\Theta \;\stackrel{!}{=}\; k,$$

which may be rewritten as

$$E[p\Theta \,|\, \Theta > \Theta_q]\; P[\Theta > \Theta_q] \; + \; p^d\, E[\Theta \,|\, \Theta \leq \Theta_q]\; P[\Theta \leq \Theta_q] \;\stackrel{!}{=}\; k/y'(x)$$

or simply

$$\alpha\, p^d + (1-\alpha)\, p_e + P[\Theta > \Theta_q]\, \underline{cov} \;\stackrel{!}{=}\; k/y'(x) \qquad \text{(FOC)},$$

where

$$p_e \;:=\; E[p \,|\, \Theta > \Theta_q],$$

$$\underline{cov} \;:=\; cov(p, \Theta \,|\, \Theta > \Theta_q) = E[p\Theta \,|\, \Theta > \Theta_q] - p_e\, E[\Theta \,|\, \Theta > \Theta_q],$$

$$\alpha \;:=\; \int_0^{\Theta_q} \Theta\, f_\theta(\Theta)\, d\Theta = E[\Theta \,|\, \Theta \leq \Theta_q]\; P[\Theta \leq \Theta_q] = 1 - E[\Theta \,|\, \Theta > \Theta_q]\; P[\Theta > \Theta_q].$$

I will make the quite natural assumption of $\underline{cov} < 0$. Observe further $0 \leq \alpha \leq 1$, hence as $\underline{cov}$ approaches zero the left hand side of (FOC) becomes a weighted average of the domestic price and the expectation of the world market price conditional on $\Theta > \Theta_q$. This conditional expectation is perfectly intuitive, since the world market price matters for the farmer only if his production exceeds his quota, i. e. if $\Theta > \Theta_q$. The right hand side of (FOC) is just the marginal cost in terms of output, hence the formula clearly reflects the conventional price–equals–marginal–cost-condition.

Let us assume the profit maximization problem to have an interior solution, i. e. the FOC is met at $x = x^*$, say. Then (FOC) implicitly defines planned output y as a function of the expected world market price, the covariance between the world market price and the stochastic component of output (both conditional on $\Theta > \Theta_q$), as well as the domestic price, and the production allowance[21]. Note that α and $P[\Theta>\Theta_q]$ depend on y:

$$\frac{\partial\alpha}{\partial y} = -\, \Theta_q^2 \, f_\theta(\Theta_q)/y(x)$$

$$\frac{\partial P[\Theta>\Theta_q]}{\partial y} = \Theta_q \, f_\theta(\Theta_q)/y(x).$$

After multiplying (FOC) by $y'(x^*)$, we compute the partial derivative of the resulting implicit function with respect to y as[22]

$$\alpha\, p^d \frac{y''(x^*)}{y'(x^*)} - p^d f_\theta(\Theta_q)\, \Theta_q^2 \frac{y'(x^*)}{y(x^*)} + (1-\alpha)\, p_e \frac{y''(x^*)}{y'(x^*)}$$

$$+\, p_e f_\theta(\Theta_q)\, \Theta_q^2 \frac{y'(x^*)}{y(x^*)} + P[\Theta>\Theta_q]\, \underline{\text{cov}} \frac{y''(x^*)}{y'(x^*)} + f_\theta(\Theta_q)\, \Theta_q\, \underline{\text{cov}} \frac{y'(x^*)}{y(x^*)}$$

$$=: \text{denom}.$$

Using (FOC) we can write this as

$$\text{denom} \;=\; k \frac{y''(x^*)}{y'(x^*)^2} \;+\; \Theta_q f_\theta(\Theta_q)\, [\Theta_q\, (p_e - p^d) + \underline{\text{cov}}]\, \frac{y'(x^*)}{y(x^*)}\,,$$

such that by virtue of the implicit function theorem we obtain the following

---

[21]Strictly speaking p_e and cov are not independent variables such as p^d and q, for they depend implicitly on y. But since they have a straightforward economic interpretation, I will treat them as if they were independent variables with the reasoning that this leads to a function which is likely to be a close approximation of the true one. In the limiting case of p and Θ being independent the approximation is exact, since then conditional and unconditional moments coincide.

[22]By assumption, the function $y = y(x)$ is one to one, i. e. it can be inverted to give $x = y^{-1}(y)$. Observe that we thus find $\frac{dy'(x)}{dy} = \frac{dy'(y^{-1}(y))}{dy} = \frac{y''(x)}{y'(x)}$.

multipliers for planned output y:

$$\frac{dy}{dp_e} = \frac{-\,(1-\alpha)y'(x^*)}{\text{denom}} \tag{1}$$

$$\frac{dy}{d\underline{cov}} = \frac{-\,y'(x^*)P[\Theta>\Theta_q]}{\text{denom}} \tag{2}$$

$$\frac{dy}{dp^d} = \frac{-\,\alpha y'(x^*)}{\text{denom}} \tag{3}$$

The nominators of these derivatives are clearly negative. The common denominator is negative, too, which we can immediately see by calculating the second derivative of the farmer's objective function:

$$\frac{d^2\ E[R(x)-kx]}{dx^2}$$

$$= y''(x)\ E[p\Theta|\Theta>\Theta_q]\ P[\Theta>\Theta_q] + \frac{y'(x)^2}{y(x)}\ \Theta_q^2 \int_0^\infty p\ f_{p,\theta}(p,\ \Theta_q)\ dp$$

$$+\ \alpha\ p^d\ y''(x) - p^d\ f_\theta(\Theta_q)\ \Theta_q^2\ \frac{y'(x)^2}{y(x)}$$

$$= y''(x)\ [\alpha\ p^d + (1-\alpha)\ p_e + \underline{cov}\ P[\Theta>\Theta_q]]$$

$$+\ (E[p|\Theta=\Theta_q] - p^d)\ f_\theta(\Theta_q)\ \Theta_q^2\ \frac{y'(x)^2}{y(x)}$$

Since it is necessary that this expression be not positive at x*, the (interior) solution of the maximization problem, we can write

$$0 \geq (E[p|\Theta=\Theta_q] - p^d)\ \Theta_q^2\ f_\theta(\Theta_q)\ \frac{y'(x^*)^2}{y(x^*)} + y''(x^*)\ [\alpha p^d + (1-\alpha)p_e + \underline{cov}\ P[\Theta>\Theta_q]]$$

$$> (p_e - p^d)\ \Theta_q^2\ f_\theta(\Theta_q)\ \frac{y'(x^*)^2}{y(x^*)} + k\ \frac{y''(x^*)}{y'(x^*)}$$

$$> [\Theta_q\ (p_e - p^d) + \underline{cov}]\ \Theta_q\ f_\theta(\Theta_q)\ \frac{y'(x^*)^2}{y(x^*)}\ +\ k\ \frac{y''(x^*)}{y'(x^*)}\ =\ y'(x^*)\ \text{denom},$$

using (FOC) and assuming[23] $E[p|\Theta=\Theta_q] > E[p|\Theta>\Theta_q]$. Since $y'(\cdot)$ is positive, we can conclude

$$\frac{dy}{dp_e} > 0, \qquad \frac{dy}{d\underline{cov}} > 0, \qquad \frac{dy}{dp^d} > 0.$$

Turning to government expenditures we can write them as

$$G(x^*) = \begin{cases} p^d\, q & \text{if} \quad \Theta > \Theta_q \\ p^d\, \Theta\, y(x^*) + p\, (q - \Theta\, y(x^*)) & \text{if} \quad \Theta \leq \Theta_q, \end{cases}$$

where I assume for simplicity that domestic needs of the commodity precisely equal the amount of quota issued. Hence expected government expenditures are given by

$$E[G(x^*)] = p^d\, q\, P[\Theta > \Theta_q] + p^d\, E[\Theta|\Theta \leq \Theta_q]\, y(x^*)\, P[\Theta \leq \Theta_q]$$

$$+ \{E[p|\Theta\leq\Theta_q]\, q - E[p\Theta|\Theta\leq\Theta_q]\, y(x^*)\}\, P[\Theta\leq\Theta_q].$$

Since consumer expenditures are constant, I will use the maximized expected value of profits minus expected government expenditures as net welfare indicator:

$$E[R(x^*)-kx^*-G(x^*)] = E[p\Theta]\, y(x^*) - E[p]\, q - k\, x^* \tag{4}$$

This formulation, of course, implicitly presupposes a single (representative) farmer. It should briefly be mentioned that there is no difficulty in allowing for a wide variety of farmers: Simply think of $y(\cdot)$, q, x^{max}, Θ, p_e, and $\underline{cov}$ as being farmer specific, that is to say, farmers may have different production functions (provided all are increasing with decreasing returns), different production quotas and acreages, and they may be affected by different risks, (where risks of neighboring farms may (and in general will) be highly correlated). The results I obtain will all be additive, i. e. they are unaffected by aggregation. It thus suffices to restrict the analysis to a single farmer[24].

---

[23]This is a very weak assumption indeed. In fact, any sensible joint density function for p and Θ with $\underline{cov} < 0$ automatically displays this property. It will be violated, however, for some extremely pathological density functions, which I therefore have to exclude by assumption. Note that the condition is still stronger than necessary, for all I need is actually $\Theta_q\, E[p|\Theta=\Theta_q] > \Theta_q\, p_e + \underline{cov}$.

[24]I have implicitly assumed administrative costs for the operation of the quota system to equal zero. Relaxing this assumption might imply that administrative costs (as a

1.3 Welfare Effects of Price Stabilization

Let us turn our attention to the question of how price stabilization on the *world* market affects *domestic* welfare. I will suppose the world market price to fluctuate in response to the stochastic shocks of countries participating in international trade. For the single country under investigation and its representative farmer, this response is described by the joint distribution $F_{p,\theta}$. In order to exclude some perversely shaped distributions, I denote the space of admissible distributions by $\boldsymbol{F}$ and for any $F_1, F_2 \in \boldsymbol{F}$ I make the following (weak) assumptions:

$$p_e := E[p\,|\,\Theta>\Theta_q] < E[p] < E[p\,|\,\Theta\leq\Theta_q] =: p^e$$

$$\underline{cov} := E[p\Theta\,|\,\Theta>\Theta_q] - p_e\, E[\Theta\,|\,\Theta>\Theta_q] < 0$$

$$\overline{cov} := E[p\Theta\,|\,\Theta\leq\Theta_q] - p^e\, E[\Theta\,|\,\Theta\leq\Theta_q] < 0$$

$$|cov_{F_1}(p, \Theta)| > |cov_{F_2}(p, \Theta)| \;\Rightarrow\; var_{F_1}(p) > var_{F_2}(p),$$

where the last moments are indexed with reference to their distributions. The first three assumptions basically express the idea that a good domestic harvest has a negative influence on the world market price. The fourth is slightly more technical to explain: It states that the dispersion of the price under distribution F_1 is larger than under distribution F_2 if the price reacts more sensitively to variations in Θ under F_1 than under F_2.

The economic interpretation of the conditional expectations p_e and p^e is very easy: p_e is the expected export price, given the farmer's production exceeds his quota, and p^e is the government's expected import price, given insufficient domestic production[25]. On an intuitive basis we would expect the discrepancy between conditional and unconditional price expectations to be the larger, the stronger the world market price responds to the realizations of Θ. Since it is suggestive to identify the price's responsiveness with respect to stochastic shocks with price instability, I use the following notion of price stabilization:

---

part of total government expenditure) might well be a function of the number of farmers. In this case the above assertion cannot be maintained.

[25]Notation is motivated by the idea that p_e is "low" and p^e is "high".

Definition:

Let $F_1 \in \boldsymbol{F}$ be the joint distribution of p and Θ. We speak of price stabilization, if F_1 is replaced by a distribution $F_2 \in \boldsymbol{F}$ such that <u>for a constant area under cultivation</u> we have

$$E_{F_1}[p] = E_{F_2}[p], \qquad E_{F_1}[p \mid \Theta \leq \Theta_q] > E_{F_2}[p \mid \Theta \leq \Theta_q],$$

$$|\underline{cov}_{F_1}| > |\underline{cov}_{F_2}|, \qquad |\overline{cov}_{F_1}| > |\overline{cov}_{F_2}|. \qquad \square$$

Price stabilization thus requires a change in the joint distribution of p and Θ, such that (provided area harvested is constant) the unconditional expectation E[p] remains unaltered, while $\underline{cov}$, $\overline{cov}$, and p^e decrease in absolute value. Then, by virtue of the identity

$$E[p] \equiv p_e\, P[\Theta > \Theta_q] + p^e\, P[\Theta \leq \Theta_q],$$

price stabilization implies that p_e increases. Similarly, using

$$\begin{aligned}
E[p\Theta] &\equiv E[p\Theta \mid \Theta > \Theta_q]\, P[\Theta > \Theta_q] + E[p\Theta \mid \Theta \leq \Theta_q]\, P[\Theta \leq \Theta_q] \\
&\equiv \underline{cov}\, P[\Theta > \Theta_q] + \overline{cov}\, P[\Theta \leq \Theta_q] + p^e\, E[\Theta \mid \Theta \leq \Theta_q]\, P[\Theta \leq \Theta_q] \\
&\qquad + p_e\, E[\Theta \mid \Theta > \Theta_q]\, P[\Theta > \Theta_q] \\
&\equiv \underline{cov}\, P[\Theta > \Theta_q] + \overline{cov}\, P[\Theta \leq \Theta_q] + p^e\, E[\Theta \mid \Theta \leq \Theta_q]\, P[\Theta \leq \Theta_q] \\
&\qquad + E[\Theta \mid \Theta > \Theta_q]\, (E[p] - p^e\, P[\Theta \leq \Theta_q]) \\
&\equiv \underline{cov}\, P[\Theta > \Theta_q] + \overline{cov}\, P[\Theta \leq \Theta_q] - p^e\, P[\Theta \leq \Theta_q]\, (E[\Theta \mid \Theta > \Theta_q] - E[\Theta \mid \Theta \leq \Theta_q]) \\
&\qquad + E[p]\, E[\Theta \mid \Theta > \Theta_q]
\end{aligned}$$

we see $E[p\Theta]$ increase as a consequence of price stabilization. Then, of course, the variance of the world market price decreases, given the assumptions on the set of admissible distributions.

Assume such a price stabilization scheme were feasible, for instance by the implementation of a buffer stock. Observe that we can rewrite the farmer's expected profits as

$$E[R(x^*) - k\, x^*]$$

$$= \{E[p\Theta\,|\,\Theta>\Theta_q]\; y(x^*) + (p^d - p_e)\, q\}\; P[\Theta>\Theta_q]$$

$$+ p^d\, E[\Theta\,|\,\Theta\leq\Theta_q]\; y(x^*)\; P[\Theta\,|\,\Theta\leq\Theta_q] - k\, x^*$$

$$= \{\underline{\mathrm{cov}}\; y(x^*) + p_e\, E[\Theta\,|\,\Theta>\Theta_q]\; y(x^*) + (p^d - p_e)\, q\}\; P[\Theta>\Theta_q]$$

$$+ p^d\, y(x^*)\; (1 - E[\Theta\,|\,\Theta>\Theta_q]\; P[\Theta>\Theta_q]) - k\, x^*$$

$$= (p_e - p^d)\; (E[\Theta\,|\,\Theta>\Theta_q]\; y(x^*) - q)\; P[\Theta>\Theta_q]$$

$$+ y(x^*)\; \underline{\mathrm{cov}}\; P[\Theta>\Theta_q] + p^d\, y(x^*) - k\, x^*$$

and expected government expenditures as

$$E[G(x^*)]$$

$$= p^d\, q\; (1 - P[\Theta\leq\Theta_q]) + \{(p^d\, E[\Theta\,|\,\Theta\leq\Theta_q] - E[p\Theta\,|\,\Theta\leq\Theta_q])\; y(x^*) + p^e\, q\}\; P[\Theta\leq\Theta_q]$$

$$= p^d\, q + P[\Theta\leq\Theta_q]\; \{(p^e - p^d)\, q + (p^d\, E[\Theta\,|\,\Theta\leq\Theta_q] - \overline{\mathrm{cov}} - p^e\, E[\Theta\,|\,\Theta\leq\Theta_q])\; y(x^*)\}$$

$$= p^d\, q + (p^d - p^e)\; (E[\Theta\,|\,\Theta\leq\Theta_q]\; y(x^*) - q)\; P[\Theta\leq\Theta_q] - y(x^*)\; \overline{\mathrm{cov}}\; P[\Theta\leq\Theta_q].$$

Using

$$E[\Theta\,|\,\Theta>\Theta_q]\; y(x^*) - q > \Theta_q\, y(x^*) - q = 0$$

$$E[\Theta\,|\,\Theta\leq\Theta_q]\; y(x^*) - q \leq \Theta_q\, y(x^*) - q = 0,$$

it is obvious that world market price stabilization unambiguously leads to both an increase in the farmer's expected profits and a decrease in expected government expenditures, provided planned output y remains at its pre–stabilization level. Thus in the short run, i. e. so long as area planted is fixed, price stabilization induces a net welfare effect equal to $\Delta E[p\Theta]\ y(x^*) > 0$.

With some additional assumptions we can strengthen this result: Suppose the markets of all countries participating in world trade to be in line with the features of the above model. Let zero profits be the equilibrium condition for competitive stockholders on the world market. Then, if exogenous, costless price stabilization is feasible, it is also Pareto–improving: In all countries do both farmers and government benefit from price stabilization, provided there is no supply response.

Unfortunately, we infer from the derivatives (1) and (2) that farmers will increase their productive efforts as a result of price stabilization. This will ensure even higher expected profits for the farmers, but it will also depress world market prices and raise expected government expenditures. Thus the sign of the change in net welfare due to an increase in planned production is unclear and may eventually counteract the positive short run effects of price stabilization.

Now observe that net welfare (4) is independent of the domestic price p^d, and recall from derivative (3) that production rises with p^d. Suppose the government keeps the consumer price at p^d, but sets the farmgate price at a lower level p^f, such that under p^f the post-stabilization FOC is met at the pre–stabilization optimal acreage x^*. It is easy to see that farmers' expected profits will then be lower than was their pre–stabilization level. However, such a policy will preserve the positive net welfare effect of price stabilization in the long run, since it prevents an expansion of area planted. Moreover, under the assumptions mentioned above, suitable decreases of farmgate prices combined with lump–sum redistributions in all countries can achieve an allocation which would – even in the long run – be Pareto–superior compared to its pre–stabilization counterpart.

Keeping the consumer price at its level p^d is, of course, done merely for ease of exposition. In fact, lowering the consumer price will in general increase consumption, and will thus at least partly counteract the increase in production induced by price stabilization. Hence a policy of decreasing both consumer and farmgate prices guided by the objective of keeping expected *excess* production at its pre–stabilization level is likely to be superior to the policy I sketched above, for farmers' expected profits will be higher than under the earlier scenario and the positive welfare effect will additionally be reinforced by the well–known triangle of consumers' surplus.

1.4 Discussion

The results of the previous section suggest that in the presence of a quota–regulated domestic market farmers will always press for price stabilization on the world market: If the farmgate price remains unaltered, world market price stabilization will lead to a higher level of expected profits. For the domestic economy, price stabilization will unambiguously be welfare increasing in the short run, while after the supply response the net effect is unclear. The government may, however, lower either farmgate prices or consumer prices or both in a suitable combination, such that price stabilization still results in higher welfare.

The intuition of this result is as follows: In an unregulated system of markets the prices on the domestic and on the world market are always identical. So long as the demand curve is downward sloping, farmers are compensated for bad harvests by fairly high prices (at least partially). Likewise, a good harvest is (partly) offset by decaying prices, i. e. the demand curve may ensure a natural stabilization of revenues and the stabilizing effect is the larger, the more elastic the demand curve is[26].

Now, if a quota system (as described above) is established, then this potentially stabilizing effect is disturbed. To see this, suppose for simplicity that the world market price and the country's harvesting conditions Θ were perfectly correlated ($\rho=-1$). Then any production exceeding the quota will be payed a rather unfavorable world market price, whereas in the case of insufficient domestic production the price will at most be p^d. Hence farmers are cut off the revenue increasing upper branch of the demand curve, but they still encounter its revenue decreasing lower branch. For government expenditures the situation is analogous: Given a good domestic production, the government is obliged to pay price p^d rather than buying cheaply on the world market, while it has to supplement bad own harvests by highly priced imports.

The notion of price stabilization I introduced earlier now implies a (absolutely) decreasing correlation between own harvests and the world market price. This can be thought of as decreasing (in absolute terms) the demand elasticity on the world market: For large own harvests the (formerly low) price will be a little higher and for bad own harvests the (formerly high) price will be a little lower than previously. This, of course, is beneficial for both farmers and government, since it reduces the revenue decreasing effect of the demand curve for the farmers and its expenditure increasing effects for the government.

---

[26]It may, however, happen that the price response will more than only offset a bad harvest.

It might be objected that the desirability of price stabilization does not rely solely on its stabilizing property, but also on the correct government response. While this assertion is doubtlessly correct, I would nevertheless defend my argument. For if we take it for granted that the farmer's response to price stabilization (i. e. his decision on area harvested) has to be taken into account, for what reason should we deny the government the possibility to readjust its instruments in accordance with its objective function (i. e. welfare maximization) as well?

This question, however, points at one of the possible shortcomings of the analysis. Assume one of the countries participating in international trade maximizes its welfare at a (in comparison to pre–stabilization) increased level of expected excess production. This will probably change expected world market prices and it will thus be conceivable that other countries suffer a welfare loss by the change in the distribution of prices. The seriousness of this issue is illustrated by the fact that almost every international commodity agreement explicitly aimed at balancing expected *excess* production[27]. Consequently, if participating countries do not take such an objective as a binding commitment, the positive welfare effects of price stabilization might be in jeopardy.

The assumption of risk neutrality has been introduced in order to bias the results against price stabilization. It is obvious that a setup with risk averse agents would tend to make price stabilization appear even more desirable. However, so long as we confine our attention to risk neutral agents, the desirability of price stabilization depends decisively on a nonzero covariance between p and Θ. In the limiting case of $\text{cov}(p, \Theta) = 0$ there would be no welfare gain by price stabilization. This amounts to saying that price stabilization is the more favorable for a certain country the larger its share of the world market is, for the more closely are p and Θ correlated[28]. A country with a small share of the world market may not be particularly ambitious to obtain price stabilization, even if its export earnings were largely due to the commodity in question. Thus under the assumption of risk neutrality the desirability of price stabilization cannot be judged with reference to how strongly a country's terms of trade are affected by price stabilization. Rather it is its share of the world market which matters.

This makes us recur to the problem of ensuring a constant expected excess production. It shows that international commodity agreements should require

---

[27]The only exceptions were the International Olive Oil Agreements, targeted at reducing *supply* fluctuations. See Gordon–Ashworth (1984) for details.

[28]A similar result is reported by Massell (1969), who finds a producer's gain from stabilization to be the greater, the larger the covariance between his individual and the whole industry's supply curve is.

countries with a large market share to reduce their farmgate prices, while countries with insignificant market shares should be allowed to keep their prices on their present level, since their supply response to price stabilization will be almost zero anyway.

There should be no doubt about the legitimacy of assuming markedly nonzero covariances, for in some product markets single countries enjoy huge market shares. For instance, Brazil's market share on the world market for coffee is approximately 25%, the Ivory Coast controls more than 30% of world's cocoa exports, the United States' share of the international wheat trade lies between 25% and 35% and as for soybeans the US even enjoys a world market position of 66% to 75% of all exports.

I would finally like to point out that the established desirability of world market price stabilization refers to a situation in which severe market distortions, namely mechanisms ensuring protected domestic markets, are prevalent. If domestic markets were unplagued by these distortions, the results might well be completely different. Yet given the present state of agricultural markets, truely free production and trade is hardly conceivable in the foreseeable future. Hence in a realistic approach of policy evaluation price stabilization should indeed be considered in the context of firm protectionist market patterns rather than under fictitious competitiveness. As there are evidently numerous ways to model domestic market distortions, world market price stabilization will probably not be desirable under all possible regimes. Note, however, that e. g. a system of unlimited intervention which some countries chose to install on a couple of important markets[29] is particularly easy to analyse in the above model. All we have to do is to introduce a distinction between domestic needs and the amount of quota issued and then let the latter tend to infinity. The result will still be the desirability of (costless) price stabilization, even without a government redistribution of the welfare gain. This under a proviso, however, to which all of these results are subject: That price stabilization feasible at all.

---

[29]For instance, the EEC did so on its wheat and beef markets.

Chapter 2: Non–Existence of Rational Expectations Equilibria

Expectations play a key role in almost all fields of economics. Lots of research has been directed at the question of *how* expectations are generated, and a variety of competing concepts has been developed. In the previous section, I identified individual expectations with the expected value (in the mathematical sense) of a random variable. This approach follows immediately from the widely accepted hypothesis that risk–neutral individuals maximize the expected value of their profits.

Using mathematical expectations as approximation to individual expectations may, however, also be taken as a simplified version of Muth's (1961) concept of rational expectations. As is well known, the seminal quality of this contribution is not attributable to a – in comparison to alternative proposals – more *realistic* expectation generating mechanism. Rather, the strength of rational expectations lies in the fact that they are *consistent* with rational, optimizing behavior.

All agents in my model, farmers, consumers, stockholders, and governments are assumed to be smart, maximizing, efficient. They are constructed like this not because their real–world counterparts are necessarily smart, maximizing, efficient, too, but because deviations from rationality cannot reasonably be motivated: In order to present a consistent analysis, we *must* suppose agents to form their expectations as efficiently as possible, for why should they choose a primitive expectation generating mechanism (adaptive expectations, for instance) if they could do better?

As Muth argues, agents which use incorrect models for forming their expectations will sooner or later experience the incorrectness and will discard the model. Thus a stationary economy presupposes that all agents generate expectations in models which are observationally equivalent to the true model. This idea can be simplified to the extent that all agents know and use the true model.

From this point of view rational expectations are the direct consequence of the *homo oeconomicus* assumption in economic models. To put it more sharply: Rational expectations are not a model assumption or a hypothesis at large, but an implication of microeconomic axiomatics. Using microeconomic methods makes it difficult, if not impossible, to consistently circumvene rational expectations. For this reason I will work with rational expectations throughout this study and I will use them in the simplified form of taking the expected value of the variable of interest.

2.1 The World Market

The analysis has so far been restricted to a single farmer in a single country. Let us now consider the free world market, where different countries exchange their excess production and where stockholders demand or supply additional quantities of the commodity. Suppose that all countries protect and regulate their domestic market by combining a quota system with a variable import levy (as described above). Let the affiliated quotas and domestic prices vary freely from country to country. Moreover, suppose that technologies and productive risks are heterogenously distributed among the countries, but that the respective assumptions of the preceding chapter still hold.

Let consumption be exogenous and predetermined by the population's dietary patterns. I relax the simplifying assumption that domestic consumption coincides with the amount of quota issued. There may rather be countries which do deliberately produce for export purposes and others which rely on imports in order to secure a sufficient amount of food supplies.

Let $c_{i,t}$ denote country i's consumption in period[30] t and let Θ_j be the random variable representing farmer j's productive risk. Denote by $y_j(\cdot)$ farmer j's production function and by $x^*_{j,t}$ his cultivated area in period t. Suppose there are N countries and M farmers. World excess production can then be written as the sum of two components: Its expected value, labeled world *systematic* excess production, and a zero–mean error term, world *accidental* excess production. The former will be denoted e_t, the latter z_t. Their formal definitions are given by

$$e_t := \sum_{j=1}^{M} y_j(x^*_{j,t}) - \sum_{i=1}^{N} c_{i,t}$$

$$z_t := \sum_{j=1}^{M} (\Theta_j - 1)\, y_j(x^*_{j,t})$$

[30]Here as well as in subsequent sections of Part I "periods" will be identified with "years".

This definition requires excess production to be completely inelastic with respect to the current world market price. This is, of course, not a truely realistic modelling choice: Consumption will, in general, display some degree of world market price responsiveness – not all countries insulate their consumers perfectly from the world market, hence world consumption may vary with the world market price. However, as demand elasticity for foodstuffs is typically low and many countries do indeed protect their agricultural markets, this price responsiveness of consumer demand is probably insufficiently small to cope with the considerable variance of production. The limiting case of complete demand inelasticity thus seems more appropriate than the competing assumption of a demand curve responsive enough to make consumption meet any level of stochastic production.

To make e_t and z_t operational we need to make some simplifying assumptions: As was shown in the analysis of the domestic market, systematic production can be interpreted as a function of $p_e := E[p|\Theta>\Theta_q]$. Since the Θ's and Θ_q's may vary among countries, e_t is formally a function of a large number of conditional expectations on the world market price. This property makes it virtually untractable. It is plausible, however, to suppose that the conditional expectations of p will be highly correlated with the world market price's unconditional expectation[31]. (Here "unconditional expectation" is to be understood as an expectation formed without *a–priori*–knowledge on the realization of Θ; it is not intended to signify the expected value of a time series. Rather, expectation operators will – unless otherwise specified – refer to expectations taken one period in advance, i. e. we have $E[\xi_t] := E_{t-1}[\xi_t]$). I will therefore suppose world systematic excess production to be a function of the unconditional expectation of the world market price, given the information of the previous period. Put formally, we have $e_t = e(\overline{p_t})$, where $\overline{p_t} := E[p_t] := E_{t-1}[p_t]$. Assume the function[32] $e(\cdot)$ to be differentiable with (in analogy to the results obtained for the domestic market) positive first derivative, $e'(\overline{p_t}) > 0$.

Similarly, the distribution of z_t does obviously depend (in a nonlinear way) on area planted and thus indirectly on conditional price expectations as well. Merely the first moment is, by construction, independent of other variables. It is to be recognized, however, that changes in the conditional price expectations influence the distribution of z_t only via their effects on area planted – a variable which is known to adjust slowly and with fairly moderate increments. As a matter of fact, hardly

---

[31]This is again an approximation which becomes exact in the limiting case of p and Θ being independent.

[32]An index t always indicates the value a variable assumes in period t. Functions are constant over time, thus they are never indexed with respect to time.

anybody who has seriously studied the issue would maintain that the distribution of the stochastic component of excess production is significantly altered by changes in conditional price expectations. Ignoring these dependencies should therefore be a reasonable approximation to reality. I will thus suppose the distribution of z_t to be completely unaffected by world market price expectations. I further simplify the setup by assuming that z_t is independent and identically distributed (i.i.d.). I denote the distribution of z_t (the measure) by $F(\cdot)$; since z_t is i.i.d. I will sometimes omit the subscript t.

So far im– and exports are completely inelastic with respect to the current world market price, their sole determinant being the domestic production–consumption balances. Yet the governments' pledge to maintain stable domestic prices does not entail the necessity for *immediate* ex– or imports. Rather, these can be shifted along the time axis by in– or decreasing stocks. Apart from state agencies, private enterprises, commercial traders, or speculators may (and do indeed) hold considerable amounts of stocks.

In obvious analogy to the theory of money demand, transactions, precautionary and speculative motives for the storage of an agricultural commodity may be singled out. Transactions and precautionary stock demand are primarily determined by the so–called "convenience yield" (see Kaldor (1939) and Working (1949)) and will, in essence, be proportional to consumption. As "speculative" I interpret all stocks accumulated with regard to both the present price and expectations of future prices[33].

In general, we will have to think of speculative stockholders as solving multi–period optimization problems. However, as Kohn (1978) has shown, it suffices to specify their stock demand equations with only two arguments, namely the current price and the expectation on next period's price. Taking into account transactions and precautionary stocks we end up with three arguments of a stockholder's stock demand function: Consumption, price and price expectation.

In the following I will suppress the argument "consumption" notationally, since it does not play a role in the intended analysis. For simplicity, I also assume storage costs, interest rates, and convenience yields to be constant over time, such that these are parameters, not arguments, of the stock demand functions. I further normalize prices to the interval [0, 1] by dividing every single price through the sum of all prices. Total stock demand s_t is then given by a mapping

[33]A truely satisfactory definition of "speculative" has – to my knowledge – not yet been found. See Orosel (1984) for a discussion of the problems related with this concept.

$$s : [0, 1] \times [0, 1] \rightarrow \mathbb{R}_0^+$$
$$(p_t, \overline{p_{t+1}}) \rightarrow s(p_t, \overline{p_{t+1}}),$$

where I denote the partial derivatives by s_1 and s_2, respectively, and assume $s_1 < 0$, $s_2 > 0$. The mapping goes from the squared unit interval to the non–negative real line, since physical stocks can never become negative.

Apart from stock demand (i. e. quantities of the commodity deliberately chosen for storage) we will have to deal with another kind of "stocks" which I will call "involuntary stocks" or "market residual". (The terminology reflects the fact that we do not know in advance if the market clears under all circumstances. Unlike physical stocks, involuntary stocks can become negative). I denote the market residual by r_t and define recursively

$$r_t := s_{t-1} + r_{t-1} + e_t + z_t - s(p_t, \overline{p_{t+1}})$$

and

$$r_1 := s_0 + e_1 + z_1 - s(p_1, \overline{p_2})$$

for a suitably chosen period 0 in which the market clears.

In this specification $s_{t-1} + r_{t-1}$ describes existing stocks, while $e_t + z_t$ is excess production. Together they form the supply side of the market. Thus, subtracting stock demand $s_t = s(p_t, \overline{p_{t+1}})$ results in the market residual. It is easy to see that this may be nonzero. For stocks and systematic excess production (i. e. $s_{t-1} + r_{t-1} + e_t$) are predetermined; they do not respond to price changes. Stock demand s_t is price elastic, but nonnegative by definition. Hence, if z_t is small enough, i. e. if there is a strongly negative shock in production, then the market cannot be equilibrated[34].

[34]Let $R \subset \mathbb{R}$ denote the (compact) range of the random variable z_t. I suppose R to be sufficiently large, such that for any value of $e(\cdot)$ there be a (possibly very small) positive probability that $e(\overline{p_t})$ and $e(\overline{p_t}) + z_t$ display different signs. Formally, I assume $E := \text{range}(\bar{e}(\cdot)) \subset R$ and $F(\{z | z < -\sup E\}) > 0$, $F(\{z | z > -\inf E\}) > 0$. This is not a very restrictive assumption, but it is still stronger than it need be.

Rearranging the above equation yields

$$r_t + s(p_t, \overline{p_{t+1}}) = s_{t-1} + r_{t-1} + e_t + z_t$$

$$= s_{t-2} + r_{t-2} + e_{t-1} + z_{t-1} + e_t + z_t$$

$$= e_t + \sum_{i=1}^{\infty} (e_{t-i} + z_{t-i}) + z_t$$

$$=: m_t + z_t, \qquad (5)$$

where the infinite sum necessarily converges, since present stocks are finite. The economic impact of this representation is described by the simple assertion that any quantity stored must once have been produced in excess of consumption. The newly introduced variable m_t reflects systematic (or mean) supply, i. e. those components of supply whose existence was to be expected prior to period t. It can be represented as a first order difference equation in the following form:

$$m_t = m_{t-1} + e_t + z_{t-1}$$

Note that it is important to carefully distinguish between systematic *excess production* e_t (the difference between production and consumption in period t) and systematic *supply* m_t (which additionally includes stocks).

We are now able to close the model by defining the process of price formation. Think of a Walrasian auctioneer who enters the market. This is a smart auctioneer, who quickly realizes that the market does not necessarily clear. He will therefore decide to somehow minimize the market residual r_t, i. e. to clear the market as much as possible. But r_t can assume negative values, thus the auctioneer prefers to consider squared values of r_t. He also realizes that r_t is a random variable and therefore his objective will be to minimize the expected value of r_t^2.

Making the expected value of r_t^2 become small requires prices (and price expectations) which make stock demand approximately equal to the predetermined quantity $m_t + z_t$, see equation (5). The price will thus depend on m_t and z_t. Since we do not know whether changes in systematic supply m_t affect prices equally strong as do the stochastic shocks z_t, I will treat m_t and z_t as distinct arguments of the price function[35]. I therefore define the set of admissible price functions by

$$P := \{p \in C \mid p : \mathbb{R} \times R \to [0, 1]\},$$

where C denotes the space of all continuous functions. Note that under supremum's metric P is closed and bounded in C but not compact[36].

Let us now turn to the rational price expectation of next period's price, $\overline{p_{t+1}}$. Suppose that the true model is known to all agents. Then, if $p(\cdot,\cdot)$ is the true price function, $\overline{p_{t+1}}$ is given as the solution of

$$\overline{p_{t+1}} = E[p(m_{t+1}, z_{t+1})]$$

$$= E[p(m_t + e(\overline{p_{t+1}}) + z_t, z_{t+1})], \tag{6}$$

where z_t is the realized value of the stochastic shock in period t, while z_{t+1} is the random variable to which the expectation operator refers.

The following lemma shows that the price expectation (interpreted as a correspondence) is well defined:

---

[35]Such a property is, of course, well known to economists. Milton Friedman's Permanent Income Hypothesis (Friedman (1957)), for instance, assesses unexpected shocks to be transitory and thus he assumes them to affect consumption differently than do longlasting changes in income. Another prominent example is Sargent & Wallace's (1975) inquiry on the optimal money supply rule, which argues that only the unexpectedness of changes in the money stock accounts for policy effects. Both viewpoints are legitimate in our context, for it is as plausible to think of an extreme accidental excess production as a temporary phenomenon as it is natural to suppose that such a shock will affect expectations differently than do foreseeable changes in the supply–demand balance.

[36]To see the latter, define the following sequence $(p_n)_{n \in \mathbb{N}}$ in P:

$$p_n(m, z) := \begin{cases} 0 & \text{if } m \leq n \\ m - n & \text{if } n < m \leq n+1 \\ 1 & \text{if } n+1 < m \end{cases}$$

Denoting supremum's metric by $d(\cdot,\cdot)$, we have $d(p_n, p_{n'}) = 1$ for all $n, n' \in \mathbb{N}$, $n \neq n'$, that is to say the sequence $(p_n)_{n \in \mathbb{N}}$ does not have a convergent subsequence. Hence P is not sequentially compact and this implies that P is not compact either.

Lemma:

For any $p \in \boldsymbol{P}$, $m_t \in \mathbb{R}$, $z_t \in R$, equation (6) has at least one solution in $\overline{p_{t+1}}$.

Proof:

For any $p \in \boldsymbol{P}$, $m_t \in \mathbb{R}$, $z_t \in R$ define

$$\begin{aligned} pex_p : [0,\ 1] &\rightarrow [0,\ 1] \\ \overline{p} &\rightarrow \int_R p(m_t + e(\overline{p}) + z_t,\ z_{t+1})\ dF(z_{t+1}) \end{aligned}$$

As pex_p is a continuous mapping of a compact interval on itself, Brouwer's fixed point theorem is applicable, i. e. there exists a $\overline{p}$ with $\overline{p} = pex_p(\overline{p})$.
Since $pex_p(\overline{p}) = E[p(m_t + e(\overline{p}) + z_t,\ z_{t+1})]$, the proof is completed. q.e.d.

In the case of multiple solutions of equation (6) we could define an arbitrary rule to pick just one of them as the derived rational expectation. For instance, in order to derive a unique price expectation we could choose the minimum of the solution set or we could pick some additional selection criterion such as minimizing the mean squared forecasting error over the solution set (see Kottmann (1989)). In fact, for non–pathological price functions equation (6) will indeed have a unique solution: Observe that if the partial derivative $p_1 := \frac{\partial p}{\partial m}(m,\ z)$ exists almost everywhere[37], it suffices to have

$$\int_R p_1(m,\ z)\ dF(z) \leq 0,$$

since this implies that pex_p is monotonously decreasing. Economically this condition requires that *on average* an increase in excess supply will not increase the price, which is obviously a very weak postulate.

In any case it should be plain that given any function $p \in \boldsymbol{P}$ we can define a function $\overline{p}_p(\cdot)$, which maps $m_t + z_t$ on $\overline{p_{t+1}}$, the solution of equation (6), (making use of the above mentioned arbitrary rule, if necessary). I call $\overline{p}_p(\cdot)$ the rational

[37]By almost everywhere (a. e.), almost surely (a. s.) etc. I always mean F–almost everywhere, F–almost surely, respectively.

expectation under p, and I will omit the index p if there is no doubt by which price function the expectation is formed. Analogously, I will sometimes replace r_t by the notation

$$r_p(m_t, z_t) := m_t + z_t - s(p(m_t, z_t), \bar{p}_p(m_t + z_t))$$

if I want to stress that for given m_t and z_t the market residual does not only depend on the actual price $p(m_t, z_t)$, but also, via the rational expectation, on the entire price function p. This function, however, is yet to be found.

We thus return to our Walrasian auctioneer. Being now able to state his minimization problem formally, we require him to pick a price function $p^* \in \boldsymbol{P}$, such that for any given $m_t \in \mathbb{R}$, p^* solves

$$\min_{p \in \boldsymbol{P}} \quad E[r_p(m_t, z_t)^2] \qquad \text{(MIN)},$$

where the expectation operator refers to the distribution of z_t on R.

(MIN) is clearly a problem from the calculus of variations, since it is nonseparable with respect to $p_t = p(m_t, z_t)$: The market residual r_t depends on the entire price function and not only on a single price p_t. A solution to (MIN) does not necessarily exist (recall that $\boldsymbol{P}$ is not compact); I will therefore have to assume it.

Note that (MIN) is simply a generalization of the conventional model of price determination by means of market clearing. For if there were a price function which would equilibrate the market under all circumstances, then this price function would certainly be a solution of (MIN). However, complete market clearing is impossible in this model due to the inelasticity of excess production. The consequences thereof I analyse in the next section.

2.2 Market Equilibrium

Traditional general equilibrium theory defines a market equilibrium by two properties: Equilibrium prices balance supply and demand, i. e. they clear the market, and they are positive and finite. In models where prices are normalized to a unit simplex the latter condition requires that all prices lie in the open unit interval (0, 1). Applied to our market with inelastic excess production and, hence, partial non–market–clearing this notion of equilibrium gives rise to the following .

Definition:

Let expectations be rational. A rational expectations equilibrium (REE) is given by a price function $p^* \in \boldsymbol{P}$ with the properties

(i) $\text{range}(p^*) \subset (0, 1)$

(ii) p^* solves (MIN) for any given $m_t \in \mathbb{R}$.

(iii) $F(\{z | r_{p^*}(m_t, z) = 0\}) > 0$ for any given $m_t \in \mathbb{R}$. □

I will call a price function "stable", if its range lies in the open interval (0, 1). Price functions which assume either of the extreme values 0 or 1 will be labeled unstable. Then, stated briefly, the above definition says that p^* is an REE if it is stable, if it ensures the best achievable allocation, and if the market clears with positive probability.

What difference does it make whether the price function is or is not an REE? Suppose that m_t is given and $p^* \in \boldsymbol{P}$ is an REE, i. e. p^* is stable. Then, since R is compact, there exist upper and lower bounds b_0 and b_1 with

$$0 < b_0 \leq p^*(m_t, z_t) \leq b_1 < 1$$

almost surely. It follows that for any given m_t and any given $\tau \geq 0$, $\tau \in \mathbb{N}$, we can find bounds by which the price is bound away from zero and one for the next τ periods. This, of course, is just what quite a range of primary commodity agreements (most of them unsuccessfully, though) has attempted to do: Finding threshold prices in between of which the actual price is to be stabilized. The existence of an REE is thus tantamount to saying that these threshold prices exist.

By contrast, if p^* were not an REE, then either the market is *always* in disequilibrium or the price function is unstable. The first possibility is not very realistic and can, for practical purposes, be discarded. More interesting is the case of an unstable price function. This would imply the existence of an m_t such that the realization of z_t might induce a price of zero or one. Hence the price might exceed every upper bound or might fall below every positive lower bound within a single period. Put differently: For any given $m_t \in \mathbb{R}$ there exists a $\tau \in \mathbb{N}$ such that the probability for the price to exceed every upper or lower bound within τ periods is positive.

Evidently, prices of zero or infinity (one) are not observed in real–world markets. But we do observe skyrocketing prices for agricultural commodities and we also observe prices well below even the most favorable variable costs of production, let alone costs of storage and handling. Thus the real–world analogue of the model–specific prices zero and one may be situations in which prices sharply rise or fall, seemingly uncontrollable until new supplies appear on the market.

I will now give a surprising additional motivation for the above equilibrium concept. The essence of Theorem 1 below is that our notion of rational expectations equilibria is equivalent to (and not merely a generalization of) the conventional equilibrium concept, in which a stable price function completely clears the market.

Theorem 1:

The price function $p \in \boldsymbol{P}$ is an REE if and only if the following conditions hold almost surely:

$$\text{(i)} \quad \text{range}(p) \subset (0, 1)$$
$$\text{(ii)} \quad r_p(m_t, z_t) = 0 \qquad \forall\, m_t \in \mathbb{R}.$$

Proof:

"$\Leftarrow$":

Let $p \in \boldsymbol{P}$ fulfill $\text{range}(p) \subset (0, 1)$ and $r_p(m_t, z_t) = 0$ a. s. for all $m_t \in \mathbb{R}$. Then $E[r_p(m_t, z_t)^2] = 0$ for all $m_t \in \mathbb{R}$, which clearly is the smallest value the objective function in (MIN) can assume for any $m_t \in \mathbb{R}$. Further, $r_p(m_t, z_t) = 0$ a. s. trivially implies $F(\{z \mid r_p(m_t, z_t) = 0\}) > 0$.

"⇒":

Let $p \in \boldsymbol{P}$ be an REE and let $m_t \in \mathbb{R}$ be given. Let

$$\boldsymbol{U} := \{u \in \boldsymbol{C} \mid u : \mathbb{R} \times R \to \mathbb{R}\}$$

be the space of continuous functions which map combinations of m_t and z_t on $\mathbb{R}$. Since R is compact, we know that there exist bounds b_0 and b_1 (depending possibly on m_t) with

$$0 < b_0 \leq p(m_t, z_t) \leq b_1 < 1$$

almost surely. Thus for any $v \in \boldsymbol{U}$ there exists a continuous, positive valued function

$$\begin{aligned} \epsilon_V : \mathbb{R} &\to \mathbb{R}_+ \\ m_t &\to \epsilon_V(m_t), \end{aligned}$$

$\epsilon_V \in \boldsymbol{C}$, such that for all $m_t \in \mathbb{R}$ we have

$$0 < p(m_t, z_t) + \epsilon_V(m_t)\, v(m_t, z_t) < 1$$

almost surely. Setting $u(m_t, z_t) := \epsilon_V(m_t)\, v(m_t, z_t)$ we have $u \in \boldsymbol{U}$. Hence for all $m_t \in \mathbb{R}$ and for all $\delta \in [0, 1]$

$$0 < p(m_t, z_t) + \delta\, u(m_t, z_t) < 1$$

holds almost surely. Since these inequalities are strict, we can find an open neighborhood of zero, V, say, $V \subset \mathbb{R}$, such that $\delta \in V$ implies $p+\delta u \in \boldsymbol{P}$ and range$(p+\delta u) \subset (0, 1)$ almost surely. Let now

$$J_u(\delta) := \int_R \left[m_t + z_t - s\left[\, p(m_t, z_t) + \delta\, u(m_t, z_t),\ \bar{p}_{p+\delta u}(m_t + z_t)\right]\right]^2 dF(z_t),$$

i. e. $J_u(\delta)$ is the value of the objective function in (MIN) for the admissible price function $p+\delta u$, where $p+\delta u$ is taken from a neighborhood of p, the solution of (MIN).

Now specifically consider

$$v(m_t, z_t) := s_1\Big[\, p(m_t, z_t),\, \bar{p}(m_t + z_t) \,\Big]\, r_p(m_t, z_t)$$

$$- \int_R s_1\Big[\, p(m_t, z),\, \bar{p}(m_t + z_t) \,\Big]\, r_p(m_t, z)\, dF(z),$$

where s_1 is the partial derivative of $s(\cdot,\cdot)$ with respect to its first argument. Define $\epsilon_v(\cdot)$ as described above and set $u(m_t, z_t) := \epsilon_v(m_t)\, v(m_t, z_t)$. As I have already noted, we have $u \in \boldsymbol{U}$.
Now examine equation (6) for the admissible price function $p+\delta u$:

$$\overline{p_{t+1}} = E\Big[\, p(m_{t+1}, z_{t+1}) + \delta\, u(m_{t+1}, z_{t+1}) \,\Big]$$

$$= E\Big[\, p(m_{t+1}, z_{t+1}) + \delta\, u\big[m_t + z_t + e(\overline{p_{t+1}}),\, z_{t+1}\big] \,\Big]$$

$$= \int_R \Big\{ p\Big[\, m_t + z_t + e(\overline{p_{t+1}}),\, z_{t+1} \,\Big] \; + \; \delta\, u\Big[\, m_t + z_t + e(\overline{p_{t+1}}),\, z_{t+1} \,\Big] \Big\}\, dF(z_{t+1})$$

$$= \int_R \Big\{ p\Big[\, m_t + z_t + e(\overline{p_{t+1}}),\, z_{t+1} \,\Big] \; + \; \delta\, \epsilon_v(m_{t+1})\, v(m_{t+1}, z_{t+1}) \Big\}\, dF(z_{t+1})$$

$$= \int_R p\Big[\, m_t + z_t + e(\overline{p_{t+1}}),\, z_{t+1} \,\Big]\, dF(z_{t+1}) \; + \; \delta\, \epsilon_v(m_t) \cdot 0$$

$$= E\Big[\, p\Big[\, m_t + z_t + e(\overline{p_{t+1}}),\, z_{t+1} \,\Big] \Big] = E\Big[\, p(m_{t+1}, z_{t+1}) \,\Big],$$

i. e. the rational price expectations under p and under $p+\delta u$, $\delta \in V$, are identical:

$$\bar{p}_{p+\delta u} \equiv \bar{p}_p$$

Therefore the derivative of $J_u(\delta)$ evaluated at $\delta = 0$ is well defined, and since p is by definition an interior solution to (MIN), we have the necessary condition

$$\frac{dJ_u(0)}{d\delta} = -2 \int_R s_1\Big[\, p(m_t, z_t), \bar{p}_P(m_t + z_t) \,\Big]\, r_P(m_t, z_t)\, u(m_t, z_t)\, dF(z_t)$$

$$= -2\, \epsilon_V(m_t)\, \mathrm{var}[\, s_1(p, \bar{p}_P)\, r_P \,]$$

$$\stackrel{!}{=} 0$$

This implies

$$r_P(m_t, z_t) = 0 \quad \text{a. s.} \qquad \vee \qquad r_P(m_t, z_t) \propto \frac{1}{s_1(p, \bar{p})} \quad \text{a. s.}$$

But $s_1(\cdot,\cdot)$ is strictly negative on the interior of its domain. Hence $r_P(m_t, z_t)$ cannot be proportional to the reciprocal of $s_1(p, \bar{p})$, since $r_P(m_t, z_t) \neq 0$ a. s. would be incompatible with p being an REE. It follows that

$$r_P(m_t, z_t) = 0$$

almost surely. Recall that m_t was chosen arbitrarily, hence the proof is completed.

q.e.d.

By virtue of Theorem 1 we immediately conclude

Theorem 2:

In the present model no REE exists.

Proof:

By assumption we have $F(\{z \mid z < -\sup E\}) > 0$. This implies $F(\{z \mid r_P(m, z) < 0\}) > 0$, hence by virtue of Theorem 1 the proof is completed. q.e.d.

The proof of Theorem 2 simply uses the fact that the market does not clear with positive probability. Theorem 1 then says that no REE exists.

2.3 The Role of Price Stabilization

The essence of the previous section may be summarized by stating that in an agricultural world market with rational expectations prices may rise or fall beyond any sensible threshold. Given the inelasticity of excess production and the fact that the market does not necessarily clear, this conclusion does not come too surprising. Does this mean that the above results are trivial?

The answer to this question is "no", as I will briefly demonstrate. Suppose expectations were a function of the current price rather than being rational, i. e. suppose we have $\overline{p_{t+1}} = \bar{p}(p_t)$. Then stock demand can be viewed as a function of the current price alone:

$$\tilde{s}(p_t) := s(p_t, \bar{p}(p_t)) = s(p_t, \overline{p_{t+1}})$$

Now specifically assume stock demand to obey to the functional form

$$s(p_t, \overline{p_{t+1}}) = f\left[\frac{\overline{p_{t+1}}}{p_t}\right],$$

where $f(\cdot)$ be strictly increasing, and specify $\bar{p}(\cdot)$ as

$$\bar{p}(p_t) := p_t + \frac{1}{4\pi}\sin^3(2\pi p_t).$$

We then have $\lim\,[\bar{p}(p_t)/p_t] = 1 < \infty$ for $p_t \to 0$, hence f is well defined for $p_t = 0$. The specification is ad hoc, but the underlying idea should be intuitive: $p_t = 0.5$ is the long run equilibrium price where no change in price is expected: $\bar{p}(0.5) = 0.5$. If the actual price is below the long run equilibrium level, next period's price will be expected to be somewhat higher (though still lower than 0.5), and if it is above, then people expect the price to decrease in the next

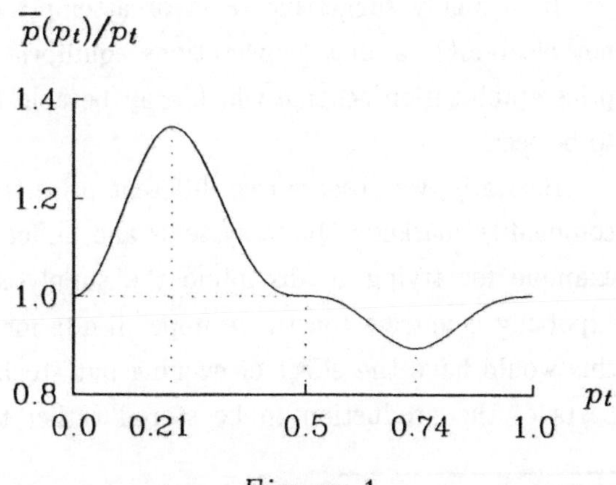

Figure 1

period (though not all the way down to the long run equilibrium level.).

Figure 1 plots $\bar{p}(p_t)/p_t$ on p_t. Since stock demand is a monotone transformation thereof, we immediately see that stock demand attains its maximum value s_t^{max} at $p_t \approx 0.21$ and its minimum value s_t^{min} at $p_t \approx 0.74$. Hence the optimal price function is given by

$$p^*(m_t, z_t) \approx \begin{cases} 0.21 & \text{if } m_t + z_t \geq s_t^{max} \\ \tilde{s}\big|_I^{-1}(m_t + z_t) & \text{if } s_t^{min} < m_t + z_t < s_t^{max}, \\ 0.74 & \text{if } m_t + z_t \leq s_t^{min} \end{cases}$$

where $I := (0.21, 0.74)$. It is easy to check that $\tilde{s}|_I$ is one to one. So long as total supply $m_t + z_t$ lies between s_t^{min} and s_t^{max}, there will always be a price between 0.21 and 0.74 such that stock demand equals total supply and the market will be equilibrated. If total supply is larger than s_t^{max}, stock demand must become as large as possible, i. e. the price must be 0.21. Conversely, if total supply is smaller than the minimum stock demand, then the price must be 0.74 in order to minimize the market residual. We hence see that p^* solves problem (MIN). (This problem takes a particularly simple form here: It is separable in p_t). Further, the range of p^* lies in the open interval (0, 1) and the market clears with positive probability. Thus p^* is a stable equilibrium price function despite the inelastic structure of excess production.

This fairly simple example shows the non–trivial character of Theorems 1 and 2. It elucidates the importance of expectations in equilibrium theory: We conclude that agricultural world markets lack equilibria in rational expectations, but they may have equilibria under more primitive expectation generating mechanisms.

It is highly suggestive to favor attempts of price stabilization when markets do not clear and rational expectations equilibria do not exist. But whether there is a price stabilization scheme which may be able to assure the existence of a REE is yet to be seen.

Basically, we observe two different price stabilization mechanisms in international commodity markets: Quota systems and buffer stocks[38]. The quota system is a typical example for trying to discipline the supply side: Quotas distributed among major exporting countries constitute upper limits for the exports of these countries. Ideally this would have the effect of evening out stochastic influences: Good harvests require parts of the production to be stored rather than exported, yet once a crop failure

[38]Combinations of both approaches are also possible.

occurs the stored quantity may be exported, provided total exports do not exceed the quota. Quota agreements depend on a consensus within the supply side only; this facilitates their negotiation. Some of the problems encountered in negotiating a quota agreement are discussed in Kaldor (1964).

Stabilizing prices by means of buffer stocks requires an international buffer stock authority which purchases large quantities when prices are depressed and sells them when they are high. If costs of storage were negligible, this might even be profitable[39]. Unfortunately, the warehousing of agricultural products is fairly expensive, see McNicol (1978, p. 51) and Newbery & Stiglitz (1981, p. 295). The buffer stock authority thus demands considerable financial contributions from the agreement's member countries. For this reason buffer stock agreements usually solicit both ex– and importing countries for participation in order to decrease costs per country. Yet support by importing countries is often less than enthusiastic. It should in this context be noted that the free–rider–problem is endemic in any effort of price stabilization.

How do we incorporate price stabilization in our model? Easily enough, for due to its very general functional forms we need not model price stabilization explicitly. For instance, a quota system, so long as it is intended to even out accidental fluctuations of production, is tantamount to a change in the distribution of z. Analogously, a buffer stock scheme alters the functional form of $s(\cdot,\cdot)$, but will most likely not affect the properties $s_1(\cdot,\cdot) < 0$ and $s_2(\cdot,\cdot) > 0$. The basic features of the model are thus unchanged by price stabilization.

Of course, price stabilization efforts do alter e. g. the structure of problem (MIN). The resulting price function will hence in general be different from the pre–stabilization price function, as the Lucas–Critique predicts. But non–market–clearing and the non–existence of rational expectations equilibria still prevail despite of stabilization efforts.

It is important to note that these results do in no way assert the ineffectiveness of price stabilization. The probabilities for extreme prices or for non–market–clearing might well be *reduced* under the new distribution or under the new functional forms. However, they will certainly not be *eliminated*, i. e. they will not become zero. This is to say that price stabilization might be partially successful, but not completely.

---

[39]In fact, so long as storage is profitable there is no need for buffer stocks, since private traders will do the job. Hence buffer stock activity is unprofitable almost by definition. A standard argument against buffer stocks even asserts that losses entailed by buffer–stock–type market intervention will be particularly large, since the existence of buffer stocks discourages private stockholders and thus requires more purchases by the buffer stock authority than had initially been anticipated (cf. Newbery & Stiglitz, 1981).

Needless to add that price stabilization might also prove counterproductive: The new functional forms induced by price stabilization will, in general, not be known a priori, and this gives rise to the possibility that they turn out to be less favorable than their pre–stabilization counterparts.

To conclude this section, I would like to point out that an abundance of possible price stabilization schemes may be formulated in terms of changing the functional forms of either the distribution of z or the behavioral relationships $s(\cdot,\cdot)$ or $e(\cdot)$. Since it is difficult to think of any proposal which would violate basic features of the model and nevertheless be economically sensible, we may infer non–market–clearing and non–existence of rational expectations equilibria under virtually any price stabilization rule. Yet how far less–than–perfect price stabilization may be able to accomplish its objectives is almost impossible to assess in a theoretical model due to the difficulties connected with the Lucas– Critique. On the other hand, the theoretical considerations clearly demonstrate that for price stabilization to have an effect at all a structural change is a necessary condition. Thus in the applied part of this study price stabilization will be tested for by using tests for structural change. Estimating the functions of interest under two different regimes is then the method for evaluating the effectiveness of price stabilization.

Chapter 3: Price Dynamics in a Linear World

The exposition of the model has so far not yet surpassed the state of two–periods–only analysis. Before turning to a multi–period analysis it may be appropriate to summarize the model of price determination that has been exposed in the previous chapter. Let for this purpose f_i, i=1, 2, 3, denote functional relationships to be specified. The model then consists of the following equations[40]:

$$e_t = f_1(\overline{p_t}), \qquad f_1'(\cdot) > 0 \tag{7}$$

$$m_t \equiv m_{t-1} + e_t + z_{t-1} \tag{8}$$

$$s_t = f_2(p_t, \overline{p_{t+1}}), \qquad \frac{\partial f_2}{\partial p_t} < 0, \quad \frac{\partial f_2}{\partial \overline{p_{t+1}}} > 0 \tag{9}$$

$$p_t = f_3(m_t, z_t), \qquad \frac{\partial f_3}{\partial m_t} < 0, \quad \frac{\partial f_3}{\partial z_t} < 0 \tag{10}$$

$$\overline{p_{t+1}} \equiv E_t[p_{t+1}] \tag{11}$$

These are three behavioral equations and two identities. The stochastic shock z_t is exogenous. The model could be supplemented by a third identity defining the market residual. However, this increases the explanatory power of the model only if we additionally impose the constraint that $f_3(\cdot,\cdot)$ solves problem (MIN). Such a constraint would be highly nonlinear and could, in practice, not be tested upon. It is therefore simply assumed that $f_3(\cdot,\cdot)$ solves problem (MIN). This assumption replaces

---

[40]Strictly speaking, the assumptions on the partial derivatives of $f_3(\cdot,\cdot)$ are new; they have not previously been made. They are economically sensible, however, and since I will use them in the sequel I take the opportunity to introduce them here.

the traditional equilibrium condition, which, as we have seen, would be inappropriate since the market does not necessarily clear.

The absence of equilibria in rational expectations is being accounted for by allowing for both a non–zero market residual and for the possibility that prices may assume any non–negative value[41]. Equation (7), describing systematic excess production, can easily be estimated since its regressor is predetermined: The price expectation has been formed in the previous period. Therefore, m_t is predetermined, too, and since z_t is exogenous we find both regressors for the price equation (10) to be predetermined as well. Stock demand, equation (9), is thus the sole simultaneous equation. It is related to the rest of the model by virtue of problem (MIN). We can, in principle, neglect stock demand so long as equation (10) is *assumed* to be a solution of (MIN). Yet as stock demand may undergo structural changes in the face of price stabilization efforts, its specification and estimation is nevertheless of considerable interest.
Let us now turn to a linearized version of the above model:

3.1 A Refined Version of the Model

An interesting feature of non–oil primary commodity markets is the more or less cyclical behavior of world market prices. Products such as cocoa, natural rubber, and sugar can serve as prime examples; for non–agricultural raw materials see e. g. the prices of copper and tin. The precise length of these cycles cannot reliably be inferred from the data without a thorough empirical investigation. It probably varies considerably between different markets, but already a short glance at price fluctuations in the past two or three decades suggests that time passing between two price peaks is at least as much as four and hardly more than ten years. If or if not such price movements can be taken to reflect an underlying systematic cycle is the question to be addressed in this section of the study.

To facilitate this task we will restrict our attention to a linearized version of the above model, already aggregated to the world market level by summing over all farmers and all countries. In order to motivate a slight modification in the specification of systematic excess production (7) I start with a linear equation describing planned (= expected) production as

---

[41]Normalizing prices to the unit interval proved to be a sensible analytical tool in the previous chapter. It is not convenient in the present one, though. Hence from now on prices will be back to normal.

$$y_t = \alpha + a_1 y_{t-1} + a_2 \overline{p_t}. \tag{12}$$

Here I introduce y_{t-1} as a seemingly new explanatory variable for y_t, where I assume the autoregressive coefficient a_1 to be smaller than, but "close" to one. The reason for this is simply that many agricultural crops (bananas, cocoa, coffee, sugar cane, and tea, for example) are perennial, such that cultivations in period t–2 not only induce planned output of period t–1, but also to a large extent predetermine expected production in period t, t+1, etc.[42]

But even in the case of annual crops (grain, oilseeds, or sugar beet) the autoregressive relationship postulated in equation (12) will be fairly strong. For expensive equipment, machines, and factory capacity complement the production of the crop. Since changes in the size of capital will usually be slow, so must be changes in expected production. Otherwise the profitability of investment and production decisions would be jeopardized.

Finally, observe that the specification of equation (12) does not at all constitute a deviation from the model exposed in the previous chapters. For there, our concern has been limited to the analysis of a two–period problem. Thus previous output decisions were implicitly incorporated in the functional form of the production function, and suppressing them notationally was perfectly legitimate since they were predetermined to the analysis. Only now, where the focus is on multi–period dynamics, do we need to mention them explicitly.

Bearing in mind the above reasoning, a_1 sufficiently close to one should not be too strict an assumption, even more so as this will turn out to be the stability condition of the model. By virtue of our results in the first chapter, I also postulate $a_2 > 0$.

For the sake of simplicity, I will slightly strengthen the assumptions on consumption: As before I take C_t to be exogenous due to fixed domestic prices, but by supposing a constant population and the absence of income effects, I now also require that consumption be constant over time: $C_t = C \quad \forall\ t$. We then get systematic excess production by

$$e_t \equiv y_t - C. \tag{13}$$

[42]The same argument applies to the production of livestock, where, for instance in the case of cattle, yesterday's size of the herd determines today's calvings and thus tomorrow's slaughterings. Markets for dairy products are affected by the same mechanism.

Combining (12) and (13) we obtain

$$e_t = \frac{\alpha}{1-a_1} + \frac{a_2\overline{p_t}}{1-a_1L} - C$$

or

$$e_t = a_0 + a_1\, e_{t-1} + a_2\, \overline{p_t}, \tag{14}$$

where $a_0 := \alpha - (1-a_1)\ C$ and L is the lag operator defined by $L\xi_t := \xi_{t-1}$. In addition, we have

$$m_t = m_{t-1} + e_t + z_{t-1} \tag{15}$$

and I assume stochastic production z to be white noise. The model is then closed by the price function

$$p_t = b_0 + b_1\, m_t + b_2\, z_t \tag{16}$$

which is the linearized solution of problem (MIN). To complete our assumptions on the parameters I assume $b_1 < 0$, $b_2 < 0$, i. e. an increase in excess supply induces a decrease in price.

We can now solve the model. Because of $|a_1| < 1$ the general solution to (14) is given by

$$e_t = \frac{a_0}{1-a_1} + \frac{a_2}{1-a_1L}\,\overline{p_t} + \Gamma a_1^t, \tag{17}$$

where Γ is an arbitrary constant. Since Γa_1^t tends to zero as t becomes large, I will simplify the analysis by working with the particular solution for which I set $\Gamma = 0$. The rational expectation of the price in period t is defined as the solution of

$$\begin{aligned}\overline{p_t} &= E_{t-1}\,[p_t] \\ &= b_0 + b_1\,[m_{t-1} + \frac{a_0}{1-a_1} + \frac{a_2}{1-a_1L}\,\overline{p_t} + z_{t-1}].\end{aligned}$$

This turns out to be

$$\overline{p_t} = \frac{(1-a_1)b_0 + a_0b_1}{1-a_1-a_2b_1} + \frac{(1-a_1L)b_1L}{1-a_1L-a_2b_1}\,(m_t + z_t) \tag{18}$$

which we can safely write in this form since $1 - a_1L - a_2b_1 = 0$ does certainly not have any roots on or within the unit circle (recall that a_2b_1 is negative). Substituting (17) and (18) in (15), we can then solve for m_t:

$$(1-L)m_t = \frac{a_0}{1-a_1} + \frac{a_2}{1-a_1L}\left[\frac{(1-a_1)b_0 + a_0b_1}{1-a_1-a_2b_1} + \frac{(1-a_1L)b_1L}{1-a_1L-a_2b_1}(m_t + z_t)\right] + z_{t-1}$$

$\Leftrightarrow$

$$\left[1 - \frac{(1-a_1L)L}{(1-a_1L-a_2b_1)}\right] m_t = \frac{(1-a_1L)}{(1-a_1L-a_2b_1)} z_{t-1} + \frac{a_0+a_2b_0}{(1-a_1-a_2b_1)}$$

$\Leftrightarrow$

$$m_t = \frac{a_0+a_2b_0}{(1-a_1-a_2b_1) - (1-a_1)} + \frac{(1-a_1L)L}{(1-a_1L-a_2b_1) - (1-a_1L)L} z_t$$

$\Leftrightarrow$

$$m_t = -\frac{a_0+a_2b_0}{a_2b_1} + \frac{(1-a_1L)L}{(1-a_1L)(1-L) - a_2b_1} z_t$$

The correctness of these transformations is immediate, since by making use of the assumption that a_1 be sufficiently close to one we see that the roots of the lag polynomial

$$(1-a_1L-a_2b_1) - (1-a_1L)L = 0$$

$\Leftrightarrow$

$$a_1L^2 - (1+a_1)L + (1-a_2b_1) = 0$$

exceed unity in absolute value[43]. Inserting in (16), we get the following representation of p_t in the time domain:

$$p_t = -\frac{a_0}{a_2} + \left[b_2 + \frac{b_1(1-a_1L)L}{(1-a_1L)(1-L) - a_2b_1}\right] z_t$$

$$=: -\frac{a_0}{a_2} + A(L)\, z_t$$

Hence we have $E[p_t] = -a_0/a_2$, i. e. by economic reasoning a_0 must be negative. In order to analyse cyclical features of p_t, we can simply suppress the constant term and confine our attention to the transformed variable $p_t + a_0/a_2$ which will obviously display the same cycle.

---

[43]To see this set a_1 equal to 1. Then the roots of the lag polynomial are complex with absolute value $\sqrt{1-a_2b_1} > 1$. By continuity, the same holds for a_1 sufficiently close to one.

3.2 Cyclical Behavior

I now derive the representation of $p_t + a_0/a_2$ in the frequency domain[44]. Since z_t is white noise its Fourier transform yields a constant spectrum of $\sigma^2/2\pi$, where σ^2 is the variance of z_t. I normalize $\sigma^2 = 2\pi$ for notational simplicity. This implies that the spectrum of $p_t + a_0/a_2$ equals its transfer function

$$T(\lambda) := A(e^{i\lambda})\,A(e^{-i\lambda}).$$

Setting

$$v(\lambda) := 2\,(1+a_1^2-2a_1\cos(\lambda))\,(1-\cos(\lambda)) + a_2^2b_1^2 - 2a_2b_1\,[1-(1+a_1)\cos(\lambda) + a_1\cos(2\lambda)],$$

we derive

$$T(\lambda) = b_2^2 + b_1^2\,\frac{(1+a_1^2-2a_1\cos(\lambda))}{v(\lambda)}$$

$$-\,2b_1b_2\,\frac{(1+a_1^2-2a_1\cos(\lambda))(1-\cos(\lambda)) + a_2b_1\cos(\lambda) - a_1a_2b_1\cos(2\lambda)}{v(\lambda)}$$

$$=: b_2^2 + \frac{u(\lambda)}{v(\lambda)}\,.$$

We would like to investigate whether the model induces "long" cycles. The longer the periodicity of a cycle the smaller is by definition its frequency. By convention we will speak of a long cycle if the transfer function $T(\cdot)$ assumes a local maximum on the open interval $(0, \pi/2)$, and of a short cycle for any other local maximum of the transfer function on $[\pi/2, \pi)$.

By the symmetry of the spectrum, we know that $T'(0) = 0$. Let us try to obtain the sign of $T'(\lambda)$ evaluated at $\lambda = \pi/2$. It suffices to analyse the nominator of this derivative. We have

[44]Readers unfamiliar with spectral analysis are referred to the books by Granger (1964), König & Wolters (1972), or Schlittgen & Streitberg (1989).

$$u'(\lambda) = 2a_1b_1^2 \sin(\lambda) - 2b_1b_2\,[2a_1\sin(\lambda)\,(1-\cos(\lambda)) + \sin(\lambda)(1+a_1^2-2a_1\cos(\lambda))]$$
$$+ 2a_2b_1^2b_2 \sin(\lambda) - 4a_1a_2b_1^2b_2 \sin(2\lambda)$$

and

$$v'(\lambda) = 2\,[2a_1\sin(\lambda)\,(1-\cos(\lambda)) + \sin(\lambda)(1+a_1^2-2a_1\cos(\lambda))] - 2(1+a_1)a_2b_1 \sin(\lambda)$$
$$+ 4a_1a_2b_1 \sin(2\lambda).$$

Hence we find

$$u(\pi/2) = (1+a_1^2)b_1^2 - 2b_1b_2\,(1+a_1^2+a_1a_2b_1)$$

$$v(\pi/2) = 2(1+a_1^2) + a_2^2b_1^2 - 2(1-a_1)a_2b_1$$

$$u'(\pi/2) = 2a_1b_1^2 - 2b_1b_2\,(a_1^2+2a_1+1) + 2a_2b_1^2b_2$$

$$v'(\pi/2) = 4a_1 + 2(1+a_1^2) - 2(1+a_1)a_2b_1.$$

The nominator of $T'(\pi/2)$ is then given by

$$T''(\pi/2) = u'(\pi/2)\,v(\pi/2) - v'(\pi/2)\,u(\pi/2)$$
$$= 4a_1(1+a_1^2)b_1^2 + 2a_1a_2^2b_1^4 - 4a_1(1-a_1)a_2b_1^3 - 4(1+a_1)^2(1+a_1^2)b_1b_2$$
$$- 2(1+a_1)^2a_2^2b_1^3b_2 + 4(1+a_1)(1-a_1^2)a_2b_1^2b_2 + 4(1+a_1^2)a_2b_1^2b_2 + 2a_2^3b_1^4b_2$$
$$- 4(1-a_1)a_2^2b_1^3b_2 - 4a_1(1+a_1^2)b_1^2 + 8a_1b_1b_2(1+a_1^2+a_1a_2b_1) - 2(1+a_1^2)^2b_1^2$$
$$+ 4(1+a_1^2)b_1b_2(1+a_1^2+a_1a_2b_1) + 2(1+a_1)(1+a_1^2)a_2b_1^3$$
$$- 4(1+a_1)a_2b_1^2b_2(1+a_1^2+a_1a_2b_1)$$

$$= 2a_1a_2^3b_1^4 + 2(1-a_1)a_2b_1^3 + 4a_1^2(1-a_1)a_2b_1^2b_2 - 4a_1a_2^3b_1^3b_2 + 2a_2^3b_1^4b_2$$

$$- 6(1+a_1^2)a_2^3b_1^3b_2 + 4(1+a_1)a_2b_1^2b_2 + (6+2a_1)a_1^2a_2b_1^3 - 2(1+a_1^2)^2b_1^2$$

$$< 2a_1a_2^3b_1^4 - 4a_1a_2^3b_1^3b_2 - 6(1+a_1^2)a_2^3b_1^3b_2$$

(all omitted terms are negative)

$$< 2a_1a_2^3b_1^4 - 16a_1a_2^3b_1^3b_2$$

(using $1+a_1^2 > 2a_1$)

$$< 2a_1a_2^3b_1^3(b_1-8b_2)$$

$$< 0 \qquad \text{if } |b_1| < 8\,|b_2|. \tag{19}$$

We thus find that $|b_1| < 8\,|b_2|$ is sufficient to ensure $T'(\pi/2) < 0$. By virtue of the intermediate value theorem we can infer the existence of a maximum of the transfer function $T(\cdot)$ in the open interval $(0, \pi/2)$ if – recall $T'(0) = 0$ – we can show $T''(0) > 0$. (Put differently, we want to show that the spectrum assumes a local minimum at $\lambda = 0$). We have

$$T''(0) = \frac{(u''v + v'u' - v''u - v'u')v^2 - 2\,v\,v'(u'v - v'u)}{v^4}$$

$$= \frac{u''v - v''u}{v^2},$$

since $u'(0)\,v(0) - v'(0)\,u(0) = 0$ follows from $T'(0) = 0$. Hence we can conclude

$$\text{sign}(T''(0)) = \text{sign}(u''(0)\,v(0) - v''(0)\,u(0)).$$

The second derivatives of $u(\cdot)$ and $v(\cdot)$ are given by

$$u''(\lambda) = 2a_1b_1^2\cos(\lambda) - 2b_1b_2\,[2a_1\cos(\lambda)\,(1-\cos(\lambda)) + 4a_1\sin^2(\lambda)$$
$$+ \cos(\lambda)\,(1+a_1^2 - 2a_1\cos(\lambda))] + 2a_2b_1^2b_2\cos(\lambda) - 8a_1a_2b_1^2b_2\cos(2\lambda)$$

$$v''(\lambda) = 2\,[2a_1 \cos(\lambda)\,(1-\cos(\lambda)) + 4a_1 \sin^2(\lambda) + \cos(\lambda)\,(1+a_1^2 - 2a_1 \cos(\lambda))]$$

$$- 2\,(1+a_1)\,a_2b_1 \cos(\lambda) + 8a_1a_2b_1 \cos(2\lambda)$$

such that

$$u''(0) = 2a_1b_1^2 - 2b_1b_2\,(1-a_1)^2 + 2a_2b_1^2b_2 - 8a_1a_2b_1^2b_2,$$

$$v''(0) = 2\,(1-a_1)^2 - 2\,(1+a_1)\,a_2b_1 + 8a_1a_2b_1.$$

Together with

$$u(0) \doteq b_1^2\,(1-a_1)^2 - 2a_2b_1^2b_2\,(1-a_1),$$

$$v(0) = a_2^2b_1^2$$

this results in

$$\begin{aligned} u''(0)\,v(0) - v''(0)\,u(0) &= 2a_1a_2^2b_1^4 - 2(1-a_1)^2a_2^2b_1^3b_2 + 2a_2^3b_1^4b_2 - 8a_1a_2^3b_1^4b_2 \\ &\quad - 2(1-a_1)^4b_1^2 + 2(1+a_1)(1-a_1)^2a_2b_1^3 - 8a_1(1-a_1)^2a_2b_1^3 \\ &\quad + 4(1-a_1)^3a_2b_1^2b_2 - 4(1-a_1^2)a_2^2b_1^3b_2 + 16a_1(1-a_1)a_2^2b_1^3b_2 \\ &\xrightarrow[a_1 \to 1]{} 2a_2^2b_1^4 + 2a_2^3b_1^4b_2 - 8a_2^3b_1^4b_2 \\ &= 2a_2^2b_1^4 - 6a_2^3b_1^4b_2 > 0. \end{aligned}$$

Hence sufficient for a local maximum of the transfer function on $(0, \pi/2)$ are two conditions, namely that a_1 be close to one and that $|b_1| < 8\,|b_2|$. The first has already extensively been discussed. The impact of the second is merely that the effect a marginal increase in systematic supply has on the world market price should not be far larger than the effect of an incremental increase in accidental supply; more precisely: It should not be more than eight times as large. It is economically plausible that this condition holds in typical agricultural product markets and I will therefore assume it. However, possible doubts about the legitimacy of this assumption in special market segments could easily be honored by means of econometric tests.

Now recall that our model was specified to be annual in periodicity. Hence the shortest cyclic movement we may observe given annual data is of two years' length. Such a cycle would correspond to the frequency $\lambda = \pi$. Analogously, the frequency $\lambda = \pi/2$ represents a four–year–cycle. Now, since we inferred (under the above conditions) the existence of a maximum of the spectrum of p_t on $(0, \pi/2)$, we can conclude that the model induces a price cycle with a periodicity of more than four years. Moreover, since T(0) was shown to be a local minimum, we have reason to see prices as realizations of a trend–free time series.

3.3 Price Cycles and Stabilization

The results of the previous section reflect surprisingly well the observations made on real–world agricultural markets and may thus be taken as indicative for the appropriateness of the chosen model. However, they also teach us something about price stabliziation, be it by means of a buffer stock or by establishing a quota system or by any other instrument in the spirit of the preceding chapter: For price stabilization, if it is to have a measurable effect at all, will result in a change of the parameters of the price function due to a different solution of problem (MIN). (This is the Lucas–Critique once again). But the basic structure of the model (in its linear approximation) is likely to remain unaltered. This is to say that despite the presence of price stabilization the parameter a_1 (the autoregressive influence in the determination of systematic production) is still likely to be close to (but smaller than) one and that, of course, the parameter a_2 (the coefficient of the expected price) is most probably still positive. Moreover, this is to say that the parameters b_1 and b_2 (the multipliers of systematic and accidental supply in the price equation, respectively) will be negative after the implementation of price stabilizing mechanisms just as they have been before.

So even in the presence of price stabilization will the price run through cycles of more than four years' length, provided the new price function does not violate the condition $|b_1| < 8\ |b_2|$. This, however, should be fairly unlikely, for if the coefficients b_1 and b_2 were indeed of different magnitude then we would rather expect the multiplier of the stochastic shock (i. e. b_2) to be larger in absolute terms than the multiplier of systematic supply, b_1. Yet even if we had reason to suspect a relationship such as $|b_1| \geq 8\ |b_2|$ it should be borne in mind that this condition is sufficient, but in no way necessary for long cycles. In fact, a closer look at inequality (19) shows quite a waste of negative terms. Numerical examples I constructed with selected configurations of parameters suggested that $|b_1|$ must be more than twentyfive times as large as $|b_2|$ in order to make the maximum of the spectrum shift to the right of $\pi/2$.

Thus we can quite safely assert that long price cycles on world agricultural markets will in general prevail even under a feasible price stabilization scheme. This is not to say that price stabilization is necessarily executed in vain, for if it were to achieve a reduction in the variance of accidental supply, then the cycle would remain, but its amplitude would be reduced. In the light of the earlier suspicion that prices might react more sensitively to stochastic than to systematic changes in supply such a reduction might in itself be desirable. It is, of course, also possible that long price cycles still exist after stabilization, but display nevertheless a significantly smaller amplitude due to coefficients of different magnitude than their pre–stabilization counterparts. Such a phenomenon could be observed if the local maximum of the transfer function would be reduced as a consequence of price stabilization.

This leads us back to the Lucas–Critique, which narrowly confines the scope of theoretical contributions to the analysis of price stabilization. For it is undisputable that any form of market intervention constitutes a fundamental change in the structure of a formerly unregulated market and thus seriously affects the underlying optimization problems of all participating agents. A comparison of pre– and post–stabilization solutions for these problems will, however, be the more difficult the more realistic the model–design is. Insofar as model parameters must be viewed as being determined by the solutions of maximization problems, do we hence lack a reasonable method of theoretical comparative–static analysis.

To my opinion, the most we can do on the theoretical level is to single out those features of the model which will most probably be unaffected by price stabilization. In this spirit, I have established the non–existence of rational expectations equilibria in the preceding and the existence of long price cycles in the present chapter. But many decisive questions with policy implications remain unanswered: Is price stabilization (at least partially) feasible, do the suggested instruments have the aspired effect or inhowfar may their operation prove counterproductive, how do people respond to the changes in the market structure, etc.? The answers to such questions depend on the market to be regulated, the institutional constraints that apply, the costs to be associated with price stabilizing efforts, the potential benefits for participating countries and, of course, the incentives to free–ride. It is thus left to empirical work and experience with price stabilizing agreements in practice to give helpful clues for these problems. I will therefore now direct my attention to an application on an important agricultural world market.

PART II

PRICE FORMATION ON THE WORLD SUGAR MARKET

Chapter 4: Characteristics of the Market

In order to empirically investigate the process of price stabilization on a specific world agricultural market, I will now address my attention to the world market for *sugar*. While this choice of product may initially appear fairly arbitrary, I hope to convince the reader of the aptitude of the sugar market as the focal point of my analysis by briefly describing the product and its market:

4.1 The Product

"Sugar" is the conventional name for a substance (crystalline or liquid) which should more precisely be labelled "sucrose"[45]. Within a wider class of mutual substitutes it has been the undisputed front runner ever since it replaced honey as the main sweetener in medieval Europe. Although sugar could easily be dispensed with from a nutritional point of view, it is regarded as a basic foodstuff throughout the world and covers about 9–10% of world caloric consumption (FAO (1977)).

Prior to 1800, sugar has exclusively been derived from sugar cane, the cultivation of which requires tropical or semi–tropical wheather conditions. Main cane–producing countries in these times were India and Java. However, boosted by the scarcity of sugar due to the British blockade of continental Europe during the Napoleonic wars, the nineteenth century witnessed the development of a technology of processing sugar from sugar beet; a crop which finds optimal growth conditions in temperate regions. This new European sugar producing industry expanded rapidly, thanks to a system of protective measures like tariffs, import quotas and production subsidies established by

[45]This is a disaccharide with the chemical formula $C_{12}H_{22}O_{11}$.

autarky–oriented governments, such that in 1900/1901 about 53% of the world sugar production stemmed from sugar beet and the remainder from sugar cane. There has been some fluctuation in this relationship since, but for the last twenty years or so the market share of sugar beet was a fairly stable 35% as opposed to 65% for sugar cane (Bartens & Mosolff (1988))[46].

Chemically, sugar from sugar cane and sugar from sugar beet are identical, i. e. both are sucrose. But sugars are available in various qualities or stages of processing. The most primitive form of sugar is *noncentrifugal* sugar, which is obtained either by letting crystallize the liquid extracted from cane or beet or by transforming it to a dark, viscous syrup (so–called fancy or edible molasse). Noncentrifugal sugar is commonly not considered to be of tradable quality; it is produced exclusively for local consumption in a couple of developing countries, primarily India and Pakistan (Zeller (1988)).

Depending on the technoloqy employed, *centrifugal* sugar can be either *raw* or *white*, where white sugar is of higher purity. By means of refining[47], raw sugar can be converted to white sugar, i. e. refined sugar always means white sugar or a liquid derivative thereof[48]. In fact, sugar from sugar beet is almost always white sugar since centrifuging and refining are integrated steps in the beet–processing industry. In contrast, sugar mills in cane producing countries usually manufacture raw sugar and the refining, if it takes place at all, is done in the country of final consumption, mostly a developed country. Given raw sugar's more favorable costs of transportation, this is a very appropriate way of handling. Consequently, (and despite of recent progress in the transportation of white sugar[49]), raw sugar is still the predominant quality in international trade.

---

[46]Percentages refer to total sugar produced. If only centrifugal sugar is considered, then the shares are approximately 40% to 60%, respectively, (ISO (1988)).

[47]The complementary product in the centrifuging and refining of sugar is blackstrap (or final) molassse, a heavy liquid from which all commercially recoverable sugar has been removed. It is of a bitter taste and inapt for human consumption. It is mainly used for livestock feed and to a lesser extent in the manufacture of industrial alcohols or other chemical products.

[48]Crystalline sugar is highly hygroscopic and hence expensive to store. However, white sugar is even more hygroscopic than is raw, thus raw sugar is usually preferred for transport or inventory purposes. Liquid sugars are rarely used for storage since they are fairly voluminous and their value–to–weight ratio is much less favorable than for sugar in crystalline form.

[49]See *Le Monde Diplomatique*: "Le Sucre sous l'Empire des Grands", March 1988.

There exist well–defined conversion rates for all sucrose–based sweeteners, crystalline or liquid, noncentrifugal, raw, or refined. These are obtained on the basis of polarization, i. e. by measuring the content of sucrose by means of a polariscope. The standard basis for raw sugar is 96 degrees polarization; the conversion rate for other sugars testing p degrees by polariscope is (2p–100)/92. Thus noncentrifugal sugar, for instance, is converted to raw value by a coefficient of 0.6, while raw sugar can in turn be expressed in terms of white sugar equivalent by multiplying its weight by 0.92. As a matter of tradition, most sugar statistics are expressed in raw value; where this is not the case, conversion is easy, so long as the quality basis is known.

This is so because sucrose is the only component of economic relevance in both beet and cane[50]. By contrast, many crops (grain or oilseeds, for instance) contain more than one exploitable component (protein and starch, or protein and fat, respectively). In accordance with different consumptive or industrial needs, cultivational efforts have successfully been directed at varying the relationship between these components, thereby producing a wide range of species of wheat, soybeans, rape, etc. and corresponding markets and prices. Conversion to a standardized crop is much more difficult in these cases due to the at least two–dimensional quality basis and – in the case of time series data – to the rapid cultivational and technical progress.

Moreover, as sucrose is a well–defined macro–molecule, it also displays a uniform flavor, irrespective of its origin. This distinguishes sugar from products like teas, coffees, or vegetable oils (let alone all kinds of meats) which are characterized by a considerable degree of heterogeneity due to flavioral discrepancies. In comparison with other agricultural products sugar thus proves to be a remarkably homogenous commodity.

4.2 Substitutes

Until the 1960's sucrose was the only sweetener of any importance, the consumption of dextrose being negligible. In recent years, however, two groups of formerly unknown sweeteners have successfully conquered certain segments of the market, particularly in developed countries. The first of these groups are the artificial, low–calorie sweeteners, which took advantage of a shift in the dietary habits in industrialized societies. Early products of this kind were saccharine and cyclamate,

[50]For the production of ethanol from sugar cane it is also the content of sucrose which matters.

characterized by about 300 times the sweetness of sugar but also by a bitter aftertaste. Later, improved palatable sweeteners have been developed, whose sweetness is about 200 times the sweetness of sucrose. The most noteworthiest among them, aspartame, accounted for significant inroads in the US market for crystalline sugar[51]. The basic weakness of the low–calorie artificial sweeteners is still their fairly costly production; according to estimates by Licht (1986) and LMC (1983) the off–factory price for aspartame ranges from 30 to 50 US–cents per pound raw sugar equivalent[52], while US production and processing costs for sugar are about 23 cts/lb from beet and 21 cts/lb from cane[53].

The second group of alternative sweeteners uses starch–containing crops for the production of isoglucose. Most popular is the manufacturing of high fructose corn syrup (HFCS) from maize, but wheat, potatoes, sorghum, or cassava can also be used[54] HFCS is a liquid sweetener and thus primarily of interest for nutritional industries, for instance in the production of soft drinks. It can be transformed to crystalline form, but this increases production costs considerably, as has been shown by Schroeder (1991). LMC (1983) gives production costs of HFCS of 12 cts/lb raw sugar equivalent for the United States, i. e. the production of HFCS is far cheaper than the production of sucrose – at least in the US[55].

Not surprisingly, US–per–capita consumption of HFCS has risen from zero in 1971 to 20.3 kg in 1986, while in the same period consumption of sucrose declined from 50.1 kg to 27.6 kg per head. The increase in the consumption of artificial sweeteners is less dramatic: Data available suggest a per capita consumption in raw sugar equivalent of 2.8 kg in 1975 and 7.7 kg in 1985 (Licht (1986)).

While other developed countries also experience a shift in consumption in favor of sugar substitutes, the quantitative effects are by far not as large as in the United States. Consumption in developing countries is even less affected by alternative

---

[51]Not quite as successful was a related product developed in Germany, acesulfame K, which is sold in the United Kingdom under the name of "Sunnet". (See FAO (1985) for details).

[52]Sugar prices and costs will always be given in terms of US–cents per pound (cts/lb), where a pound is a US–pound equal to 0.454 kg.

[53]These are costs for the US–Mainland. Costs for sugar from sugar cane in Hawaii are significantly lower; LMC (1983) compute less than 17 cts/lb.

[54]As of yet, maize appears to be the only profitable source for the production of isoglucose, while other crops – technologies still being developed – are not yet competitive. A detailed study is provided by Schroeder (1991).

[55]Schroeder (1991) obtains similar results for southern areas of the EEC. Note that in order to control the expansion of isoglucose, the EEC decided to introduce production quotas in 1981.

sweeteners, either because these states do not dispose of the necessary technological equipment or because government–controled sugar prices are too low to make sugar substitutes competitive. (Recall the analysis by Bale & Lutz (1981), for the second point).

To complete the section on sugar substitutes, I will finally briefly mention noncentrifugal sugar. This may take the reader by surprise, since, as has been noted earlier, noncentrifugal sugar can simply be viewed as sucrose in a low–quality–stage of processing. However, all data I will be using in the sequel relate to centrifugal sugar exclusively; hence the crude products must be classified as substitutes.

The scarce information we have about noncentrifugal sugar basically suggests that its impact on international trade is negligible. Zeller (1988) rightly points out the importance of noncentrifugal sugar as a production reserve for centrifugal sugar in times of shortages. This is obviously a substitution effect, but it is as obviously captured in the data, since the newly produced sugar is centrifugal. In what follows, "sugar" will always denote centrifugal sugar.

In total, centrifugal sugar made up about 82% of the 1982 consumption of sweeteners throughout the world, while starch–based sweeteners accounted for 2% and non–centrifugal sugar for 7% (Hoff & Lawrence (1985)). Given the close substitutability between sugar and alternative sweeteners, we can expect their prices to be highly correlated. More importantly, in view of the market shares of sugar and its substitutes, the price of the former is most likely a major determinant for the prices of the latter, but the converse is hardly conceivable. Hence sugar is presumably a commodity well suited for a partial equilibrium analysis.

4.3 The Market

As I have noted in Part I, agricultural products display strongly protected domestic markets and the sugar market constitutes a prime example for such policies. There is strong evidence for my earlier assertion that both production and consumption of sugar are inelastic with respect to the current world market price, and a detailed account of it will be given in a later section. Yet for the purpose of this introductory description I will focus on market features other than protectionist in nature.

Sugar from either beet or cane is presently produced in more than a hundred countries with a total production in 1986 of slightly above hundred million metric tons raw value[56]. This constitutes approximately a 50% increase from the 1967 level of about 65 million tons. Table 1 gives a survey of the most important sugar producing nations for these years.

Table 1

Production of Sugar

	1967			1986		
Rank	Country	Production in 1000 mt	% of World Production	Country	Production in 1000 mt	% of World Production
1	SU	9188	13.8	EEC	14126	14.1
2	EEC	8394	12.6	SU	8660	8.6
3	CUB	6236	9.4	BRA	7999	8.0
4	USA	5539	8.3	IND	7594	7.6
5	BRA	4220	6.3	CUB	7467	7.4
6	MEX	2412	3.6	CHI	5960	5.9
7	AUS	2398	3.6	USA	5676	5.7
8	IND	2174	3.3	MEX	4068	4.1
9	SAF	1732	2.6	AUS	3439	3.4
10	CHI	1609	2.4	THA	2718	2.7

Source: ISO, Statistical Bulletin.

[56]Unless explicitly stated otherwise, the weight of sugar will always be expressed for raw value equivalent and tons will always denote metric tons (mt).

Cane is primarily cultivated in developing countries (Cuba, Brazil, Mexico, India, China, Thailand, the Philippines, etc.). The most important developed cane producer is Australia, but the United States and Japan also derive parts of their production from sugar cane.

Sugar cane is a perennial crop, the first harvest (virgin cut) being due 15 – 18 months after planting, and another following every twelve months. (In equatorial and some other tropical countries two cuts per year are possible). The yield declines steadily after the virgin cut, such that a new plantation is preferred after about four years by large and technically well equipped rural enterprises. Small labor–intensive farms in developing countries have much longer growth cycles of between eight and fifteen years[57], see for instance Scott (1981) for Australia, Rose (1980) for Brazil, and Wolffram & Beckers (1989) for Mauritius.

Due to the perennial character of sugar cane, area harvested adjusts very slowly to price changes. This effect is often reinforced by the capacity requirements of sugar mills: In order to operate profitably, sugar mills need large supplies; a fact often blamed for the existence of monoculturally structured regions in cane producing countries (Rieder & Egger (1983)). Farms willing to switch crops may then undergo pressures from sugar mills not to do so, particularly in countries with a dubious record of civil liberties. However, long term contracts between farmers and mills do also contribute to productive rigidity.

Sugar beet producers of importance are the EEC[58], the Soviet Union, China, and the United States, where the latter two also grow large amounts of cane. Unlike cane, sugar beet is an annual crop, harvested seven or eight months after sowing. It is therefore often maintained (e. g. Hoff & Lawrence (1985)) that beet allows producers to adjust supply more rapidly in response to price changes than does cane. This is basically correct, but should not be overemphasized. For the harvest of sugar beet typically occurs in a very limited period of time and requires the use of expensive machines in order to efficiently pursue the business. Since these are not only costly but also crop–specific, we can expect their capacity to be quite influential with

---

[57]This considerable variation is not necessarily attributable to suboptimal behavior, for the decision of when to plant a new generation of sugar cane obviously depends on farm–specific capital–labor–input ratios, which can be fairly heterogenous already on a national basis. Even more so do relative prices differ when compared internationally.

[58]All EEC data in this thesis refer to the territory of the EEC–10 in 1981 (Belgium, Denmark, France, Great Britain, Greece, Ireland, Italy, Luxemburg, the Netherlands, West Germany), regardless of the Community's true membership at the time of data collection.

Table 2

<u>*Consumption of Sugar*</u>

	1967			1986		
Rank	Country	Consumpt. in 1000 mt	% of World Consumpt.	Country	Consumpt. in 1000 mt	% of World Consumpt.
1	EEC	10316	16.2	SU	13378	13.3
2	SU	9971	15.6	EEC	10762	10.7
3	USA	9662	15.2	IND	8749	8.7
4	BRA	2921	4.6	USA	7112	7.1
5	IND	2377	3.7	CHI	6700	6.7
6	JAP	2197	3.4	BRA	6572	6.5
7	CHI	1953	3.1	MEX	3534	3.5
8	MEX	1643	2.6	JAP	2767	2.8
9	CAN	1087	1.7	SAF	1383	1.4
10	ARG	843	1.3	PHI	1177	1.1

Source: ISO, Statistical Bulletin.

respect to output decisions. Hence, since changes in the structure of capital are slow, production decisions will be much stickier than the life cycle of the crop might initially suggest. Also, along the lines of my earlier argument, sugar factories depend crucially on sufficient supplies during the three–month–long campaign, such that institutional supports (contracts, quotas, price guarantees) are likely to suppress the price responsiveness of beet growers.

Turning to world consumption, we note an increase from 62 million tons in 1967 to more than 100 million tons in 1986. The level of world per caput consumption has remained static at about 20 kg, however; apparently as a result of two offsetting trends: A decline of per caput consumption in developed countries in response to a change in dietary patterns and as a consequence of substitution in favor of HFCS and artificial sweeteners was counteracted by rising per caput consumption in a couple of developing (particularly oil exporting) countries due to income effects (FAO (1985)). The relative importance of the ten top sugar consuming countries is displayed in Table 2.

It is easily seen that the largest producers of sugar are also the largest consumers of sugar. Typically, 75% – 80% of world sugar production is consumed in its country of origin. This implies that international trade is presently limited to about 20 to 25 million tons raw value.

For the sake of completeness, Table 3 ranks the largest net exporters of sugar. The market shares displayed therein may be deceptive for some countries, since they were computed as the ratio of *net* exports to total world exports (world *net* exports are zero by definition). Thus those exporters, which also imported some sugar in 1967 or 1986 actually enjoy a larger market share than shown in Table 3. This is of particular importance for the EEC, whose total exports in 1986 were 4.2 million tons, from which 1.7 million tons of imports[59] were subtracted. In 1967 the ten countries of the 1981–EEC added up to be a net *importer* of sugar.

The International Sugar Organisation (ISO) distinguishes two types of exports: Exports under special arrangements and (as the residual) exports to the free market[60]. The definition of "special arrangements" was agreed upon in Articles 34 to 39 and Articles 29 to 33 of the International Sugar Agreements (ISAs) of 1968 and 1977, respectively. The basic idea of these provisions is the exclusion of exports traded at a long term negotiated rather than the free world market price from the price stabili–

[59]These were mainly due to the Lomé Accord, see below.

[60]The same distinction holds for imports.

Table 3

Net Exports of Sugar

	1967			1977			1986		
Rank	Country	Net Exports in 1000 mt	% of World Exports	Country	Net Exports in 1000 mt	% of World Exports	Country	Net Exports in 1000 mt	% of World Exports
1	CUB	5683	28.1	CUB	6238	22.1	CUB	6703	24.8
2	AUS	1848	9.2	AUS	2965	10.5	AUS	2710	10.0
3	PHI	1003	5.0	PHI	2575	9.1	BRA	2554	9.4
4	BRA	1001	5.0	BRA	2487	8.8	EEC	2496	9.2
5	SAF	816	4.0	THA	1675	5.9	THA	2049	7.6
6	DOM	673	3.3	SAF	1325	4.7	SAF	874	3.2
7	TAI	570	2.8	DOM	1117	4.0	MAU	662	2.4
8	MAU	564	2.8	ARG	958	3.4	SWA	498	1.8
9	MEX	557	2.8	EEC	953	3.4	DOM	481	1.8
10	FIJ	336	1.7	MAU	674	2.4	FIJ	315	1.2

Source: ISO, Statistical Bulletin.

zing mechanisms of the ISA's. Arrangements defined to be "special" include

a) The Commonwealth Sugar Agreement (CSA)

This Agreement was established in 1951 with the objective of ensuring the supply of sugar in the United Kingdom and maintaining a stable price for the exporting members[61]. A key element of the CSA were the so–called "negotiated price quotas", which allowed the exporting nations to sell a specified quantity of sugar at a favorable price to the British Sugar Corporation Ltd[62]. Both prices and quotas were renegotiated every three years. A yearly total of roughly 1.7 million metric tons of negotiated price quotas was distributed for instance in the early 1970's and the prime beneficiary thereof were the West Indies with 737.000 mt or 42% of all quotas. Mauritius, Australia, and Fiji also enjoyed fairly large negotiated price quotas, which accounted for another 22%, 19%, and 8% of British quota–covered imports[63].

Theoretically, Great Britain could expect to obtain about two thirds of its imports at the price negotiated in the CSA. However, as Gemmil (1976) notes, in years such as 1974, when prices rose rapidly in the free market, the United Kingdom nevertheless had to pay far higher prices in order to secure its supply of sugar. After Great Britain joined the EEC in 1973 the CSA was not renewed and became inoperative with the end of 1974.

b) The ACP–Sugar Protocol

The Commonwealth Sugar Agreement was succeded by the "Protocol No. 3 on ACP Sugar" as a part of the Convention of Lomé[64], signed by the EEC and thirteen

---

[61]Exporting members were Australia, Fiji, British Honduras, India, Mauritius, the West Indies (Antigua, Barbados, Guyana, Jamaica, St. Kitts–Nevis–Anguilla, Trinidad and Tobago), Swaziland, East Africa (Kenia, Tansania, Uganda), and Southern Rhodesia. The latter was excluded from the Agreement after its unilateral declaration of independence in 1965.

[62]Developing exporters were paid a higher price than was Australia, the sole developed exporting member of the CSA. This higher price included a variable component which was designed to be related to the current world market price. An extensive description of the CSA is given in Ahlfeld (1970).

[63]An analysis of the income transfers due to the CSA can be found in Strangmann (1981).

[64]The Convention of Lomé also replaced the treaties of Jaunde and Arusta, by means of which the EEC had formerly aided developing countries.

African, Caribbean, and Pacific (ACP) states[65] in February 1975. Again, quotas (totalling 1.4 million tons raw value) were allotted to regulate imports of sugar to the EEC, and the price agreed upon was the EEC intervention price paid to domestic farmers[66]. The distribution of quotas, however, was drastically altered as opposed to the CSA: Mauritius, Swaziland, Fiji, and Belize (formerly British Honduras) were granted considerable increases in quotas, while Australia (as a developed nation) was excluded from the Agreement and the quota of the West Indies was cut by about 40% (Hagelberg & Harries (1976)). Presently, Mauritius enjoys by far the largest single quota (530.000 mt or 37% of the quota total), followed by Fiji (178.000 mt or 13%), Guyana (171.000 mt or 12%), Jamaica (129.000 mt or 9%), and Swaziland (127.000 or 9%). Further, some non–CSA states (Congo, Malawi, Madagascar, and Surinam) also received import allowances to the Common Market.

Unlike the CSA the ACP Sugar Protocol does not aim at ensuring supply in the EEC. In fact, in 1975 the EEC had already reached self–sufficiency on its sugar market and considerable excess production of sugar was perceivable within a short time (McGregor (1978)). Thus ACP sugar imports have in general merely been refined in the EEC and then re–exported to the free world market[67]. (This procedure has recently been critically examined by Wolffram & Beckers (1989)). The ACP Sugar Protocol thus largely proves to be an aid to developing countries aimed at achieving income transfers rather than a conventional trade contract[68].

c) The US Sugar Act

The US Sugar Act was initiated in 1934 and has experienced quite some stormy times since. Its basic idea is the allotment of quotas to particular foreign suppliers as

[65]Similar agreements with India, Belize, St. Kitts–Nevis–Anguilla, and Surinam are formally not a part of the Lomé Accord. However, since these are virtually identical in spirit, I will not mention them explicitly. ACP and Lomé will henceforth refer to these agreements, too.

[66]The CSA's negotiated price was fob, while the price granted to ACP–countries is cif. Due to high freight rates, this difference is not negligible.

[67]The refining mainly takes place in Great Britain, where large capacities are available. Proposals to dispense with the import of ACP–sugar have hence always encountered strong British resistance since this would endanger the British sugar–refining industry.

[68]Again, the income effects are examined by Strangmann (1981).

well as to domestic producers; both are paid the US domestic price for quota–covered sugar. Hence this amounts to a preferential treatment whenever the US domestic price exceeds the world market price[69].

Prior to the Cuban revolution of 1959, Cuba was the main beneficiary of the US Sugar Act, contributing 3 million tons to the annual US import total of 4.2 million tons. But in response to the nationalization of American property in Cuba the Eisenhower Administration tried to undermine Fidel Castro's regime economically by banning all imports of Cuban sugar in July 1959. The resulting shortfalls were made up for by increasing the quotas allocated to other foreign suppliers and by encouraging domestic producers.

Sugar covered by the US Sugar Act was as much as 9 million tons in the early 1970's. Out of that, about 55% was produced by domestic farmers (including Puerto Rican farmers) and about 45% was delivered by more than thirty foreign nations. Most important importers were those which had benefited from the embargo of Cuba: Expressed as a percentage of total import quotas (i. e. total of quota issued to foreign suppliers) the Philippines' share was 26%, the Dominican Republic's 13%, Mexico's 12%, Brazil's 11%, and the West Indies' and Australia's 4% each (Licht (1972)).

With the end of 1974 the US Sugar Act expired and no support program was in force during 1975 and 1976. But when sugar surplusses developed, Congress voted for a new sugar legislation, the Food and Agriculture Act of 1977, which provided price supports for domestic producers only. The absence of country–specific import quotas then enabled efficient sugar exporting nations such as Thailand to make inroads into traditional market shares at the expense of the Philippines, Peru, and smaller supplying countries (see the analysis by Zeller (1988)). However, in May 1982 a country–by–country quota system on all US sugar imports was reimposed which basically restituted the pre–1975 market shares and again granted preferential prices to foreign suppliers[70].

In the face of a steady decline of US sugar consumption and the rise of HFCS, this new United States Sugar Act aimed at preserving the level of domestic production – an aim which could only be accomplished by halving permissible imports. As the United States was still the second largest importer of sugar, this

[69]See Gemmill (1976) for more information on the economic mechanisms of the US Sugar Act.

[70]Note that the ISO lists imports under these newly introduced quotas as imports from the free world market, since the last codified definition of special arrangements was given in the ISA of 1977, when no US Sugar Act was in force. By analogy to the ISA of 1968, of course, US imports under the new US Sugar Act should not be labeled "free market imports".

constituted a major shock to the free world market (Hoff & Lawrence (1985)). A good review of the developments in the US sugar market can be found in Manegold & Sommer (1986).

d) Exports by Cuba to Socialist Countries

After the suspension of Cuban exports to the USA in 1959 the Soviet Union and other socialist countries replaced the United States as the main importer of Cuban Sugar. This was mainly a politically motivated decision, since the Soviet Union's imports now clearly exceeded her domestic needs: Despite an increase in stocks of 900,000 mt and an increase in annual consumption of almost two million tons, Soviet exports of sugar rose by 500,000 mt from 1959 to 1961 and – domestic production still expanding – by one million tons from 1959 to 1969. Hence with the beginning of the seventies the Soviet Union was a major exporter of sugar, although domestic production trailed consumption by at least one million tons. Later, Soviet planners took account of projected Cuban imports and Soviet production declined.

Little seems to be known about the sugar accord between Cuba and the Soviet Union. Basically, it appears to be a rouble–valued barter by which Cuba receives petroleum and machinery in exchange for sugar (Statistisches Bundesamt (1987)). Unlike the special arrangements mentioned earlier, there is no evidence of fixed quotas; rather both prices and quantities are readjusted from time to time following negotiations on a bilateral basis. Gemmill (1976), without giving further reference, reports a linkage between the contracted price and movements of world sugar prices; however, a comparison of published contracted prices (expressed, questionably enough, in US cts/lb) and world market prices (Statistisches Bundesamt (1987)) does not lend strong support for this assertion.

Apart from that, the nonconvertibility of the rouble might also have contributed to the International Sugar Organization's decision to exempt Cuban sugar exports to socialist countries from its definition of the free market. This, however, gave rise to considerable problems when countries with the status of an importing member of the ISA re–exported Cuban sugar to the free market. Due to this experience, the exact provisions differ slightly between the ISA of 1968 (see Articles 36 and 39) and the ISA of 1977 (see Articles 31 to 33), but the general idea was that exports of Cuba to Bulgaria, Czechoslovakia, East Germany, Hungary, Mongolia, Poland, Romania, the Soviet Union, Albania, China, North Korea, (North) Vietnam, and Yugoslavia were considered to be attributable to special arrangements and thus unrelated to the free market. □

Similar in spirit to the special arrangements mentioned above (but not counted as such by the ISO) are bilateral agreements and long–term contracts, whose pricing provisions protect both buyer and seller against extreme short–run price shifts. Information on these agreements is scarce and few authors care to at least acknowledge their existence. Those who do, do usually not attempt to evaluate their quantitative effects (see Hoff & Lawrence (1985)) and I will do likewise[71]. Instead, I merely point out that the ISO's definition of the free market probably overestimates its true size, even if this definition is modified to take the US Sugar Act of 1982 into account.

It should be apparent that for the purpose of this study exports to the free market[72] are of key interest, while total exports are not. Table 4 lists the most important *free market net exporters.* In addition to 1967 and 1986 I also give the ranking for 1977, which is representative for those years (1975 – 1981) in which the US Sugar Act was not in force, i. e. in which all US imports were truely free market imports.

We easily infer from Tables 3 and 4 that Cuba is far less important an exporter if reference is confined to the free market. Conversely, not only the EEC's relative importance, but also her net export performance increases in this case. This is mainly due to the re–export of ACP–sugar. Note that in 1986 the EEC is the largest exporter to the free world market while it has still been a net importer in 1967, the year in which the Community's Common Agricultural Policy (CAP) was initiated. Another remarkable development is the rise of Thailand, whose sugar exports were virtually nil prior to 1970, but which has become a major exporter since.

Some authors (Frohn (1984) and Zeller (1988), for instance) single out the so called ABCE–countries (Australia, Brazil, Cuba, the EEC) as the dominant exporting nations. Tables 3 and 4 show that this classification deserves modification: Thailand and the Philippines are undisputably of top importance, and it seems generally difficult to draw a clear–cut borderline between larger and smaller exporting nations.

In fact, the world sugar market is a fairly polypolistically structured market. Whether this can already be inferred from the selection of cumulative market shares

---

[71]Abbot (1990), however, presents some figures on long–term contracts between Australia and a selection of her trading partners.

[72]I modify the International Sugar Organisation's definition of "special arrangements" to also include the US Sugar Act of 1982. Thus "free market" will in the sequel refer to "free market" in the sense of the ISO *minus* any trade covered by the 1982 US Sugar Act.

Table 4

Net Exports of Sugar to the Free Market

Rank	1967			1977			1986		
	Country	Net Free Market Exp. in 1000 mt	% of World Free Mark. Exports	Country	Net Free Market Exp. in 1000 mt	% of World Free Mark. Exports	Country	Net Free Market Exp. in 1000 mt	% of World Free Mark. Exports
1	CUB	1752	19.3	AUS	2965	14.3	EEC	3870	23.8
2	AUS	1317	14.5	PHI	2575	12.4	AUS	2612	16.0
3	SU	1052	11.6	BRA	2487	12.0	BRA	2350	14.4
4	SAF	783	8.6	EEC	2362	11.4	THA	2027	12.4
5	BRA	552	6.1	THA	1675	8.1	CUB	1472	9.0
6	TAI	498	5.5	CUB	1483	7.1	SAF	839	5.2
7	CZE	426	4.7	SAF	1325	6.4	SWA	354	2.2
8	POL	380	4.2	DOM	1117	5.4	CZE	350	2.1
9	CHI	338	3.7	ARG	958	4.6	GDR	345	2.1
10	ROU	209	2.3	TAI	595	2.9	GUA	253	1.6

Source: ISO, Statistical Bulletin.

displayed in Table 5 is perhaps a matter of personal taste: While it is obvious that no single country enjoys excessive market power, it might be objected that there is a potential for the formation of cartels, since a coalition of three could control about 40% of the market and two more would increase this share to about 60%. But it should be borne in mind that even cartels are not likely to operate successfully: As the examples of Thailand and the EEC teach, formerly negligible sugar exporters might take advantage of price differentials and rapidly expand their production.

Table 5

Cumulative Market Shares for Sugar Exporters

(in percent)

	1967		1977		1986	
	total net exports	free market net exports	total net exports	free market net exports	total net exports	free market net exports
CMS(1)	28.1	19.3	22.1	14.3	24.8	23.8
CMS(2)	37.3	33.8	32.6	26.7	34.8	39.8
CMS(3)	43.3	45.4	41.7	38.7	44.2	54.2
CMS(5)	51.3	60.1	56.4	58.2	61.0	75.6
CMS(10)	64.7	80.5	74.3	84.6	71.4	88.8

<u>Note:</u> CMS(i) denotes the cumulative market share of the top i exporting nations, i = 1, 2, 3, 5, 10.

It might, however, be inadequate to confine our attention to country-specific market shares. For while it is true that production and trade of sugar underlies governmental controls in almost all countries[73], the actual handling of sugar is often

[73]Rieder & Egger (1983) cite as exceptions Belize and the Dominican Republic, where large enterprises (Tate & Lyle, Gulf & Western, respectively) are still quite influential in the sugar economy.

Table 6

Net Imports of Sugar from the Free Market

Rank	1967			1977			1986		
	Country	Net Free Market Imp. in 1000 mt	% of World Free Mark. Imports	Country	Net Free Market Imp. in 1000 mt	% of World Free Mark. Imports	Country	Net Free Market Imp. in 1000 mt	% of World Free Mark. Imports
1	JAP	1667	19.5	USA	5271	27.0	JAP	1818	10.1
2	CAN	917	10.7	JAP	2785	14.2	CAN	1183	6.6
3	EEC	353	4.1	CHI	1276	6.5	SU	1113	6.2
4	IRQ	351	4.1	SU	1081	5.5	IND	1013	5.6
5	MOR	342	4.0	CAN	973	5.0	PAK	752	4.2
6	ALG	318	3.7	IDS	545	2.8	EGY	744	4.1
7	MAL	276	3.2	ALG	492	2.5	KOR	687	3.8
8	USA	269	3.1	IRQ	479	2.4	IRN	652	3.6
9	SWA	255	3.0	MAL	396	2.0	CHI	591	3.3
10	CEY	249	2.9	NIG	382	2.0	NIG	578	3.2

Source: ISO, Statistical Bulletin.

left to private enterprises. Most important of these are the French–owned "Sucres et Denrées" and the British "Tate & Lyle" with an annual transshipment of approximately three million tons of sugar each. Next come the American company "Phillip Brothers" (2 million tons) and two more British houses, "Ed. F. Man" (1.5 million tons), and "C. Czarnikow" (0.8 million tons). Their volume of trade is quite impressive if compared with the export performance of the top exporting nations, and it is conceivable that they exert some sort of market power despite the presence of institutional regulations. Yet inasmuch as this is the case, they also reduce the market power of sugar–trading nations such that the market may actually become more, rather than less, competitive thanks to the existence of private trading companies[74].

Imports of sugar are again to a large extent determined by special arrangements and consequently the Soviet Union, the USA, and the EEC are among the top importing nations. Of more interest is a ranking of imports from the free market only, where Japan, Canada, and – since the mid–seventies – the Soviet Union turn out to be the front runners (Table 6). In years in which no US Sugar Act was in force, the USA was by far the largest importer, for instance in 1977. We also note that heavily populated states like China and India (but also Pakistan and Egypt) sometimes have massive import requirements, presumably due to insufficient domestic harvests. Apart from these countries all other importers are characterized by fairly small market shares and their exact ranking is of little interest.

4.4 Prices

Price quotations for the residual sugar market, i. e. the world market after deduction of special arrangements and bilateral contracts, are recorded on a daily basis at three commodity exchanges in New York, London, and Paris. The most important of these is the New York Coffee and Sugar Exchange, where the price of contract No. 11 (raw sugar in bulk, fob Caribbean ports and stated in US cts/lb) is widely regarded as the representative price. Trade in London is also in terms of raw sugar, while Paris is a white sugar exchange.

For the purpose of the International Sugar Organization another important price has been defined as the "ISA Daily Price", a weighted average of the New York contract No. 11 price and the London daily price, fob Caribbean ports. Manegold &

[74]The power of transnational corporations in the non–fuel primary commodity industries is analysed in detail by Girvan (1987).

Sommer (1986) carried out a comparison of different world sugar prices and found all spot prices to be highly intercorrelated, with the price for white sugar being slightly higher than for raw (as one would expect). There is also some trade in futures (these exist for up to 18 months ahead), and Manegold & Sommer's presentation suggests that New York futures prices are not exposed to factors causing significant deviations from the spot price. This is less clear for futures prices in London and Paris, but Manegold & Sommer seem unable to explain why European futures might behave differently.

Following Manegold & Sommer's analysis it is tempting to speak of "the" world market price so long as any of the above spot prices is being referred to. For convenience, all actual expect). There is also some trade in futures (these exist for up to 18 months ahead), and Manegold & Sommer's presentation suggests that New York futures prices are not exposed to factors causing significant deviations from the spot price. This is less clear for futures prices in London and Paris, but Manegold & Sommer seem unable to explain why European futures might behave differently.

Real World Market Prices for Sugar and Oil

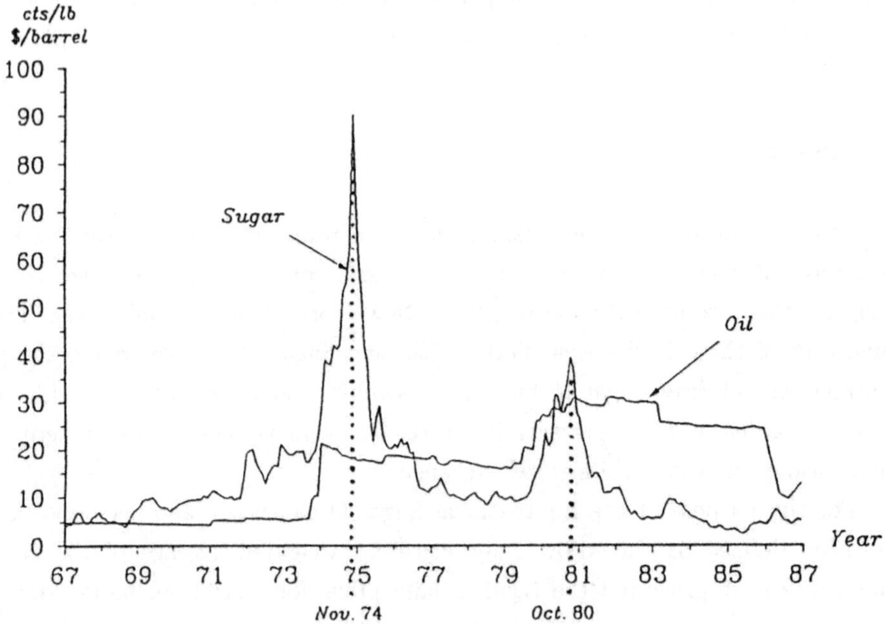

Figure 2

Following Manegold & Sommer's analysis it is tempting to speak of "the" world market price so long as any of the above spot prices is being referred to. For convenience, all actual sugar prices in this study are taken from the International Monetary Fund's "International Financial Statistics", where the IMF published monthly averages of the New York contract No. 11 price until 1975 and the ISA Daily Price thereafter[75]. Unless otherwise specified, all Dollar–valued prices have been deflated by dividing through US Consumer Price Index (1980=100), also extracted from the above source.

The volatility of sugar prices is stunning: Taking monthly values from 1967 to 1986 the real price fluctuates between a maximum of 90.11 cts/lb in November 1974 and a minimum of 2.41 cts/lb in June 1985. Two major price peaks occurred during these years, the first in November 1974, the second in October 1980. They almost coincided with the oil price shocks, but unlike oil prices sugar prices fell as quickly as they had risen. Moreover, the 1974 sugar price boom began in December 1971 (sugar prices more than doubled from November 1971 to February 1972) and (nominal) prices were already at a then–time record high of 9.81 cts/lb in July 1973, shortly before the Yom–Kippur War shook the Middle East and initiated OPEC's first oil embargo. (Figure 2 depicts real monthly prices for sugar and crude petroleum[76]).

In Figure 3 (nominal sugar prices from 1955 to 1985) we even find four price peaks and each of these seems to coincide with times of major political tensions: In 1956 the war in the Middle East (invasion of the Suez Canal) and the Hungarian uprising, in 1962/63 the Cuba Crisis and the assassination of President Kennedy, and finally the oil price shocks of the seventies. This has led some authors (for instance Rieder & Egger (1983)) to interpret a price boom as a response to political instability. Yet the appropriateness of this supposition remains obscure, since sugar prices were unimpressed by the events of 1959 (Cuban Revolution and Chrustchev's Berlin Ultimatum), 1967 (War of Six Days), or 1968 (assassinations of Robert Kennedy and Martin Luther King, Tet Offensive in Vietnam, revolutionary atmosphere in Paris). Further, not only did the 1972 – 1974 price surge start a long time before the first oil embargo, but also is the 1962/63 price boom not particularly well explained by political tensions, since its main upswing occured *after* the Cuba Crisis, while Mr Kennedy's assassination coincided with the starting point of the preceding downswing. Thus neither oil prices nor political turmoils seem able to satisfactorily

[75]Prices from these two sources are so very similar that switching the data basis should not affect the quality of the time series.

[76]Prices for Saudi Arabian light crude petroleum fob Ras Tanura, deflated by the US Consumer Price Index. Data sources are the IMF's *International Financial Statistics.*

Figure 3

World Sugar Prices, 1955 – 1985

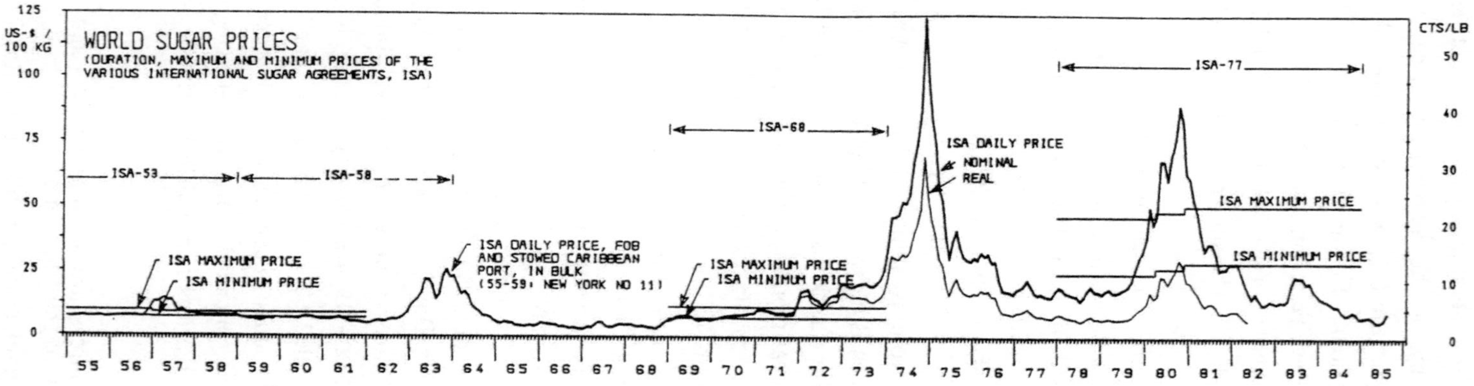

Source: Manegold & Sommer (1986)[77]

[77]Real prices have been computed by dividing through the United Nations' Index of Export Unit Values of Manufactures (1970=100), thus real prices in Figure 3 differ considerably from real prices in Figure 2. Since June 1982 the index is no longer available.

explain world sugar price booms. Rather, factors immanent to the market should be taken into account.

There have been various attempts to reduce the fluctuations of world sugar prices, the earliest dating back as far as 1864. Some of them (the Brussels Sugar Convention of 1902 or the London Sugar Agreement of 1937) have operated fairly well, others have failed to achieve their objectives. An appraisal of internationally coordinated efforts to stabilize the world sugar market is provided by Gordon–Ashworth (1984).

Past World War II four International Sugar Agreements with market stabilization provisions have been in force: The 1953 and the 1958 ISA operated consecutively during the period from 1954 to 1961[78], the 1968 Agreement covered the years 1969 to 1973, and the 1977 ISA was designed for 1978 to 1982 and later extended until 1984. All of them sought to maintain prices between predetermined levels by means of export quotas and stock provisions. None of them succeeded to do so, though: Even the 1977 ISA with its broadened range of admissible prices resulted in an embarrassing failure, cf. Figure 3.

4.5 The Data

The International Sugar Agreement of 1968 established an administrative body, the International Sugar Organisation, in order to monitor the performance of the Agreement (Article 3 of the 1968 ISA). Member countries were encouraged to transmit all relevant statistics on production, consumption, exports, imports, and stocks to the ISO. But also quite a few non–member–countries (the most prominent example is the EEC) were cooperative enough to provide information on their sugar economy. All available data were published on a monthly basis by the Statistics Division of the ISO in its "Statistical Bulletin".

For the purposes of this study the high volatility of sugar prices makes it appear appropriate to work with data of such a low periodicity. (By the same reasoning other authors have done likewise, cf. Wymer (1975) and Hagelberg (1978)). I fixed the time from 1967 to 1986 as the period of investigation; a total of twenty years and 240 observations. The period thus includes the International Sugar Agreements of 1968 and 1977 as well as three subperiods without market regulations on behalf of the

[78]The ISA of 1958 was initially intended to last until 1963. However, the US refusal to import Cuban sugar disarrayed a market already plagued by latent excess supplies, such that quota renegotiations in 1961 failed to reach an agreement and the ISA became inoperative in 1962.

ISO[79]. As subperiods with and without market control keep changing, it is less likely that a long–term parameter shift in the market is falsely interpreted as an effect of the International Sugar Agreements.

Apart from that, confining my attention to the period from 1967 to 1986 was motivated by the fact that 1967 marked the starting point of the EEC's Common Agricultural Policy, (i. e. aggregating the EEC's member countries would have been inappropriate prior to 1967) and by the accession of Portugal and Spain[80] to the EEC in 1986; two countries with a previously poor record of sugar statistics[81].

The choice of countries to be included in this study was mainly determined by weighing two factors, namely the availability of monthly data and the relative importance of these countries for the world sugar market. Seventeen exporting countries (Argentina (ARG), Australia (AUS), Brazil (BRA), Colombia (COL), Cuba (CUB), the Dominican Republic (DOM), the EEC, Fiji (FIJ), Guyana (GUY), India (IND), Mauritius (MAU), Mexico (MEX), the Philippines (PHI), South Africa (SAF), Swaziland (SWA), Taiwan (TAI), and Thailand (THA)) as well as four importing nations (Canada (CAN), Japan (JAP), the Soviet Union (SU), and the United States (USA)) were eventually selected[82]. All of these have a neat record of their exports and imports and in the rare cases where single observations are missing, these have been replaced by plausible estimates[83].

With the exception of Cuba and the Soviet Union all other countries also provide monthly data on production, consumption, and stocks. However, sometimes these collections are not as complete as are the export and import data and then

---

[79]Besides the Agreements of 1968 and 1977, ISA's have been negotiated in 1973 and 1984. These latter Agreements had no economic clauses; their main objective was the maintenance of the administrative apparatus of the ISO. I will sometimes write that no Sugar Agreement was in force at a certain time. This is to be understood in the sense that no ISA with economic provisions was in force at that time.

[80]Portugal and Spain joined the Community in 1986, but EEC sugar data for this year (as published by the ISO) still exclude the Iberian countries.

[81]Of course, the EEC's territorial definition changed considerably between 1967 and 1985: The United Kingdom, Ireland and Denmark joined the Community in 1973, and 1981 witnessed Greece do likewise. However, as opposed to Portugal and Spain, sufficient data for these countries prior to their accession are available, and adding them to the data for the EEC in its respective state of membership allows the construction of a data set consistent for the EEC–10.

[82]Unfortunately, China could not be included in this study, the main reason being the lack of monthly data on exports and imports.

[83]If no other extraneous information was available, data of a higher periodicity were uniformly split into monthly data.

information is limited to bimonthly, quarterly or even annual data for certain subperiods. In order to obtain monthly estimates for the missing observations I chose the following method, applicable to both production and consumption data (but not for stocks!): For each country, all available monthly figures were regressed on monthly dummies and these were used to split the data of higher– than–monthly periodicity into monthly values.

It is not possible to treat stock data accordingly, since these do not only follow a seasonal pattern, but may also depend on market regulating mechanisms established by the ISAs (quotas, maximum and minimum stock provisions, etc.). But given a complete collection of data on production, consumption, and net exports, stock levels are easily reconstructed by virtue of the stock identity, if disappearance is assumed to be zero.

In the cases of Cuba and the Soviet Union *all* monthly values for production, consumption, and stocks are missing. Cuba provides quarterly values instead, the Soviet Union confines herself to annual data. As these two countries are of key importance for the world sugar market, it deemed necessary to nevertheless include them in this study, and a procedure for deriving monthly estimates was called for. The approach chosen is heuristic and runs as follows:

Quarterly shares of Cuban and neighboring Dominican production were compared and their coefficient of correlation was found to be quite high (0.87). Thus monthly weights for Dominican production were used to split Cuban quarterly into monthly data. Consumption data could not be treated analogously, since there was no significant correlation for the quarterly weights. But the Cuban weights were all very close to 0.25, hence I simply divided the quarterly figures by three in order to obtain estimates of monthly sugar consumption. By virtue of the stock identity I could then compute approximate monthly stock levels.

Because of the annuity of production and consumption data, things were more difficult for the Soviet Union. Moreover, no geographically comparable region was at hand which suggests itself as much for the reconstruction of monthly data as does the Dominican Republic for Cuba. The best I could think of was to compute the monthly weights of production in the EEC and use these to disaggregate Soviet production data.

At first this approach appears rather adventurous, even though apparently more than 90% of Soviet sugar beet is grown in regions of continental climate (Licht (1981)). But apart from what is generally characteristic of northern hemisphere countries, it would certainly go too far to assume that weather conditions in the EEC allow conclusions to be drawn on how the weather is like in the Soviet Union. On the other hand, the timing of the harvest of sugar beet is much more crop– than wheather–specific. To illustrate this point, let us compare the monthly weights for production of sugar in Canada[84] with the analogous values for the EEC. Although there can be no doubt that wheather conditions are virtually independent in these countries, the weights display a coefficient of correlation of 0.96. I took that as a justification for the use of European weights in the disaggregation of Soviet production data.

Consumption data were obtained by dividing the annual values by twelve. Stock data would then follow by the stock identity, but fortunately they are not needed for the purposes pursued in this study.

By these methods I obtained a sufficient set of basic data for the twenty–one countries in question. I undertook some further manipulations, though:

Disappearance for instance, the residual of the stock identity, was often zero from January to November, but nonzero in December. I then changed stock data such that disappearance is distributed evenly throughout the year. It also occured that there was a large disappearance in one year and precisely the same disappearance with the opposite sign in a later period. In this case stock levels were altered such that these diappearances cancelled.

A disappearance of zero usually indicates that one out of the four accounts production, consumption, net exports, and stocks has been computed rather than independently verified. As Licht (1984) and Ahlfeld (1987) note, stocks or consumption are most likely to be computed, since their direct measurement is more difficult than the recording of production or net exports. As far as the data published by the ISO are concerned, it appears that at least partly it is consumption that has been computed as the residual of the stock identity: Some countries display consumption data with a counterintuitively high degree of fluctuation[85]. Since one would expect the population to consume rather smoothly, a high volatility of consumption is likely to indicate statistical inaccuracies. I have therefore decided to smooth all consumption data by working with three–months moving averages. This procedure should not greatly affect data which have been correctly reported (since they should already be fairly smooth), but it might substantially improve others. For

---

[84]Canada, the EEC, and the Soviet Union are the only nations in this study which derive their sugar (almost) exclusively from beet.

[85]This is most apparent in the case of Canada, where a (small) *negative* value is reported for consumption in November 1977. This is not a typographical error on the part of the ISO, since the negative value precisely fulfills the stock identity. Besides, monthly values add up to the published amount of annual consumption.

the purpose of this study, I will always treat the smoothed or estimated data as if they were the original ones.

After these manipulations, I constructed data for an aggregate "rest of the world" (ROW): Net exports are easily determined by the requirement that world net exports be zero each month[86]. Data for consumption and production were derived as follows: The ISO publishes *annual* consumption and production data for the regions Europe, North America, Central America, South America, Asia, Africa, and Oceania. For each region, I estimated *monthly* weights from the respective countries under explicit consideration in this study. After subtracting their annual data from the regional accounts, I used these weights to split the remaining annual figures into monthly estimates. Stock data followed by the stock identity.

All available data (both in levels and in logarithms) were finally seasonally adjusted by regressing them on twelve monthly dummies[87]. Unless explicitly stated otherwise, production, net exports, consumption, and stocks will in the sequel always refer to the residuals of these regressions. Price data, however, do not display a seasonal pattern, hence they were left unaltered.

Notation is simple: PRO denotes production, CON consumption, NEX net exports (net imports, if negative), and STO denotes stocks. Composite abbreviations refer to country–specific data, i. e. ARGSTO denotes Argentinian stocks, ROWNEX and WORPRO are net exports of the rest of the world or world production, respectively. See the list of abbreviations. If a variable is used in natural logarithms, this is indicated by a prefix LN, i. e. LNBRACON is the natural logarithm of Brazilian consumption. Lags, if any, are given in parenthesis, for instance LNAUSSTO(–i) denotes the natural logarithm of Australian stocks lagged i periods. The use of annual data will explicitly be stated in the text; it does not seem worthwhile to make notation distinguish between different periodicities, since only once will we make use of annual, rather than monthly data.

The ISO does not publish data for crop areas. Instead, these have been extracted from the FAO's Production Yearbooks. For sugar *cane* the distinction between "area harvested" and "area under cultivation" is quite important; only the former is of

---

[86]This, of course, presupposes that exports by one country are reported as imports by another country within the same month, which, given delay caused by shipment, is rather unlikely. The inaccuracy may be small, however, since such errors occur in every month and thus partly cancel.

[87]For Cuban and Soviet data this procedure results in the fact that monthly data on production and consumption which have just been constructed as described above are again modified. One might alternatively have deseasoned the original quarterly data and split them evenly into estimates for seasonally adjusted monthly values. Which of these methods is superior I do not know.

interest for production functions. The FAO generally publishes "area harvested", yet unfortunately some (fairly rare) errors occur and the published values actually refer to "area under cultivation". In comparison with data published in other sources (statistics provided by F. O. Licht or the Statistisches Bundesamt) some of these mistakes could be detected and were tacitly corrected. Crop areas for Taiwan have exclusively been taken from *Länderberichte* by the Statistisches Bundesamt, since the FAO stopped to publish statistics for Taiwan after its exclusion from the United Nations in 1971.

Alongside with areas, the FAO reports annual production data. These are virtually identical with the respective ISO–values for the years from 1975 to 1986, but for earlier years the two sources are not necessarily fully compatible. In the estimation of production functions I will therefore regress the FAO production data on the FAO acreages, since it seems desirable to use data from the same data source within one regression.

To sum up, the world sugar market commends itself for empirical work out of the following reasons: Sugar is a remarkably homogenous and well defined commodity. The few substitutes that exist have a comparably small volume of trade which does allow for a partial equilibrium approach. The market is fairly competitive; there are neither exporting nor importing countries which exert excessive market power. Sugar prices are extremely volatile[88] and hence the most natural target for price stabilization efforts. Periods with and without market regulating mechanisms alternate several times. The market has been consistently monitored by the ISO; data published are, though less than perfect, sufficient for the construction of a reasonable data set to be used in regression analysis.

---

[88]The sugar price is in fact the most volatile primary commodity world market price. See Hwa (1979) and Newbery & Stiglitz (1981).

Chapter 5: Quantitative Analysis of the World Sugar Market

The main objective of this chapter is the specification and estimation of the three relationships of immediate economic interest in the world sugar economy, namely the functions describing systematic excess production, stock demand, and price determination (cf. the introduction to Chapter 3). Sections 5.5 to 5.8 are devoted to this purpose. However, some preliminary investigations are indispensible. These include

a) obtaining an estimate for the unobservable *systematic* component of sugar production

and

b) testing the key assumption of completely world market price inelastic systematic excess production.

Sections 5.3 and 5.4 will deal with these issues.

The methodology employed in this chapter will predominantly be time series econometrics. Readers unfamiliar with the theory of *stationary* time series may consult books such as Box & Jenkins (1970), Fuller (1976), or Schlittgen & Streitberg (1989). On the field of *nonstationary* processes, particularly on processes with a unit root, these references also provide some help but do not cover the latest developments, for research has been very intense in recent years (and is still ongoing). As *testing* for unit roots and for cointegration will play a considerable role in the following analysis, I start this chapter with a brief discussion thereof (Section 5.1 and 5.2). Good surveys of the main issues can be found in Perron (1988) and Park & Phillips (1988, 1989). Following the widely accepted terminology in the literature I will speak of an integrated process of order k (an I(k)–process), if the time series of the k–th differences is a stationary, invertible process (an I(0)–process).

5.1 Testing for Unit Roots

The importance of unit root processes in economics is widely recognized ever since Hall (1978) presented both theoretical and empirical evidence for their relevance in consumption data[89]. Constructing tests for unit roots, however, proved to be a difficult issue since the distribution of conventional test statistics is (even asymptotically) non–standard. The pioneering work by Fuller (1976) and Dickey & Fuller (1981) provided critical values for the case of autoregressive processes driven by Gaussian i.i.d. innovations. Tests for more general models (including, for instance, MA–representations) have in the sequel been constructed by Said & Dickey (1984) and Phillips (1987); extensions of the Phillips–tests are due to Phillips & Perron (1988) and Perron (1988). Unlike the original Dickey–Fuller tests, these latter tests are only asymptotically valid; their finite sample distributions appear intractable.

A Monte Carlo investigation by Schwert (1989) concludes for both the Said–Dickey and the Phillips–Perron tests that convergence to the limiting distribution can be very slow if the time series is generated by an autoregressive integrated moving average (ARIMA) process with a strong *negative* autocorrelation of the error term. Schwert illustrates this with an ARIMA(0,1,1) of the form $y_t = y_{t-1} + \epsilon_t - \Theta\, \epsilon_{t-1}$. If the MA–parameter Θ is large and positive ($\Theta = 0.5$ or $\Theta = 0.8$), then simulations show disastrous results for the level of the Phillips–Perron tests even if the sample size is as large as 1000. The Said–Dickey tests perform fairly well if long autoregressive approximations are used (fitting fifteen lags for 250 observations, for instance); fewer lags again result in severe distortions in the level of the tests for large MA–parameters ($\Theta = 0.8$). In the case of negative MA–parameters, however, both types of tests are relatively close to their levels: The Said–Dickey tests appear to be slightly better than the (possibly mildly conservative) Phillips–Perron–tests.

Thus so long as we may legitimately consider a time series to be the realization of an ARIMA process, Schwert's study unambiguously suggests the use of the Said–Dickey procedure. However, preliminary investigations I undertook on the sugar market data indicated some degree of heteroskedasticity particularly in the estimated error terms of price and stock data. This would constitute a violation of the ARIMA–assumption which is essential to the Said–Dickey tests. The Phillips–Perron tests, on the other hand, allow for a much more general class of error processes including mildly heteroskedastic ones, such that they seem more appropriate for this particular set of data. I have therefore decided to use the Phillips–Perron tests in

---

[89]For a cautiously dissenting voice see Sims (1988), see also Sims et al. (1990).

testing for a unit root unless there is evidence for a strongly negative first–order autocorrelation in the error terms. If I had reason to suppose that this might be the case, I fitted an MA(1) process for the errors. The estimated MA–parameter usually turned out to be very small and in fact *never* exceeded 0.2. Thus I inferred from Schwert's study that the Phillips–Perron tests should be approximately accurate.

Now assume that a given time series with T observations is suspected to be I(1). We can write the process in the representation

$$y_t = \alpha\, y_{t-1} + u_t,$$

where u_t is a invertible, zero–mean error process[90]. We have $\alpha = 1$ under the null hypothesis[91]. Three different test statistics are then usually advocated: The conventional F– and t–statistics and a test relying on the value of T (a–1) (where a is the estimate of α)[92]. Said & Dickey (1984) work directly with these statistics. Phillips & Perron (1988), on the other hand, use transformations thereof in order to cope with the effects of the residual processes and show that the distributions of the transformed statistics converge to the distributions tabulated by Fuller (1976) and Dickey & Fuller (1981).

Of key importance in these transformations is a consistent estimate of the variance of the cumulated error process. This is obtained using spectral density estimators and a lag window with a truncation parameter l. Perron (1988) points out that the specific choice of window (I use a Parzen window) may be of less importance than the choice of l. In all of my tests I have therefore checked the sensitivity of the results to various values of l ranging from $l = 1$ to $l = 100$. I have generally found values of l between 3 and 10 to induce fairly stable test statistics, while more extreme values of l behave increasingly unreliable[93]. Hence in the tables I will give the test statistics of the Phillips–Perron tests for $l = 3$, $l = 5$, and $l = 10$.

---

[90]Such a representation is possible for any I(1) process. For instance, denote an arbitrary ARIMA(p,1,q) by $(1-L)\,A(L)\,y_t = B(L)\,\epsilon_t$. Then we can write this in the desired form as $y_t - y_{t-1} = B(L)/A(L)\,\epsilon_t =: u_t$, where α is set equal to one. Of course, any I(0) process admits the same representation. For if an ARMA(p,q) is given by $A(L)\,y_t = B(L)\,\epsilon_t$, then just set $\alpha = 0$ and write $y_t = B(L)/A(L)\,\epsilon_t =: u_t$.

[91]Actually, the null is $|\alpha| = 1$. For the sake of simplicity, I do not explicitly consider the case of $\alpha = -1$.

[92]Under the null a converges with rate T, not with rate $\sqrt{T}$, to its probability limit. See Fuller (1976).

[93]Schwert (1989), without further justification, uses two values of l: $l_4 := \text{int}\{4(T/100)^{1/4}\}$ and $l_{12} := \text{int}\{12(T/100)^{1/4}\}$. In our analysis, where we have $T = 240$ for most of the time series, this would amount to $l_4 = 4$ and $l_{12} = 14$.

For a single null hypothesis we thus get nine different (but highly correlated) test statistics. I will reject the null if at least one of them is significant at its 5% level. While there is no doubt that this (slightly) distorts the level of the test, my justification is that a somewhat increased true level effectively counteracts the (following Schwert (1989)) mildly conservative nature of the Phillips–Perron tests.

Unit root tests always require that a certain alternative be specified. Of particular importance is the question of whether or not the alternative presupposes the (stationary) time series to fluctuate around a linear deterministic trend. Tests whose alternatives include a trend have generally lower power than have their trend–free counterparts. Since it is highly desirable to be able to distinguish between random walks and trend stationary time series, Perron (1988), in his critique of a testing strategy advanced by Dickey, Bell & Miller (1986), recommends the following approach to testing the unit root hypothesis:

Specify the alternative with a trend and compute the appropriate transformed test statistics for the F–test, the t–test, and the coefficient test T(a–1), denoted by $Z_1(F)$, $Z_1(t)$, and $Z_1(a)$, respectively. If rejection (at the 5% level, say) is possible, then there is no need to go further. If the null cannot be rejected, this may be attributable to the poor power properties of these statistics compared to those in an alternative without trend. Thus another transformed F–statistic, $Z_2(F)$, is used to test the null that the process – while still being I(1) – does neither include a drift (i. e. a non–zero constant term) nor a linear trend[94]. In case this null cannot be rejected either, analogous unit root tests are carried through against (stationary) alternatives which do not include a trend term and the corresponding test statistics will be denoted $Z_3(F)$, $Z_3(t)$ and $Z_3(a)$.

In a recent paper, Perron (1989) argues that many macroeconomic time series formerly believed to be random walks might rather be stationary around a linear trend with a one–time change in the level or the slope of the trend function. He identifies the Great Crash of 1929 or the 1973 oil price shock as potential causes for such a structural change and recommends the following testing strategy:

Regress the time series under investigation on a constant, a linear trend, and one or two dummies reflecting the structural change. (Perron defines his Model A to include a dummy for the constant, Model B to include a dummy for the slope of the trend term, and Model C to combine both approaches). The residuals of this so–called "detrending regression" are then tested under the null of being I(1). The test statistics are again transformations of the conventional t–statistic or of a, the

---

[94]Transformed t–tests would also be possible, but the test statistics would not be invariant with respect to the initial observation in finite samples.

regression estimate of the first order autoregressive parameter α. They will be denoted $Z_i(t)$ and $Z_i(a)$, respectively, where i = A, B, C indicates the choice of model in the detrending regression. Perron derives the asymptotic distribution of these statistics; the critical values turn out to depend on the relative time of the structural shift in the sample and on the choice of Model A, B, or C.

While the matter has – to my kowledge – not yet been studied, it is suggestive to suspect slow convergence of Perron's (1989) test statistics in the presence of high first order MA–parameters (recall Schwert's (1989) paper). Therefore, when applying this test I have always checked the estimated errors for positive MA–parameters, but in fact I never encountered any larger than 0.1.

5.2 Testing for Cointegration

A linear combination of (nonstationary) I(1)–variables may well be stationary; the variables are then called "cointegrated" and the vector of coefficients defining the stationary linear combination is referred to as the "cointegrating vector". (This vector need, however, not be unique). The concept of cointegration was advanced by Granger (1981) and has, as Engle & Granger (1987) point out, an important equilibrium interpretation since it admits a model representation which is closely related to the so–called error correction models.

Tests for cointegration are generally performed under the null of no cointegration for a given set of time series[95]. Most tests are based on the results of what is labelled the "cointegrating regression", a simple static OLS regression of one of thc nonstationary variables on the others. Tests for cointegration very much resemble unit root tests; their basic idea is simply a unit root test applied to the error process of the cointegrating regression[96]. The difference results from the fact that the true disturbances are not available and the estimated residuals must be used in their place. Thus, since OLS picks residuals such that their sum of squares is minimized, the null would too often be rejected if the critical values of the unit root tests were applied. Rather, in order to avoid liberal test procedures, tests for cointegration must use a different set of critical values.

[95]A null of cointegration is far less advantageous, cf. Phillips & Ouliaris (1988a).

[96]As is easily seen, cointegration requires that the error process of the cointegrating regression be stationary.

Engle & Granger (1987) suggest a total of seven tests for cointegration and use simulations to compute critical values for a bivariate system of time series with 100 observations. Their power investigation concludes that if the true system is first order autoregressive, then a Durbin–Watson–based test and a Dickey–Fuller–type test procedure (shorthand: DF–test) work best, while for higher order systems the Augmented Dickey–Fuller test (ADF) should be used. A subsequent study by Engle & Yoo (1987) provides critical values for the DF– and ADF–tests for various numbers of variables and observations. It argues that the DF–test is likely to be conservative in higher order systems with a small number of observations, but that the difference between the DF– and the ADF–test becomes negligible in large samples. The ADF–test, on the other hand, may not be fully efficient unless the true lag structure of the errors is known. Engle & Yoo (1987) strongly criticize the Durbin–Watson– based test, since it requires different critical values for different error processes even with as much as 200 observations.

It was left to Phillips & Ouliaris (1988a) to establish the asymptotic distribution theory for the ADF–test. They also examine the limiting distribution of the unit root tests $Z_3(t)$ and $Z_3(a)$ if applied to the residuals of a cointegrating regression. (The test statistics of these tests are precisely the same as those of $Z_3(t)$ and $Z_3(a)$, but the critical values are not. To indicate the difference, I will drop the subscript, whenever $Z_3(t)$ and $Z_3(a)$ are used as tests for cointegration, i. e. then I will refer to them as $Z(t)$ and $Z(a)$, respectively). Phillips & Ouliaris (1988a) show ADF and $Z(t)$ to be asymptotically equivalent but to have slower rates of convergence than $Z(a)$ under the alternative of cointegration. Thus they infer that $Z(a)$ should have superior power properties in large samples and provide extensive tables of critical values for both the $Z(t)$ and the $Z(a)$ test.

Some completely different approaches to testing the null of no cointegration exist. I mention a method derived by Johansen (1988), who estimates cointegrating vectors using maximum likelihood techniques and constructs likelihood ratio tests. His procedure is of limited use for our purposes, however, since it relies on the assumption of Gaussian disturbances – a prerequisite which is, as we will see later, hardly ever met on the world sugar market. Further, Phillips & Ouliaris (1988b) advance tests based on estimates of the innovations' spectral density matrix at zero frequency. A necessary condition for cointegration is that this matrix be singular. The number of its latent roots equal to zero is in fact the number of linearly independent cointegrating vectors and the associated latent vectors are the cointegrating vectors themselves.

Using these theoretical results, Phillips & Ouliaris (1988b) construct a test statistic based on the minimum latent root of the spectral density matrix at the origin and another one based on the ratio of the minimum latent root to the average of all latent roots. They state that these tests perform well in both Monte Carlo investigations and in empirical, macroeconomic applications.

My experience with these tests leads to a far less favorable judgment. I applied the minimum latent root test and the latent root ratio test to various sets of potentially cointegrated variables related to this study, and the results have been very unsatisfactory throughout. The apparent deficiency of the procedure presumably lies in the estimation of the spectral density matrix at zero frequency. Following suggestions by Phillips & Ouliaris (1988b) I used a Daniell periodogram window to smooth the estimate in a small neighborhood of the origin. It turned out that the test statistics then depend decisively on the width of this window (and it is quite conceivable that the same type of problem will arise with other choices of spectral windows). For smoothing over a large vicinity of the origin (with typically non–singular spectral density matrices at non–zero frequencies) usually resulted in not even near–singular matrix estimates at frequency zero. Narrow spectral windows, however, produced highly unreliable estimates and it did not seem advisable to base a test thereon.

I hence confine my attention to the DF–, ADF–, Z(t)–, and Z(a)–tests, all of which make use of the cointegrating regression. As far as the appropriate normalization of the cointegrating vector is concerned, I follow Engle & Yoo (1987) in their view that estimating the cointegrating regression by OLS already gives the natural normalization for this vector. (If there is more than one linearly independent cointegrating vector, then OLS will pick just one of them). I will always set up the cointegrating regression such that it regresses a variable modeled to be endogenous on a set of explanatory variables.

In my setup, the ADF–tests provides for four extra lags in the error process. The Z(t)– and Z(a)–statistics will again be evaluated for different values of the truncation parameter l, since the optimal l is unclear a priori.

Applying more than one statistic to the null of no cointegration will again distort the level of the tests. But the practical work shows all statistics to be highly correlated, so the actual level may be only slightly higher than the nominal 5% required to reject the null. In fact, the sometimes conservative nature of the DF–test (Engle & Yoo (1987)) tends to reduce this distortion.

5.3 Estimation of Production Functions

We will now proceed to estimate the relationships of interest in the world sugar economy. Before turning to the estimation of production functions as a means of decomposing actual production in its systematic and stochastic components, a few words should be said about *how* regressions in this study were performed[97]:

The criteria of specification and regression evaluation are as follows:. My initial choice of regressors has always been determined by theoretical considerations. A regressor with undisputable explanatory power from the theoretical point of view but with an (at the 5%–level) insignificant regression coefficient was not excluded from the regressor matrix unless its affiliated t–statistic displayed an absolute value smaller than one. For a given set of regressors I have generally tested various functional forms and tried to pick the one which gave rise to satisfactory statistics for the specification tests, i. e. the CPT, the Durbin–Watson–, Goldfeld–Quandt–, Chow–, Rainbow–, and Reset test (see Appendix A.1). An alternative specification yielding a higher $\overline{R}^2$ was welcome if it did not violate these prerequisites – if it did, it was discarded.

Unfortunately, the idea of "satisfactory statistics" makes us encounter the problem of multiple testing (Hillier (1991)). The joint distribution of the specification tests is not known, but it is clear that they are neither independent nor perfectly correlated. Thus under what I will call the "composite null" of a correct specification the probability for a single test to reject at its 5%–level, say, is obviously larger than 5%. For instance, take the four F–tests (Chow, Goldfeld–Quandt, Reset, and Rainbow) as well as the white noise tests (Durbin–Watson and CPT) and assume them to be independent. Then, under the composite null (no structural change, no heteroskedasticity, no non–linearities, no serial dependence) the probability of no test signalling a rejection at its (isolated) 5%–level is $(0.95)^6 = 0.735$, in other words, even if the composite null is true, at least one of the six tests would reject at its conventional 5%–level with a probability larger than 25%.

There are – to my knowledge – no exact methods available to cope with the problem of multiple testing. Krämer & Sonnberger (1986) discuss some very general approaches, but these do not seem very satisfactory. Hillier (1991) suggests a solution

---

[97]I used the GAUSS Mathematical and Statistical System (versions 1.49B and 2.0) for the computations. Programs for a couple of non–parametric tests have kindly been provided by Prof. Herbert Büning, Free University of Berlin; all other procedures and routines not supplied with the conventional GAUSS package have been written by myself. I have in particular supplemented the GAUSS OLS–procedure by some diagnostic test subroutines. Details on these tests are given in Appendix A1.

for a very particular set of F–tests inapplicable to our problem. As this is not very promising, I will use the following rule of thumb instead:

Let us confine our attention to the six tests mentioned above[98]. Assume the two white noise tests to be perfectly correlated and assume the same for Reset and Rainbow. Assume all other tests to be independent. (The first two assumptions overestimate the true dependencies, the last one underestimates them). Then the six tests shrink to actually four independent tests, i. e. the probability of at least one test being significant at its 5%–level is equal to $1 - (0.95)^4 = 0.185$. Put differently, in order to ensure a five percent level for the composite test, there should be no rejection of the composite null unless one of the isolated tests displays a P–value of less than 0.013, since we have $(1 - 0.013)^4 \approx 0.95$. For convenience, I round this value down to 1%. (Similarly, in order to ensure a 1% level for the composite test, the level of the isolated tests should be fixed at 0.25%). I will hence reject the composite null for the specification tests whenever a single test is significant at the 1% level.

With this reasoning in mind, we may now focus on the actual estimation of country–specific production functions. I have argued in Part I that exogenous shocks, due to e. g. wheather conditions or crop diseases, heavily influence the production of sugar and other agricultural commodities. I have moreover suggested to model these shocks as a zero–mean stochastic component of output, which is to be distinguished from the systematic component. However, these two cannot be discriminated a priori, i. e. the stochastic component of sugar production is not directly observable. Hence it must be estimated from available production data.

The main determinant of sugar production is area harvested. Other input requirements (labor, machines, fertilizer, herbicides, and pesticides) are usually proportional to acreage. Yet due to technical progress, their effects may not be constant over time. Thus let PRO denote production, AH area harvested and ρ the rate of technical progress, and let AH and ρ be non–stochastic. Then production in period t might be modeled as:

$$\mathrm{PRO}_t = \beta_1\,(1+\rho)^t\,\mathrm{AH}_t + u_t, \tag{20}$$

where u_t is a zero–mean disturbance[99].

---

[98]It should be plain that tests rejecting the null of normal disturbances do not lead to a rejection of the model, since there is nothing wrong with non–normal error terms – they just require bootstrap procedures for the parametric F–tests.

[99]I have pointed out in Part I that multiplicative risk is the preferred way of modeling. This approach is clearly incorporated in (20), since all we assume about u_t is an expected value of zero. Thus if Θ denotes multiplicative risk with $E[\Theta] = 1$,

A function of this kind, however, is nonlinear and thus difficult to estimate without knowledge on the distribution of u_t. For small values of ρ a reasonably good linear approximation of (20) would be given by

$$PRO_t = \beta_1 \,(1+t\rho)\, AH_t + u_t \tag{21}$$
$$= \beta_1 AH_t + \beta_1 \rho \,(t\, AH_t) + u_t,$$

where, of course, the parameters β_1 and ρ are identified.

Due to additional country–specific regressors or particular error processes, the final specifications of the production functions evidently differ from country to country, but thanks to (21) they all share the general form

$$PRO_t = \beta_0 + \sum_{i=1}^{B} \beta_i x_{ti} - \sum_{i=1}^{C} \gamma_i \epsilon_{t-i} + \epsilon_t \tag{21'}$$

where the x_{ti}'s are exogenous regressors such as area harvested or area harvested times a linear trend variable and ϵ_t is an independent error term[100]. I allow for a moving average representation of the disturbances ($\gamma_i \neq 0$, $i \in \{1...C\}$) which might, due to the perennial character of the cultivations, be adequate for cane producing countries. For instance, hurricanes in tropical countries may have devastating effects on sugar cane plantations and in this case not only the current but also next year's harvest (to a lesser extent, though) may be diminished. Similarly, crop diseases harm-

---

then setting

$$u_t := (\Theta-1)\, E[PRO_t] = (\Theta-1)\, \beta_1\, (1+\rho)^t\, AH_t$$

is clearly compatible with the model exposed in Chapter 1. More generally, we could write this heteroskedastic process in the form

$$u_t := f(t, AH_t)\, (\Theta-1)$$

where $f(\cdot,\cdot)$ is an arbitrary deterministic function. Consequently, for the GLS–regressions that are to follow I specified the variance of the disturbances as an increasing function of t and AH_t.

[100]Throughout this thesis β_i's and b_i's will denote true coefficients and their estimates, respectively. Simultaneously, $\sqrt{\beta_1}$, β_2, $\sqrt{b_1}$, and b_2 symbolize true and estimated values of the skewness and kurtosis of a residual distribution. This ambiguity is tolerated since it is attributable to widely accepted notational conventions. No serious confusion should arise, though; the correct meaning of the symbols will always be clear from the context.

ful in one year may still affect the plant in the next. Thus if there is correlation among the errors, it should be positive, i. e. we can expect γ_1 to be negative. Of course, merely ϵ_t is the stochastic component of output in period t, for ϵ_{t-1} is then already a fixed and known determinant of production.

Table 7 gives a survey of the actually specified production functions. The periodicity of all variables is annual[101]. The notation is self–explaining: ARGPRO is sugar production in Argentina, ARGAH is area harvested in Argentina, ARGEPS(–1) is an Argentinian error term lagged one period, and so forth. CNST, of course, is a constant term and TREND denotes a linear trend.

For Brazil, BRAALC, the production of alcohol from sugar cane, had to be included in the regression. In the case of the EEC the rate of technical progress is known to be approximately 3% (BML (1989)). Since the estimation of (21') resulted in coefficients which imply too large a rate of technical progress ($\hat{\rho} \approx 5.2\%$), I preferred to take the known value of 3% as given and estimate the then linear specification (20), i. e. EECTP is a proxy for technical progress and contains terms of the form $(1 + 0.03)^t$.

Most difficult is the specification of the production function for the Soviet Union since her data on production and on area harvested are virtually uncorrelated. (A regression of type (21') yielded a negative $\overline{R}^2$). A closer examination of the area data reveals a peculiar, almost sinusoidal time path, whose extreme values always coincide with the end of the respective five–year–plan. I hence suspect the data on area harvested published by the FAO to be *planned* rather than *actual* acreages. If this were true, then one would expect the discrepancy between planned and actual areas to be small at the beginning of a five–year–plan and large at its end at least if the five–year–plan aimed at drastically altering sugar beet cultivation, as it appears to be the case for the eighth, nineth, and eleventh five–year plan. With this reasoning I

[101]This gives a total of 20 observations – certainly not enough to apply unit root tests based on asymptotic arguments. Dickey & Fuller (1981), however, provide critical values for a sample size as little as 25. I used these to test the annual data for the presence of unit roots and was often unable to reject the null. But this is uninformative, since power investigations by Dickey & Fuller (1981, Table VIII) demonstrate an extremely poor performance of their tests in small samples. Their smallest sample is 50 observations, though, i. e. more than twice as many as we have available in our context. With fifty observations and against a stationary alternative with an autoregressive coefficient of 0.8, for instance, the empirical power of the best Dickey–Fuller test is 0.3, while for an autoregressive coefficient of 0.9 it is 0.1. The statistic relevant to our problem (Φ_3 in their notation) displays an empirical power of 0.17 and 0.08, respectively. So with even much fewer observations than 50, power will become almost negligible and this is why I dispense with the unit root tests as far as my annual data are concerned and rather assume stationarity.

Table 7

Specifications of Production Functions

Equation #	Depend. Variable	Explanatory Variables β_0	β_1	β_2	β_3	MA-term γ_1	Method of estimation
(22)	ARGPRO	—	ARGAH	—	—	ARGEPS(-1)	it. OLS
(23)	AUSPRO	—	AUSAH	—	—	—	OLS
(24)	BRAPRO	—	BRAAH	BRAAH*TREND	BRAALC	—	GLS
(25)	CANPRO	—	CANAH	—	—	—	GLS
(26)	COLPRO	—	COLAH	COLAH*TREND	—	—	GLS
(27)	CUBPRO	—	CUBAH	—	—	CUBEPS(-1)	it. OLS
(28)	DOMPRO	—	DOMAH	—	—	DOMEPS(-1)	it. OLS
(29)	EECPRO	CNST	—	EECAH*EECTP	—	—	GLS
(30)	FIJPRO	—	FIJAH	—	—	—	GLS
(31)	GUYPRO	CNST	GUYAH	GUYAH*TREND	—	—	GLS
(32)	INDPRO	CNST	INDAH	INDAH*TREND	—	—	GLS
(33)	JAPPRO	—	JAPAH	JAPAH*TREND	—	—	OLS
(34)	MAUPRO	—	MAUAH	MAUAH*TREND	—	—	OLS
(35)	MEXPRO	—	MEXAH	MEXAH*TREND	—	MEXEPS(-1)	it. OLS
(36)	PHIPRO	—	PHIAH	—	—	—	OLS
(37)	SAFPRO	—	SAFAH	—	—	—	OLS
(38)	SUPRO	—	SUAH	SUAH*TREND	SUPLAN*(1+ρ*TREND)	—	it. OLS
(39)	SWAPRO	—	SWAAH	SWAAH*TREND	—	—	OLS
(40)	TAIPRO	CNST	TAIAH	TAIAH*TREND	—	—	OLS
(41)	THAPRO	—	THAAH	THAAH*TREND	—	—	GLS
(42)	USAPRO	CNST	USAAH	USAAH*TREND	—	—	GLS
(43)	ROWPRO	CNST	ROWAH	ROWAH*TREND	—	—	OLS

constructed SUPLAN, a dummy variable, which contains the first five elements of a moderately increasing sequence[102], positive for the eighth and the eleventh, negative for the nineth, and zero for the tenth five–year–plan.

SUPLAN thus is intended to account for the errors of Soviet planners. Put differently, it is hoped that for an unknown constant α actual area harvested is roughly approximated by (SUAH + α SUPLAN). (21) then takes the form

$$SUPRO_t = \beta_1\,(1+t\rho)\,(SUAH_t + \alpha\,SUPLAN_t) + u_t \qquad (38)$$

$$= \beta_1\,SUAH_t + \beta_1\,\rho\,(t\,SUAH_t) + \alpha\,\beta_1\,[(1+t\rho)\,SUPLAN_t] + u_t$$

which can (and has been) estimated by iterative OLS[103], see below.

Table 7 also reveals the method of estimation. While OLS was the basic approach, quite a few regressions displayed heteroskedasticity; in this case GLS was used. Due to the limited number of observations it has not been possible to use an adaptive estimator in the spirit of Robinson (1987). Instead, I usually specified the variance of the error process as a linear function of time or of area harvested and premultiplied the regression equation with the square root of the inverse of the resulting covariance matrix. In some rare cases this procedure was not able to sufficiently correct the apparent heteroskedasticity. I then resorted to the use of simple concave or convex functions in place of the linear specification.

GLS was not employed in the presence of serial correlation of the error terms, since that was to be captured by the MA–representation. Whenever an MA–disturbance was encountered, estimation proceeded by means of iterative OLS, the basic approach of which is as follows[104]: First estimate the regression without the

---

[102]The so–called Fibonacci–sequence: 1, 2, 3, 5, 8, 12, etc.

[103]Alternatively one could estimate this in the form

$$SUPRO_t = \beta_1\,SUAH_t + \beta_1\rho\,(t\,SUAH_t) + \alpha\beta_1\,SUPLAN_t + \alpha\beta_1\rho\,(t\,SUPLAN_t) + u_t,$$

which would – in the presence of four regressors and three parameters – require restricted least squares.

[104]The procedure is slightly different in the estimation of the Soviet production function, equation (38): In the first step, set $\rho = 0$ for the third regressor and run the regression. Compute an estimate for ρ by dividing the regression coefficient of the second regressor by the regression coefficient of the first, i. e. set $\rho = b_2/b_1$ for the third regressor and rerun the regression. Then proceed with the new coefficient estimates as described above until convergence is reached.

MA–term. Lag the estimated residuals, insert them in the regressor matrix and reestimate the regression. Use the new residuals to run a third regression and proceed like that until coefficient estimates and residuals converge[105].

Since areas harvested are fixed for one year, the regressions have been computed with annual data. Using monthly data and eleven seasonal dummies would also have been possible, but it is not clear whether much is gained by this approach. The unevitable cost would have been the use of data from different sources (production data from the ISO, areas harvested from the FAO), which, as noted earlier, are not necessarily compatible.

Regression results are shown in Table 8. There are two regressions with fairly low $\overline{R}^2$'s: In the case of Mauritius this is due to hardly any variance in area harvested, and the reasons for the Soviet Union have been mentioned above.

All estimated coefficients display the expected sign and most of them are significant at the 1%–level. Significant coefficients for the constant term in some of the regressions may indicate that the estimated relationship is but a linear approximation to the true one. Serial correlation of the error terms is encountered in cane producing countries only. The distribution of the error terms seems to be approximately Gaussian for most countries, the exceptions being Swaziland and ROW (See Table A2.1 in the Appendix). The specification tests, whose results are given in Table A2.2, do not reject the hypothesis of model adequacy and only few tests would reject their null if they were taken separately.

On the basis of the above regressions we get a picture of systematic and accidental production in the sense of the theoretical exposition in Part I. For each country and each (economic) year I computed the ratio of the estimated error term to total production. Multiplying these percentages with the original[106] data on *monthly* production immediately yields an estimate of monthly accidental production in each country.

Evidently, this procedure relies on the rather questionable assumption that a harvest is uniformly good or bad throughout the (economic) year. But the error involved may turn out to be fairly small, since for most countries the bulk of the harvest takes place in only two or three consecutive months. For these months the stochastic influence will be quite adequately estimated through the annual data. For the remaining months harvesting conditions are possibly less well approximated, but in face of the usually tiny quantities produced no large errors are to be expected.

[105]Interestingly, it seems that this procedure converges only for *invertible* MA–processes.

[106]Production data prior to seasonal adjustment.

Table 8

<u>*Regression Results: Coefficients, t–values, $\bar{R}^2$*</u>

Equation #	Depend. Variable (# of observ.)	Estimated Coeff. of Explanatory Var. (t-values) b_0	b_1	b_2	b_3	Estim. MA-coeff. c_1	$\bar{R}^2$
(22)	ARGPRO	—	4.72**	—	—	-0.55*	0.78
	(21)	—	(42.2)	—	—	(-2.40)	
(23)	AUSPRO	—	11.13**	—	—	—	0.91
	(21)	—	(112.5)	—	—	—	
(24)	BRAPRO	—	2.80**	0.11**	-0.96**	—	0.86
	(21)	—	(33.9)	(6.60)	(-7.50)	—	
(25)	CANPRO	—	4.38**	—	—	—	0.60
	(21)	—	(49.0)	—	—	—	
(26)	COLPRO	—	2.50**	0.11**	—	—	0.94
	(21)	—	(43.5)	(17.1)	—	—	
(27)	CUBPRO	—	5.43**	—	—	-0.44	0.50
	(21)	—	(36.6)	—	—	(-2.08)	
(28)	DOMPRO	—	6.12**	—	—	-0.88**	0.75
	(21)	—	(41.6)	—	—	(-5.60)	
(29)	EECPRO	2787**	—	3.67**	—	—	0.87
	(21)	(7.71)	—	(15.0)	—	—	
(30)	FIJPRO	—	6.65**	—	—	—	0.56
	(21)	—	(33.2)	—	—	—	

* = significant at the 5%-level
** = significant at the 1%-level

<u>Note:</u> b_0 is the coefficient of the constant term,
b_1 is the coefficient of area harvested,
b_2 is the coefficient of area harvested times technical progress,
b_3 is a coefficient of additional regressors.

Table 8
(cont'd)

Regression Results: Coefficients, t–values, $\bar{R}^2$

Equa-tion #	Depend. Variable (# of observ.)	Estimated Coeff. of Explanatory Var. (t-values)				Estim. MA-coeff.	$\bar{R}^2$
		b_0	b_1	b_2	b_3	c_1	
(31)	GUYPRO	199.8**	3.24**	-0.11**	---	---	0.63
	(21)	(4.10)	(3.28)	(-6.10)	---	---	
(32)	INDPRO	-3341*	2.53**	0.06**	---	---	0.88
	(21)	(-2.32)	(4.00)	(4.71)	---	---	
(33)	JAPPRO	---	5.71**	0.14**	---	---	0.86
	(21)	---	(22.7)	(7.33)	---	---	
(34)	MAUPRO	---	7.51**	0.05	---	---	0.15
	(21)	---	(20.1)	(1.72)	---	---	
(35)	MEXPRO	---	4.22**	0.12**	---	-0.49*	0.74
	(21)	---	(19.4)	(7.01)	---	(-2.23)	
(36)	PHIPRO	---	5.16**	---	---	---	0.72
	(21)	---	(42.8)	---	---	---	
(37)	SAFPRO	---	8.63**	---	---	---	0.62
	(21)	---	(45.9)	---	---	---	
(38)	SUPRO	---	2.60**	-0.03**	158.4**	---	0.31
	(21)	---	(24.2)	(-3.09)	(3.18)	---	
(39)	SWAPRO	---	10.62**	0.15*	---	---	0.93
	(21)	---	(12.1)	(2.6)	---	---	

* = significant at the 5%-level
** = significant at the 1%-level

<u>Note:</u> b_0 is the coefficient of the constant term,
b_1 is the coefficeint of area harvested,
b_2 is the coefficient of area harvested times technical progress,
b_3 is a coefficient of additional regressors.

Table 8
(cont'd)

Regression Results: Coefficients, t–values, $\bar{R}^2$

Equa-tion #	Depend. Variable (# of observ.)	Estimated Coeff. of Explanatory Var. (t-values) b_0	b_1	b_2	b_3	Estim. MA-coeff. c_1	$\bar{R}^2$
(40)	TAIPRO	161.0	6.94**	-0.05*	---	---	0.70
	(20)	(1.66)	(6.81)	(2.20)	---	---	
(41)	THAPRO	---	2.41**	0.12**	---	---	0.93
	(21)	---	(5.89)	(4.12)	---	---	
(42)	USAPRO	1284	4.56**	0.05**	---	---	0.64
	(21)	(1.51)	(4.08)	(4.04)	---	---	
(43)	ROWPRO	-16991*	7.34**	-0.06	---	---	0.84
	(21)	(-2.30)	(4.39)	(-1.81)	---	---	

* = significant at the 5%-level
** = significant at the 1%-level

<u>Note:</u> b_0 is the coefficient of the constant term,
b_1 is the coefficient of area harvested,
b_2 is the coefficient of area harvested times technical progress,
b_3 is a coefficient of additional regressors.

I denote stochastic production by the symbol Z, i. e. the country–specific data are given by ARGZ, AUSZ, etc. Summing over all countries and ROW results in world accidental production WORZ. The regression of WORZ on seasonal dummies yields only coefficients with t–values far smaller than 1; therefore WORZ has not been seasonally adjusted. Subtracting accidental from total production[107] gives systematic production. After seasonal adjustment this variable is denoted by SYS, i. e. WORSYS, ARGSYS, AUSSYS, and so forth.

[107]Again, this is production prior to seasonal adjustment.

5.4 Protected Domestic Markets and the Inelasticity of World Systematic Excess Production

A key assumption of the theoretical exposition in Part I asserted systematic excess production (i. e. systematic production minus consumption) to be independent of the current (= unlagged) world market price. This is not really a disputed assumption in the literature, since it is in accordance with the work of many authors who either find extremely low elasticities of supply and demand or use long mean lags for the price variable.

Since production is generally considered to be predetermined, most authors focus on the elasticity of consumption; Wymer (1975) reports –0.03, Hwa (1985) estimates –0.02 and Sturgiss et al. (1987) find –0.01. Hwa also gives 0.02 as a (long run) estimate of the elasticity of production. Long term elasticities estimated by Adams & Behrman (1976) (see Table 9) result in a slightly more complicated picture: Centrally planned economies display distinctively non–zero elasticities but have very long mean lags. Demand elasticities of other countries are virtually zero, while the corresponding supply elasticities are somewhat higher (mean lags of approximately two years, as one would expect, given the perennial character of sugar cane).

Table 9

Estimated Price Elasticities for the World Sugar Market

	Demand		Supply	
	elasticity	mean lag in years	elasticity	mean lag in years
Developed Countries	-0.03	3.8	0.15	1.7
Less Developed Countries	-0.05	0.6	0.19	2.5
Centrally Planned Econ.	-0.47	5.2	0.71	2.7

Source: Adams & Behrman (1976)

Thus previous work strongly suggests low short run elasticities, yet this cannot directly be taken as support for the assumption of independence between systematic excess production and the world market price, since these estimates were in fact derived under the alternative hypothesis and do not refute this alternative. However, it might be worthwhile to have a closer look at the domestic sugar markets in order to study inhowfar institutional constraints insulate these markets from the world market.

Information on domestic market distortions is taken from a couple of sources, mainly Statistisches Bundesamt (*Länderberichte*), OECD (1988), Lawrence & Hoff (1985), and Manegold & Sommer (1986). Another account of protectionism and national support policies can be found in the book by Abbot (1990, pp. 293–306). For some countries included in this study I have not been able to obtain particulars of their domestic sugar markets, but their degree of intervention is not likely to be much different from what we see below:

a) Argentina

The domestic sugar industry benefits from price supports and surcharges on imports, while exports are taxed, making excess production unattractive unless it is destined for preferentially priced markets. The government fixes a minimum price for sugar cane and a maximum price for refined sugar. Imports are duty–free whenever domestic prices threaten to exceed this maximum price. Rigid price controls or price freezes have frequently been encountered in the government's fight against hyperinflation.

b) Australia

The consumer price for sugar is calculated on the basis of a government–fixed formula, while production is regulated by quotas issued to the sugar mills (mill peaks) and then translated into cane quotas (farm peaks). A commercial company maintaining a state–authorized monopoly markets the export of raw sugar. The Central Sugar Board distributes the proceeds from exports and domestic markets between growers and millers according to a fixed–price formula for cane. The OECD-calculated "producer subsidy equivalent" (PSE) for sugar averaged at about 20% in 1984 to 1986, the "consumer price equivalent" (CSE) was approximately 17%[108].

[108]The OECD (1987, ch. II, Note 1) defines the PSE as "the payment that would be required to compensate farmers for the loss of income resulting from the removal of a

c) Brazil

The Sugar and Alcohol Institute (IAA) tightly regulates production and marketing of both sugar and alcohol. In the presence of a fixed domestic price, planting and milling quotas are set for both uses. The IAA is the sole exporter and owns all export storage and handling facilities. Investments in plant modernization are boosted by generous government–designed credit plans, whose nominal interest rates are considerably less than the rate of inflation, i. e. real interest rates are negative. Lawrence & Hoff (1985) state that this may imply negative production costs of about 4 cts/lb in Brazil's efficient central–south region. As in the case of Argentina, tight price controls as a measure to fight hyperinflation also distort the market.

d) Canada

Producers benefit from a joint support program sponsored by the Federal Government and the provincial governments of Alberta and Manitoba. Subsidies are based on 75% of the current costs of production plus 20% of the previous fifteen–year–average price. The average PSE for 1984 to 1986 was 36.8%, while the CSE was slightly below 30%.

e) Cuba

Production, distribution, and exports of sugar are entirely controlled by the government. Both consumer and producer prices are fixed and kept low. Inofficial markets with flexible prices exist for many (particularly for rationed) commodities; whether this is also the case for sugar I do not know.

f) Dominican Republic

The Dominican Sugar Institute, a body composed of representatives from the government, producers, and labor, supervises the industry and issues different milling

---

given policy measure. Expressed as a percentage it represents that part of the value of output accounted for by assistance of various kinds". The CSE "corresponds to the implicit tax on consumption resulting from a given policy measure (market price support element of the PSE) and to any subsidies to consumption". The OECD (1988) does not provide CSEs disaggregated with respect to different products. Therefore, CSEs given in this thesis always relate to subsidies for all agricultural crops, PSEs, however, relate solely to sugar.

quotas for the domestic, US, and world markets. The Government Price Stabilization Institute (INESPRE) monitors consumption prices for a couple of vital foodstuffs. It operates like a buffer stock authority whose objective it is to prevent prices higher than a given threshold.

g) EEC

The Common Organization of the Market in Sugar (COMS) assigns quotas (so–called A– and B–quotas[109]) to the member countries. These apportion them to the appropriate sugar factories in their territories, and they in turn contract with the individual farmers. There is a fixed price for sugar beet, the "basic price". For production within the A–quotas farmers receive 98% of the basic price. B–quota production is paid only 68% (under certain conditions only 60.5%) of the basic price, and C–sugar, i. e. sugar in excess of even the B–quota, must be exported to the world market without any government supports.

A– and B–sugar is granted export subsidies if the world market price is higher than the domestic price, and exports are taxed in the reverse case. The COMS also sets a white sugar intervention price, which is the basis for the consumer price. A variable import levy is imposed on all imports, charging the difference between the world market price and the intervention price (minus costs of transportation). This levy can become negative if the world market price is high, such that the domestic price is in fact fixed at the level of the intervention price. The OECD estimates the PSE for sugar at 74.7% (!) in the 1984 to 1986 average, while the CSE is 34%.

h) India

The government pursues a policy of price supports for producers and offers special assistance to small famers as far as irrigation, marketing, and storage is concerned. Consumption prices of sugar are also fixed by the government. However, several inofficial markets exist and less than 50% of India's population participates in the monetary part of the economy, anyway.

[109]The basic idea of A– and B–quotas is as follows: A–quotas sum to roughly the expected domestic consumption. Together with the quantities covered by B–quotas self–sufficiency should be guaranteed even under the most unfavorable weather conditions.

i) Japan

Government control of sugar production is executed by the Sugar Price Stabilization corporation (SPSC), a quasi–government organization. Domestic producers are subsidized and imported sugar is subject to a variable duty in accordance with certain minimum, maximum, and target prices. Consumer price ranges are reestablished each year. From 1984 to 1986 the sugar PSE averaged at 71.8% and the CSE was about 45%.

j) Mauritius

The Mauritius Sugar Syndicate administers the production of sugar and fixes farmgate as well as consumer prices. The former decline degressively, i. e. small farms receive higher prices than do large. Consumer prices are fairly stable at a level slightly higher than the average world market price of about 9 cts/lb. The impetus of world market prices for Mauritian sugar producers is particularly small since more than 80% of the normal sugar exports are imported by the EEC under the Lomé Convention.

k) Mexico

Under the auspices of the Compañia Nacional de Subsistencia Populares (CONASUPO) the government established a system of guaranteed farmgate prices in order to secure a sufficient supply of basic foodstuffs. The CONASUPO also handles most of the ex– or imports of sugar. Consumer prices are fixed, although there are frequent readjustments which take account of rapid inflation.

l) Philippines

Using a quota system the government–controlled Sugar Quota Administration (SQA) allocates total production quantities to the sugar mills. In addition, a trade quota system is administered by the SQA, which regulates export allowances.

Raw sugar prices for export, direct domestic use, and industrial use are controlled by the Government Price Control Council, subject to Presidential approval. A centralized sugar trading company monitors all exports since late 1972.

m) South Africa

The Sugar Industry Central Branch and the South African Sugar Association distribute grower quotas among individual farmers. Retail prices are controlled by the Ministry of Economic Affairs and are roughly twice as high as the average world market price. Small growers also receive assistance through an industry equalization fund. The domestic price is protected against the fluctuations of the international market by a (possibly negative) variable levy.

n) Soviet Union

Soviet sugar production is centrally planned, using a system of guaranteed prices, procurement quotas, subsidies, and bonuses for meeting the production targets. The consumption price of sugar is fixed, but unlike many other foodstuffs sugar has never been rationed in the period from 1967 to 1986.

o) Taiwan

The Taiwanese sugar industry is entirely controlled by the Taiwan Sugar Corporation (TSC), a private company which owns and operates plantations producing about one third of all Taiwanese sugar cane. Two thirds are produced by farmers under contract to the TSC. These contracts establish guaranteed minimum prices for private sugar production.

p) Thailand

The Thai government manipulates the wholesale and retail prices of refined sugar in order to keep the farmgate price of cane at attractive levels. Main interventionary instruments include a business tax on domestic sugar sales and sugar export premiums. Consumption prices of a number of basic foodstuffs are fixed by the government; whether this also covers sugar I do not know.

q) USA

US sugar production is regulated by a tight quota system which, under the US Sugar Acts, applies to both domestic and foreign producers. Imports not covered by quotas are prohibited. A price support program relying on purchases in the case of excess supplies ensures the existence of a minimum price considered remunerative to domestic farmers. Consumers, on the other hand, are not protected against supply shortages, i. e. the domestic price may rise considerably in cases of insufficient production. The 1984 – 1986 PSE was 76%, the CSE only about 15%. □

The above exposition demonstrates the existence of severe market distortions in all of the countries considered. Since the objective of these distortions appears to be the disconnection of the domestic from the world market price, the independence of these prices is in fact the appropriate null hypothesis.

Unfortunately, tests based on domestic and world market prices are not very advantageous. Note first that domestic prices are frequently but a single instrument of government intervention; therefore, other measures such as subsidies, quotas, favorable loans, tax reductions, levies, etc. would be neglected. So long as these were constant over time this would not matter, but more often than not will they constitute a *changing* body of non–price instruments. In this case domestic prices are uninformative. Information on domestic prices is also scarce; *annual* data provided by the Statistisches Bundesamt and the ISO Yearbook for a couple of countries are often incomplete and do not seem to be very reliable. Moreover, the use of asymptotic distributions for certain test statistics is problematic with at most twenty observations.

I thus prefer to test the null using monthly data on systematic excess production (denoted EXC := SYS – CON) and the corresponding real world market prices, PR. I will use two very different sorts of tests: On the one hand two non–parametric correlation tests[110] relying on Spearman's (rank based) coefficient of correlation, r, and on Kendall's τ, and on the other hand a test for Granger–causality which basically is a parametric F–test[111].

Let us first turn to the non–parametric tests. Their underlying probabilistic model supposes the combinations of systematic excess production and world market price to be *independent* drawings from a constant joint distribution. Time series data like EXC and PR clearly violate this assumption[112]. However, under a null of

---

[110]Büning & Trenkler (1978, pp. 250–265) provide an extensive discussion of these tests.

[111]See Granger (1969) and Kirchgässner (1981).

[112]Little is known about the exact distribution of non–parametric tests applied to time series data. Serfling (1968) obtained the asymptotic distribution of the Wilcoxon test for strongly mixing processes and Kohne (1981) did the same for the sign test. In both cases the asymptotic distributions coincide with their analogues for independent data.

independence for the *time series* EXC and PR it follows immediately that EXC_t and PR_t are independent for any value of t. Let us therefore simply assume to be ignorant about the time structure of the joint observations (EXC_t, PR_t) and treat them like independent drawings. Then, of course, due to time dependencies in the process of data generation, it may appear as if EXC_t and PR_t were correlated even though – this is the null – the time series are indeed independent. But this is merely to say that the critical values of the tests are inexact: The tests become liberal if applied to time series data. In view of the fact that we expect the maintenance of the null, we may legitimately use the tests since a liberal setup biases the tests against the null.

I will test the null not only for contemporaneous but also for lagged prices (with lags of six, twelve, eighteen, and twenty–seven months) in order to take time lags attributable to crop growth or administrative lags in the mechanisms of government intervention into account. The shorter lags (six to twelve months, for new sugar cane plantations even eighteen months) are supposed to capture the effects of farmers' price expectations at the time of planting. These expectations do, of course, strongly depend on the then–time world market price. The longer lags (eighteen and twenty–seven months) reflect the possibility that governments may more or less slowly adjust domestic prices and production incentives to changing world market conditions. Since these adjustments must be in effect (or at least unrevocably be announced) at the time of planting, and since the average time for the crop to mature might be set at about nine months, the presumed administrative lag would be nine or eighteen months, respectively[113].

The tests are specified against the alternative of positive correlation between world systematic excess production[114] and the real world market price. They are applied to the twenty–two countries[115] and to the aggregate WOREXC. For the former we again have a composite null hypothesis (e. g. "There is no positive correlation between EXC and PR in any of the twenty–two countries"). Assuming the test statistics of the different countries to be independent under the null, a

---

[113]This reasoning clearly shows that we cannot expect the maintenance of the null if tested with lagged prices. Seemingly significant statistics rejecting the null must be cautiously received, however, since the tests together with their conventional critical values are apparently liberal.

[114]Most of the EXC series display a distinctive trend. Hence prior to testing with the non–parametric correlation tests, the EXC data were detrended by regressing them on a deterministic trend. So "EXC" in Table 10 actually denotes the residuals of this regression. For PR detrending did not appear appropriate. In Table 11, EXC is back to normal.

[115]By "the twenty–two countries" I mean the twenty–one countries under explicit consideration plus the aggregate "rest of the world".

five–percent level of significance requires to reject the null if the P–value of a single country's test statistic is smaller than 0.0025, for $(1 - 0.0025)^{22} \approx 0.95$. In the case of WOREXC, of course, the null is rejected for P–values smaller than 0.05.

The results of the tests are displayed in Table 10. Neither Spearman's r nor Kendall's τ are given, since they are difficult to interpret unless they assume values close to 0 or 1. Instead, I show the corresponding P–values determined under the asymptotic normal distribution of the test statistics. For convenience, I also give the conventional (Pearson–type) coefficient of correlation, denoted ρ.

In general, the P–values for Spearman's r and Kendall's τ are very close. The null hypothesis cannot be rejected for EXC and unlagged PR, despite low P–values for ROW: In fact, the probability that one out of the twenty–two test statistics is smaller than 0.013 (Spearman) or 0.006 (Kendall) is still about 25% or 12%, respectively. Also, the test statistic for the world total is far from its 5% level.

However, for quite a few countries (Argentina, Australia, Brazil, Canada, the Dominican Republic, the EEC, India, Japan, the Philippines, South Africa, Thailand, the United States) P–values decrease considerably, if the alternative is specified with lagged PR. We find indeed both the composite null and the null for the world total rejected for all lags tested, the rejection in the composite case being due to extreme test statistics for the rest of the world (lags of six, twelve, and eighteen months) or for Japan (lag of twenty–seven months). Apart from Japan, many other countries display very low P–values, especially when the lag of twenty–seven months is tested; note the results for Brazil, Canada, the EEC, India, Japan, Thailand, and the United States. Most of these countries have western–oriented free market economies, incidentally.

On the other hand, a strong minority of countries (Colombia, Cuba, Fiji, Guyana, Mauritius, Mexico, the Soviet Union, Swaziland, and Taiwan) appears to be perfectly insulated from the world market. For some of these countries (like Cuba or the Soviet Union) this is not surprising in view of the fact that their economic system is centrally planned. For others, their export structure (large share of ACP–exports for Fiji, Guyana, Swaziland, and Mauritius; special export arrangements between Cuba and the Soviet Union) may serve as a possible explanation for this phenomenon.

So far the tests precisely confirm our initial suspicion: Systematic excess production for sugar is independent of (or at least uncorrelated with) the current world market price, but reacts to lagged prices. Judging from the above P–values it appears that lags of between six and twelve months on the one hand and twenty–seven lags on the other hand tend to be slightly more influential than the lag of eighteen months. This might be taken as evidence for the two distinct ways of how

Table 10

Tests for Positive Correlation

Null Hypothesis: Independence of EXC and PR, EXC and PR(−6)

Country	EXC versus PR			EXC versus PR(-6)		
	Pearson's ρ	P-values for		Pearson's ρ	P-values for	
		Spearman's r	Kendall's τ		Spearman's r	Kendall's τ
ARG	0.11	0.936	0.941	0.02	0.789	0.826
AUS	-0.04	0.232	0.246	0.00	0.068	0.068
BRA	0.00	0.422	0.450	0.05	0.190	0.191
CAN	0.09	0.318	0.333	0.07	0.073	0.110
COL	-0.07	0.968	0.974	-0.12	0.987	0.988
CUB	-0.07	0.817	0.855	-0.10	0.899	0.922
DOM	-0.04	0.612	0.643	0.04	0.267	0.296
EEC	0.09	0.310	0.309	0.23	0.052	0.049*
FIJ	0.00	0.062	0.047*	0.00	0.344	0.316
GUY	-0.02	0.574	0.588	-0.01	0.743	0.753
IND	-0.01	0.664	0.667	0.04	0.257	0.195
JAP	-0.02	0.637	0.671	0.19	0.091	0.101
MAU	0.03	0.776	0.759	-0.05	0.835	0.840
MEX	-0.01	0.357	0.372	-0.06	0.853	0.849
PHI	0.03	0.941	0.939	0.11	0.525	0.527
SAF	-0.06	0.958	0.959	-0.02	0.938	0.942
SU	-0.11	0.975	0.982	0.06	0.980	0.978
SWA	0.01	0.412	0.374	-0.03	0.450	0.425
TAI	-0.09	0.999	0.999	-0.03	0.999	0.999
THA	-0.09	0.597	0.702	-0.04	0.314	0.409
USA	0.19	0.744	0.782	0.27	0.230	0.287
ROW	0.13	0.013*	0.006**	0.21	0.000**	0.000**
WOR	0.07	0.453	0.466	0.25	0.014*	0.013*

Table 10

(cont'd)

Tests for Positive Correlation

Null Hypothesis: Independence of EXC and PR(−12), EXC and PR(−18)

Country	EXC versus PR(-12)			EXC versus PR(-18)		
	Pearson's ρ	P-values for Spearman's r	P-values for Kendall's τ	Pearson's ρ	P-values for Spearman's r	P-values for Kendall's τ
ARG	0.07	0.384	0.410	0.16	0.130	0.135
AUS	0.09	0.043*	0.034*	0.10	0.136	0.123
BRA	0.02	0.091	0.077	0.01	0.066	0.054
CAN	0.00	0.117	0.137	0.08	0.035*	0.044*
COL	-0.18	0.973	0.976	-0.11	0.868	0.860
CUB	-0.08	0.865	0.893	-0.16	0.904	0.926
DOM	-0.02	0.106	0.102	0.09	0.467	0.461
EEC	0.28	0.107	0.105	0.02	0.164	0.177
FIJ	-0.07	0.326	0.359	0.00	0.514	0.540
GUY	-0.06	0.577	0.580	-0.05	0.742	0.741
IND	0.05	0.093	0.075	0.09	0.048*	0.055
JAP	0.20	0.015*	0.018*	0.11	0.017*	0.015*
MAU	0.01	0.849	0.827	0.03	0.929	0.936
MEX	-0.14	0.995	0.996	-0.10	0.992	0.993
PHI	0.17	0.176	0.118	0.19	0.188	0.154
SAF	0.11	0.757	0.779	0.08	0.300	0.323
SU	-0.20	0.999	0.999	-0.10	0.987	0.977
SWA	0.04	0.365	0.379	-0.02	0.369	0.380
TAI	0.08	0.894	0.909	0.09	0.730	0.673
THA	-0.03	0.100	0.137	0.06	0.024*	0.027*
USA	0.29	0.188	0.196	0.17	0.335	0.353
ROW	0.27	0.000**	0.000**	0.22	0.002**	0.001**
WOR	0.30	0.012*	0.012*	0.26	0.035*	0.031*

Table 10

(cont'd)

<u>*Tests for Positive Correlation*</u>

Null Hypothesis: Independence of EXC and PR(−27)

	EXC versus PR(-27)		
Country	Pearson's ρ	P-values for	
		Spearman's r	Kendall's τ
ARG	0.09	0.054	0.059
AUS	0.06	0.401	0.411
BRA	0.14	0.024*	0.025*
CAN	0.09	0.003**	0.004**
COL	-0.13	0.895	0.899
CUB	-0.06	0.820	0.843
DOM	0.14	0.604	0.649
EEC	0.31	0.015*	0.018*
FIJ	-0.06	0.925	0.924
GUY	-0.04	0.806	0.812
IND	0.15	0.028*	0.023*
JAP	0.08	0.001**	0.002**
MAU	0.02	0.951	0.950
MEX	-0.11	0.998	0.998
PHI	0.21	0.615	0.650
SAF	0.09	0.145	0.155
SU	0.06	0.865	0.830
SWA	-0.02	0.675	0.668
TAI	0.18	0.396	0.373
THA	0.12	0.024*	0.014*
USA	0.15	0.023*	0.022*
ROW	0.08	0.092	0.096
WOR	0.36	0.003**	0.003**

lagged world market prices affect systematic excess production: They largely determine the farmers' world market price expectation and they motivate changes in the government–set domestic production incentives. However, it remains to be borne in mind that the tests are presumably liberal (due to the time series strucure of the data) and conclusions from the seemingly significant statistics may be premature.

Thus it remains to be seen, whether similar conclusions can be drawn from a test which explicitly takes the time series structure of the data into account. I will, as already mentioned, apply a test for Granger–causality to regression equations which specify (lagged or unlagged) values of PR as possibly causal variables for systematic excess production. Thereby I follow the setup exposed e. g. in Kirchgässner (1981, pp. 41–45): EXC is regressed on lagged endogenous variables (I used EXC(–1) and EXC(–2)) and on (in my case: six) consecutive values of PR[116].

With the same reasoning as for the non–parametric tests I specify a wide variety of groups of lagged prices as possibly causal variables. For each country five regressions are tested, the first including PR and PR(–1) up to PR(–5) as regressors, the second PR(–6) up to PR(–11), and so forth. The fifth regression then tests the influence of the regressors PR(–24) up to PR(–29). Formally, the regression equation can be written as

$$\begin{aligned} EXC = {} & \alpha_0\, CNST + \alpha_1\, EXC(-1) + \alpha_2\, EXC(-2) + \beta_1\, PR(-j) + \beta_2\, PR(-j-1) \\ & + \beta_3\, PR(-j-2) + \beta_4\, PR(-j-3) + \beta_5\, PR(-j-4) + \beta_6\, PR(-j-5) + u, \end{aligned}$$

where $j \in \{0, 6, 12, 18, 24\}$ and u is an error term. The Granger test then consists of an F–test testing the null $\beta_1 = \beta_2 = \beta_3 = \beta_4 = \beta_5 = \beta_6 = 0$. Since we again have a composite null hypothesis for the twenty–two countries, it is obvious that the same significance requirements as for the non–parametric tests apply for the country–specific test statistics of the Granger tests. For the world aggregate, of course, we still reject the null whenever the P–values are smaller than 5%.

The results of these tests are given in Table 11. It is obvious that the null of no causality cannot be rejected for EXC and the most recent prices, since the lowest

---

[116] I tested all EXC–series for the presence of a unit root using the Phillips–Perron tests. Without any exception, the null was rejected and the significance level of the test statistics was mostly far beyond 1%. I do not give the detailed results since the Granger tests are the only application in this thesis where the stationarity of the *country–specific* EXC–data plays a role. The results for WOREXC are reported in Section 5.7. Whether or not PR is I(1) is less clear (see the respective test statistics in Table 12); if it were, then the above regression would still make sense if the vector $(\beta_1, \ldots, \beta_6)'$ cointegrates the PR–variables. I will abstain from a thorough investigation of this question since this leads us far off our intended analysis.

Table 11

Granger Tests for Causality

Null Hypothesis: Grouped Values of PR are not Causal for EXC

EXC	P-values for F-tests testing coefficients of				
	PR up to PR(-5)	PR(-6) up to PR(-11)	PR(-12) up to PR(-17)	PR(-18) up to PR(-23)	PR(-24) up to PR(-29)
ARG	0.157	0.321	0.398	0.022*	0.769
AUS	0.633	0.245	0.984	0.256	0.606
BRA	0.689	0.292	0.998	0.398	0.626
CAN	0.201	0.487	0.485	0.335	0.384
COL	0.171	0.109	0.451	0.321	0.306
CUB	0.453	0.991	0.913	0.792	0.869
DOM	0.540	0.675	0.064	0.096	0.006**
EEC	0.282	0.819	0.609	0.485	0.100
FIJ	0.891	0.853	0.694	0.471	0.931
GUY	0.035*	0.269	0.588	0.820	0.548
IND	0.513	0.610	0.360	0.263	0.091
JAP	0.643	0.629	0.012*	0.422	0.661
MAU	0.799	0.290	0.969	0.021*	0.822
MEX	0.557	0.183	0.254	0.885	0.055
PHI	0.236	0.433	0.134	0.139	0.010**
SAF	0.185	0.000**	0.050*	0.177	0.697
SU	0.987	0.893	0.770	0.898	0.838
SWA	0.855	0.353	0.867	0.360	0.781
TAI	0.923	0.393	0.448	0.493	0.402
THA	0.330	0.807	0.773	0.936	0.275
USA	0.601	0.106	0.016*	0.285	0.392
ROW	0.298	0.425	0.281	0.788	0.658
WOR	0.101	0.410	0.383	0.043*	0.006**

P–value for the twenty–two countries is Guyana's 0.035 (while all others are much larger)[117] and the P–value for the world total is also well above the 5%–level of significance. For the next group of lagged prices, however, the composite null is rejected due to an extremely low P–value for South Africa. This is, incidentally, the only time where the composite null cannot be maintained: Despite some fairly low P–values for Japan and the United States (PR(–12) up to PR(–17)), for Argentina and Mauritius (PR(–18) up to PR(–23)), and for the Dominican Republic and the Philippines (PR(–24) up to PR(–29)), none of these is low enough to reject the composite null at the 5%–level. Yet P–values obtained for the world aggregate clearly signal a causal relationship between the two groups of prices with the longest lags and current excess production: For PR(–18) up to PR(–23) the statistics are significant at the 5%–level and for PR(–24) up to PR(–29) we even find significance at the 1%–level.

So we are left with the same conclusions as in the case of the non–parametric tests: Systematic excess production seems to be unaffected by the current world market price or by prices lagged less than half a year. On the other hand, there is evidence for a causal relationship if prices are lagged for between six and eleven months or between eighteen and twenty–nine months (where the very long lag of between two years and two years and a half is most strongly supported). Since these latter results coincide so nicely with the evaluation of Spearman's and Kendall's test, we may feel encouraged to drop the earlier established reservation on behalf of the liberal nature of these tests. The common interpretation that applies is, as already pointed out, to view shorter lags as an outflow of farmers' world market price expectations, while the longer ones are attributable to slow adjustments of government–set domestic production incentives to changing world market conditions.

5.5 Prices ...

The preceding section argues that systematic excess production in the world sugar market is likely to be completely inelastic with respect to the current world market price. The market thus displays – not unexpectedly – the properties assumed for the theoretical exposition of Part I. As mentioned earlier, modeling the world market for sugar as a residual market with completely inelastic excess production leaves us with three relationships of economic interest: Stock demand as the sole price elastic

[117]The probability for at least one of the twenty–two statistics to have a P–value of 0.035 or smaller is equal to $1 - (1-0.035)^{22} \approx 54.3\%$.

component of the market, systematic excess production in response to lagged prices, and, last but not least, the price itself.

Following the theoretical considerations of Part I, the world market price will depend on world accidental production WORZ and on systematic excess supply, the sum of period t's systematic excess production and period t–1's stocks. However, alongside the considerable increase in world sugar consumption from 1967 to 1986, world stock levels grew at approximately the same rate. The above notion of world systematic excess supply now displays a strong positive trend, which I eliminate by dividing through the level of actual consumption. After seasonal adjustment, the variable

$$WORM_t := (WORSTO_{t-1} + WOREXC_t) \;/\; WORCON_t$$
$$= (WORSTO_{t-1} + WORSYS_t) \;/\; WORCON_t \;-\; 1$$

denotes the version of world systematic excess supply appropriate for this study.

Another modification of the theoretical setup deems reasonable: Sugar is but one out of a broad range of agricultural products, which, being alternative crops on the production side and sometimes substitutes on the consumption side, are characterized by a more or less interdependent system of prices. The price of wheat, as one of the major crops with undisputable importance in both human consumption and animal foodstuffs, is widely regarded as a cornerstone of this system. This is why the price of wheat not only signals the relative scarcity of wheat, but also serves as an indicator for senses of unrest in agricultural markets in general. Being sometimes subject to politically motivated restrictions in trade (recall grain embargos against the Soviet Union in the 1970's), the price of wheat is also sensitive to international tensions and may transmit their repercussions to other agricultural markets. I therefore include the (real) price of wheat, PRWH, or, in logarithms, LNPRWH, as an explanatory variable in the regression analysis of the real world market price of sugar[118].

In modeling the process of price formation a view at Figure 4 may be helpful. It depicts LNPR together with its potential explanatory variables WORM, WORZ, and LNPRWH[119].

---

[118]Price data refer to US Hard Red Winter (ordinary protein wheat) and were extracted from the IMF's *International Financial Statistics.* The US Consumer Price Index was used to deflate nominal prices.

[119]In Figure 4 the *negative* of WORM and WORZ is shown, since these variables are presumably negatively correlated with LNPR. The time series have been subject to affine transformations in order to improve their graphical presentation. The unit length of the y–axis is hence uninformative and not given.

Apparently, LNPR and WORM are closely related. Sugar prices were very low in 1967 and 1968, when systematic excess supply was high, but increased steadily from 1969 to 1973, as a result of declining excess production. While WORM remained approximately constant at an exceptionally low level during 1974, sugar prices continued to boom in late 1973/1974, reflecting skyrocketing wheat prices. However, while the wheat market cooled down a little after the politically tumultuous winter of 1973/1974 (first oil crisis), the unprecedented upsurge of prices in the sugar market

LNPR and its Determinants

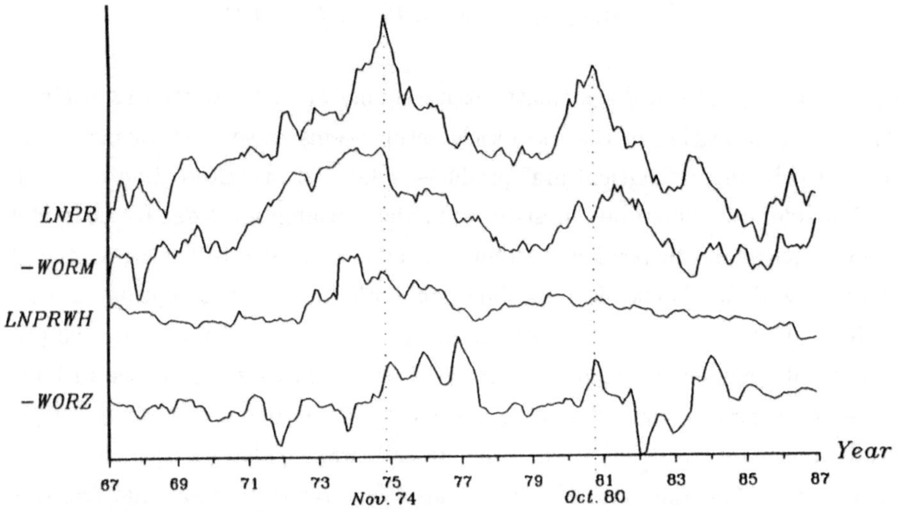

Figure 4

was yet to continue, a development, which, in my eyes, can only be attributed to a series of extremely bad harvests (note the decline in WORZ) during all of 1974.

With the beginning of 1975, systematic excess supply began a long period of recovery, which lasted well until the spring of 1979, and simultaneously wheat prices began approaching their pre–1973 levels. Consequently, sugar prices also fell, and two more, clearly discernible times of bad harvests in late 1975 and late 1976 were apparently unable to forcefully counteract this tendency.

In 1979 the trend was reversed when systematic excess supplies began to deteriorate once more. The situation never grew as tight as it had been in 1973, though, and prices did hence not even come close to their 1973/1974 level. Still, another half a year of unfortunate harvests in the summer and fall of 1980 made sugar prices peak in October 1980. This again was probably reinforced by wheat prices, which experienced two minor surges in the falls of 1979 and 1980. 1981, however, witnessed much better wheather conditions and harvests improved considerably, such that sugar prices began to fall despite a persistent shortage of systematic supplies. The latter was overcome in 1982 and systematic excess supplies have remained at a more than satisfactory level for the rest of the sample period, with sugar prices being consequently fairly depressed. The only noteworthy exception is probably due to another major decrease in WORZ during all of 1983; here again the records note a rather tiny rise in sugar prices.

This discussion suggests that the basic price movements in the world sugar economy can be attributed to the three explanatory variables mentioned above. In particular, the stunning simultaneity of oil and sugar price booms seems to be quite a coincidence, but hardly more than that: Homemade supply shortages and unfortunate wheather conditions causing poor harvests can be singled out as major determinants of skyrocketing sugar prices.

This is not to say that the oil price shocks did not have repercussions on the world sugar market. They may in fact well have fueled speculative activities there (as they have possibly done in other primary commodity markets) and I provide for this possibility by including the price of wheat in the regression. But it is extremely unlikely that the political tensions would have resulted in such significant sugar price peaks, had the situation not simultaneously been characterized by tight supplies.

Figure 4 leaves little doubt about the appropriateness of studying the logarithms, rather than the levels of the real world market price: LNPR and WORM fluctuate very closely. Of course, one might also imagine a regression of PR on exp{WORM} and other regressors. I have experimented with such alternative functional forms, but LNPR as a linear function of WORM, WORZ, and LNPRWH clearly dominated all others and therefore I chose the representation given in Figure 4.

Before starting to estimate this relationship, we have to examine whether the variables are stationary time series[120]. As Table 12 shows, LNPR appears to be I(1). If

[120]For all time series used in this thesis, the unit root tests indicate stationarity for their first differences at extremely high significance levels. I will henceforth not explicitly mention this issue nor give the respective test statistics, since only the non–stationarity of the first differences would come as a surprise result.

Table 12

Tests for Unit Roots

Model: $y_t = \mu$ CNST $+ \alpha\, y_{t-1} + \beta$ TREND $+ u_t$

Note: $Z_1(\cdot)$ tests (μ, α, β) as H_0: $(\mu, 1, 0)$ against H_1: (μ, α, β)
$Z_2(\cdot)$ tests (μ, α, β) as H_0: $(0, 1, 0)$ against H_1: (μ, α, β)
$Z_3(\cdot)$ tests (μ, α, β) as H_0: $(0, 1, 0)$ against H_1: $(\mu, \alpha, 0)$

Var.	Trunc. Param.	$Z_1(F)$	$Z_1(t)$	$Z_1(\alpha)$	$Z_2(F)$	$Z_3(F)$	$Z_3(t)$	$Z_3(\alpha)$	
	3	2.99	-2.37	-10.70	1.99	2.61	-2.29	-10.27	
PR	5	3.31	-2.51	-12.06	2.21	2.96	-2.43	-11.64	accepted
	10	3.65	-2.65	-13.52	2.44	3.33	-2.58	-13.13	
	3	3.28	-2.14	-6.99	2.19	2.32	-1.82	-5.89	
LNPR	5	3.32	-2.22	-7.73	2.22	2.43	-1.92	-6.67	accepted
	10	3.38	-2.28	-8.31	2.26	2.54	-2.01	-7.37	
	3	2.86	-2.26	-7.65	1.99	2.22	-2.04	-6.80	
WORM	5	3.01	-2.34	-8.49	2.08	2.40	-2.14	-7.62	accepted
	10	2.99	-2.33	-8.36	2.07	2.38	-2.13	-7.56	
	3	5.25	-3.24	-20.64	3.50	5.10*	-3.19*	-20.14*	
WORZ	5	6.31*	-3.55*	-24.90*	4.21	6.14*	-3.5**	-24.3**	rejected
	10	6.30*	-3.55*	-24.87*	4.20	6.13*	-3.5**	-24.3**	
	3	1.92	-1.87	-7.90	1.38	1.55	-1.67	-6.86	
LNPRWH	5	2.01	-1.92	-8.34	1.44	1.64	-1.73	-7.27	accepted
	10	1.96	-1.89	-8.10	1.41	1.59	-1.70	-7.07	

* = significant at the 5%-level
** = significant at the 1%-level

this were true, then at least one of the explanatory variables WORM, WORZ, and LNPRWH should also be non– stationary. In fact, see again Table 12, the unit root hypothesis cannot be rejected for WORM and for LNPRWH, while WORZ is apparently stationary[121].

We thus need to test whether LNPR, WORM and LNPRWH are cointegrated, i. e. strictly speaking we test the null of no cointegration. Since LNPR is the endogenous variable, the standard type of cointegrating equation would be specified in the following form:

$$\mathrm{LNPR}_t = \beta_1\ \mathrm{WORM}_t + \beta_3\ \mathrm{LNPRWH}_t + u_t, \tag{44}$$

where u_t, of course, is a zero–mean error process.

It does, however, seem advisable to include the (stationary) time series WORZ as a regressor in the cointegrating regression. While this is useless from the theoretical point of view (since cointegration can only occur between variables which are nonstationary), two reasons for doing so may nevertheless be advanced: First, if the variables are cointegrated, then an error–correction form of LNPR may be specified in which the equilibrium errors (i. e. the residuals of the cointegrating regression) are used as regressors. Since the equilibrium concept supposes LNPR to respond to WORZ as well as to WORM and LNPRWH, the residuals of the cointegrating regression can only legitimately be used in the error–correction specification of LNPR if the explanatory variable WORZ is included in the cointegrating regression. Second, it is interesting to compare the coefficients of WORM and WORZ in order to determine whether accidental supply shocks do indeed have effects of different magnitude as opposed to their systematic counterparts. While such a comparison can in principle also be carried out with WORZ as a regressor in the error–correction form of LNPR, common sense suggests that the coefficients to be compared should not be estimated in two separate regressions, if they can consistently be estimated in only one[122].

---

[121]In the case of WORZ the $Z_1(\cdot)$ tests (those which specify an alternative with trend) reject the null at the five percent level of significance; hence testing could have stopped at this step. However, since a trend was not discernible, I also computed the $Z_3(\cdot)$ statistics, the power of which is believed to be higher due to a trend–free alternative. Not surprisingly, some of these statistics reject at the 1%–level of significance, making the argument even stronger.

[122]The conditions for a consistent estimate of WORZ in the cointegrating regression or in the error correction form are identical, namely they require that WORZ and the residuals of the respective regression be contemporaneously uncorrelated. See Theorem 3.1 in Park & Phillips (1989).

Table 13

<u>*Tests for Cointegration*</u>

Null Hypothesis: Variables are not Cointegrated

Results of Cointegrating Regressions							Test Statistics					
Equation #	Dep. Var. (# of observ.)					DW / $\bar{R}^2$	Dickey-Fuller	Augmen. Dickey-Fuller	Trunc. Param. l	Z(t)	Z(α)	Null
(44)	LNPR (240)	variable	WORM	—	LNPRWH	0.170 / 0.719	-3.36	-4.16*	3	-3.71*	-26.13*	rejected
		coefficient	-0.76	—	0.88				5	-3.88*	-28.81*	
		t-value OLS	-12.85	—	7.26				10	-3.91**	-29.22*	
(45)	LNPR (240)	variable	WORM	WORZ	LNPRWH	0.178 / 0.734	-3.43	-4.02	3	-3.79*	-27.27	rejected
		coefficient	-0.76	-1.11	0.84				5	-3.94*	-29.68*	
		t-value OLS	-13.21	-3.81	7.06				10	-3.93*	-29.46*	

* = significant at the 5%-level
** = significant at the 1%-level

I will hence also apply the tests for cointegration to a cointegrating regression of the form

$$\mathrm{LNPR}_t = \beta_1\ \mathrm{WORM}_t + \beta_2\ \mathrm{WORZ}_t + \beta_3\ \mathrm{LNPRWH}_t + v_t, \qquad (45)$$

where $v_t := u_t - \beta_2\ \mathrm{WORZ}_t$, u_t from (44). As the critical values for cointegration tests depend on the number of regressors[123], I will use the critical values for three regressors when testing equation (45), i. e. I will treat WORZ as if it were I(1). This setup clearly tends to make the test conservative, since a stationary variable can explain less of LNPR's variance than a nonstationary regressor can and hence the null is less likely to be rejected. Incidentally, a conservative nature of the tests counteracts their – due to multiple testing – inflated level.

Test statistics and the results for the cointegrating regressions are given in Table 13. Let us discuss the regression results first:

In both regressions all variables display the expected sign. In accordance with theoretical considerations we see that the inclusion of the stationary variable WORZ in the cointegrating regression hardly changes the estimated coefficients for the I(1) regressors. As regression (45) shows, the estimate for the coefficient of WORZ is far larger (in absolute terms) than the estimate for the coefficient of WORM; in fact, the former is about 150% of the latter. Yet the difference is not large enough to be significant; a formal F–test would not be able to reject the null of equality for these coefficients[124]. Hence, while there is evidence for supply shocks to have a larger effect on the price if they are unanticipated rather than anticipated, we conclude that the hypothesis of equal multipliers cannot unequivocally be discarded.

Indicating the significance levels of the estimated coefficients is in general not possible for cointegrating regressions since OLS is not the efficient method of estimation[125] (note the low Durbin–Watson statistic), i. e. the true standard erors are larger than those obtained from the usual computer output. Thus the OLS–based t–values suggest higher–than–actual levels of significance. West (1988) offers a partial

---

[123]The critical values increase in absolute value as the number of regressors becomes larger.

[124]However, this may merely be a problem of the F–test's power. Apart from that, an F–test is not the appropriate test in the presence of serially correlated errors in the first place.

[125]This is to say that OLS does not minimize the estimated coefficient vector's covariance matrix. Of course, the OLS–estimate of a cointegrating vector converges very quickly to its probability limit, i. e. at rate $T^{1-\delta}$ (for any $\delta > 0$) rather than at rate $\sqrt{T}$, where T is the number of observations. See Stock (1987).

solution by demonstrating asymptotically normal distributions for the estimated coefficients of I(1)–regressors under the precondition that the expected value of the regressors' first differences be non–zero. This is to say that the nonstationary regressors must display a non–zero drift – a requirement not met for any of the cointegrating regressions in this study. Also, Stock (1987) analyses the matter for cointegrated variables and finds the estimators' asymptotic distributions to depend very sensitively on various nuisance parameters. He tabulates distributions for selected sets of parameters, but none of these is apt for our purposes. I therefore simply give the usual OLS–type t–values and caution the reader to base inference on them.

Turning to the results of the cointegration tests displayed in Table 13, we note that the apparent disadvantage embodied in the inclusion of WORZ in the cointegrating regression is a presumable loss of power for the tests (see my earlier arguments on the tests becoming conservative). However, even if WORZ is included in the cointegrating regression, then the null of no cointegration can still be rejected for the Phillips–Ouliaris tests. In case it is not, some of these test statistics allow rejections even at the 1%–level, and the ADF rejects at the 5%–level. Thus as a whole, cointegration can clearly be inferred.

We may hence specify and estimate an error correction form of LNPR. The error correction term, i. e. the residuals of regression (45) will be denoted ECLNPR and Δ represents the difference operator[126]. Using OLS, I obtained the following regression equation:

$$\underset{}{\Delta LNPR} = -\underset{(-3.54)}{0.08^{**}}\, ECLNPR(-1) + \underset{(5.50)}{0.33^{**}}\, \Delta LNPR(-1) + \underset{(1.85)}{0.21}\, \Delta LNPRWH + E_{46}$$

$$\overline{R}^2 = 0.174 \qquad DW = 1.979 \tag{46}$$

E_{46} denotes the estimated errors of equation (46)[127] and t–values are given in parenthesis. A constant term was insignificant and has therefore been omitted. The error–correction term displays the negative sign expected in view of the equilibrium interpretation of cointegrated variables; the coefficient is highly significant. Also significant is $\Delta LNPR_{t-1}$, indicating – as we will verify in the next section – that an autoregressive specification of LNPR will comprise two lags. The unlagged change in wheat prices serves as a third regressor with immediate economic appeal; it is,

[126]The difference operator is defined by $\Delta y_t := y_t - y_{t-1}$.

[127]In the sequel E_i, $i \in \mathbb{N}$, will always denote the estimated residuals of equation (i).

however, not significant (at the 5%–level) with its t–statistic corresponding to a P–value of 0.064.

The tests for normality (see Table A2.3) reject the null; the distribution of the error terms is clearly skewed to the right and has higher than normal kurtosis. The specification tests (Table A2.4) have satisfactory test statistics with the exception of the Rainbow test, which clearly signals a non–linearity. I have been unable to find a more appealing specification of the error–correction form of LNPR; checking different kinds of scatter plots did not reveal a discernible non–linearity. Still we should confine our interpretation of the estimated equation to a first order approximation of the true, presumably non–linear function.

5.6 ... and Price Expectations

Both stock demand and systematic excess production rely decisively on (unobservable) price expectations. With the same reasoning as in Part I, I will use the concept of rational expectations (Muth (1961)) for the generation of data on expected (real) prices.

Unfortunately, the appropriate time horizon for price expectations is unknown. Arbitrarily enough, I will employ two types of expectations; three and nine months in advance. The first of these, denoted PREX3, is destined to be a proxy for the price expectation of stock holders with speculative motives: As mentioned earlier, carrying physical stocks of sugar is fairly expensive and consequently prices in the near future will be of prime interest to stockholders. PREX9, the rational expectation of the real world market price nine months in advance, is likely to be adequate for the production decisions of beet growing farmers and approximately adequate for cane producers whose harvests occur either once or (in equatorial countries) twice a year.

Now suppose we used the above price function (46) for the derivation of the rational price expectation. In the annual model of Part I, the stochastic component of production is a zero–mean i. i. d. process, but this is not the case for the applied work using monthly data. Rather, WORZ is a serially correlated time series; a feature which is clear since, if the harvest in, say, August is good, then the harvest in September is likely to be pretty good, too. Similarly, WORM and LNPRWH are characterized by clearly discernible intertemporal dependencies. Therefore, the derivation of price expectations would first require the derivation of corresponding expectations on WORZ, WORM, and LNPRWH. Errors made in the estimation of these initial expectations would then carry over and add up in the generation of the final price expectations.

In view of these difficulties, it seems much easier and equally appropriate to use a direct ARIMA–specification of the world market price in order to derive price expectations. (This would be what one might label a *weakly* rational price expectation). Using Schlittgen & Streitberg's (1989, pp. 230 – 235) correlation table, it turns out that for the regression residuals to be white noise either of the following autoregressive models should be fitted:

$$\Delta y_t = \alpha \, \Delta y_{t-1} + \eta_t \tag{47}$$

$$y_t = \alpha_1 \, y_{t-1} + \alpha_2 \, y_{t-2} + \epsilon_t, \tag{48}$$

where η_t and ϵ_t are white noise error terms and y represents either PR or LNPR[128]. Since the first differences are stationary, running regression (47) by OLS yields a consistent estimate of α, provided

$$\lim_{T \to \infty} \frac{1}{T} \sum_{t=1}^{T} E\,[\Delta y_{t-1} \, \eta_t] = 0,$$

a condition which η_t trivially fulfills if it is white noise. Rewriting (48) as

$$y_t = (-\alpha_2) \, \Delta y_{t-1} + (\alpha_1 + \alpha_2) \, y_{t-1} + \epsilon_t, \tag{48'}$$

we get a regression model with one stationary and – under the null of a unit root – one nonstationary regressor. Estimating (48') by OLS is of course completely equivalent to estimating (48) by OLS. Yet in form (48') the model fulfills the assumptions of Theorem 3.1 in Park & Phillips (1989); thus by virtue of their theorem we know that the coefficient estimates in regression (48') (and hence in (48)) are consistent if and only if

$$\lim_{T \to \infty} \frac{1}{T} \sum_{t=1}^{T} E\,[\Delta y_{t-1} \, \epsilon_t] = 0.$$

This is to say that the conditions for consistent estimation in models (47) and (48) are precisely the same, i. e. from the consistency viewpoint it does not matter whether the regressions are run in differences or in levels. However, model (47)

---

[128]A constant term was found to be insignificant under (47) and (48).

presupposes the existence of a unit root, while model (48) does not. Since not to reject the null of a unit root does not imply verification of this null, model (48) is obviously more appropriate in our context, for it would also be valid if the alternative of a stationary process were true.

For the derivation of the price expectation I thus use model (48) with y = LNPR. The motivation for the use of logarithms lies in the apparent presence of strong heteroskedasticity in the error process of the levels (signalled by the Goldfeld–Quandt test). Also, price expectations are, of course, always positively valued, yet price expectations derived from an ARIMA representation of PR do not automatically fulfill this constraint, primarily during the period of extremely depressed world market prices in 1985. This problem, too, can easily be circumvened by using logarithms[129].

The regression equation then takes the following form:

$$\underset{}{\mathrm{LNPR}} = \underset{(21.23)}{1.306^{**}}\ \mathrm{LNPR}(-1) - \underset{(-5.003)}{0.308^{**}}\ \mathrm{LNPR}(-2) + E_{49}, \qquad (49)$$

$$\overline{R}^2 = 0.970 \qquad DW = 1.943$$

where the regression was estimated by OLS. Both coefficient estimates are highly significant and extremely close to the unit root postulate of adding up to one. I will henceforth loosely refer to LNPR as being I(1), just as if these regression results were a verification of the unit root hypothesis. For some similar series I will do likewise. In the Appendix we find further test statistics: The null of normality is rejected; the actual distribution seems to be skewed to the right and to display fatter tails (Table A2.3). The test statistics of the specification tests are quite satisfactory both for the composite null and taken separately (Table A2.4).

By means of (49) we can easily derive the rational expectation *on the logarithm* of the world market price. However, this is not very helpful, since the expectation on the level rather than the logarithm of future prices is commonly thought to be influential to economic behavior. Thus rewrite (49) in the following form:

$$\mathrm{LNPR}_t = (\alpha_1 L + \alpha_2 L^2)\ \mathrm{LNPR}_t + \epsilon_t, \qquad (49')$$

---

[129]It might be worth a try to cope with this heteroskedasticity by specifying an ARCH–model (Engle (1982)) for PR. However, this would not resolve the problem of possibly negative price expectations. Moreover, little is gained for our analysis since I will only very rarely make use of the time series PR: For the overwhelming majority of regressions that are to come, LNPR will be the appropriate regressor. But sure enough ARCH–models would inflate the size of the thesis even further and this does not seem desirable.

where ϵ_t is i.i.d. and L is the lag operator. Then period t's rational expectation of PR three months ahead is given by

$$E_t[PR_{t+3}] = E_t[\ \exp\{LNPR_{t+3}\}\ ] = E_t[\ \sum_{i=0}^{\infty} \frac{(LNPR_{t+3})^i}{i!}\ ] \approx E_t[\ \sum_{i=0}^{12} \frac{(LNPR_{t+3})^i}{i!}\ ]. \quad (50)$$

The last expression is the expectation of a twelve–term Taylor expansion of $\exp\{LNPR_{t+3}\}$. This approximation is virtually exact for normal world market prices (prices lower than 30 cts/lb), but even for expected world market prices as large as 100 cts/lb the approximation error is less than one promille of the true value. We thus need to determine $E_t[(LNPR_{t+3})^i]$, i = 1, ..., 12. Setting

$$E_p := E_t[LNPR_{t+3}] = (\alpha_1^3 + 2\alpha_1\alpha_2)\ LNPR_t + (\alpha_1^2\alpha_2 + \alpha_2^2)\ LNPR_{t-1}$$

and

$$u := (\alpha_1^2 + \alpha_2)\ \epsilon_{t+1} + \alpha_1\ \epsilon_{t+2} + \epsilon_{t+3},$$

some fairly messy algebra yields the following expressions[130]:

$$E[(LNPR_{t+3})^2] = E_p^2 + E[u^2]$$

$$E[(LNPR_{t+3})^3] = E_p^3 + 3\ E_p\ E[u^2] + E[u^3]$$

$$E[(LNPR_{t+3})^4] = E_p^4 + 6\ E_p^2\ E[u^2] + 4\ E_p\ E[u^3] + E[u^4]$$

$$E[(LNPR_{t+3})^5] = E_p^5 + 10\ E_p^3\ E[u^2] + 10\ E_p^2\ E[u^3] + 5\ E_p\ E[u^4] + E[u^5]$$

$$E[(LNPR_{t+3})^6] = E_p^6 + 15\ E_p^4\ E[u^2] + 20\ E_p^3\ E[u^3] + 15\ E_p^2\ E[u^4] + 6\ E_p\ E[u^5] + E[u^6]$$

$$E[(LNPR_{t+3})^7] = E_p^7 + 21\ E_p^5\ E[u^2] + 35\ E_p^4\ E[u^3] + 35\ E_p^3\ E[u^4] + 21\ E_p^2\ E[u^5] + 7\ E_p\ E[u^6] + E[u^7]$$

---

[130] E_p and u are, of course, time dependent. A respective index is suppressed for notational convenience.

$$E[(LNPR_{t+3})^8] = E_p^8 + 28\,E_p^6\,E[u^2] + 56\,E_p^5\,E[u^3] + 70\,E_p^4\,E[u^4]$$

$$+ 56\,E_p^3\,E[u^5] + 28\,E_p^2\,E[u^6] + 8\,E_p\,E[u^7] + E[u^8]$$

$$E[(LNPR_{t+3})^9] = E_p^9 + 36\,E_p^7\,E[u^2] + 84\,E_p^6\,E[u^3] + 126\,E_p^5\,E[u^4] + 126\,E_p^4\,E[u^5]$$

$$+ 84\,E_p^3\,E[u^6] + 36\,E_p^2\,E[u^7] + 9\,E_p\,E[u^8] + E[u^9]$$

$$E[(LNPR_{t+3})^{10}] = E_p^{10} + 45\,E_p^8\,E[u^2] + 120\,E_p^7\,E[u^3] + 210\,E_p^6\,E[u^4]$$

$$+ 252\,E_p^5\,E[u^5] + 210\,E_p^4\,E[u^6] + 120\,E_p^3\,E[u^7] + 45\,E_p^2\,E[u^8]$$

$$+ 10\,E_p\,E[u^9] + E[u^{10}]$$

$$E[(LNPR_{t+3})^{11}] = E_p^{11} + 55\,E_p^9\,E[u^2] + 165\,E_p^8\,E[u^3] + 330\,E_p^7\,E[u^4]$$

$$+ 462\,E_p^6\,E[u^5] + 462\,E_p^5\,E[u^6] + 330\,E_p^4\,E[u^7]$$

$$+ 165\,E_p^3\,E[u^8] + 55\,E_p^2\,E[u^9] + 11\,E_p\,E[u^{10}] + E[u^{11}]$$

$$E[(LNPR_{t+3})^{12}] = E_p^{12} + 66\,E_p^{10}\,E[u^2] + 220\,E_p^9\,E[u^3] + 495\,E_p^8\,E[u^4]$$

$$+ 792\,E_p^7\,E[u^5] + 924\,E_p^6\,E[u^6] + 792\,E_p^5\,E[u^7]$$

$$+ 495\,E_p^4\,E[u^8] + 220\,E_p^3\,E[u^9] + 66\,E_p^2\,E[u^{10}] + 12\,E_p\,E[u^{11}]$$

$$+ E[u^{12}]$$

Estimates for the realization of the MA–process u are easily obtained from the regression coefficients and residuals of (49'), and since an MA–process is stationary by definition it is then straightforward to estimate the moments $E_t[u^i]$, $i = 2,\ldots,12$. The underlying assumption[131] of this procedure is, of course, the existence of the twelth order moments for the white noise process (ϵ_t). An estimate of E_p is at hand for all periods (except the very first one) and hence the approximation (50) to the true

---

[131]Actually, this assumption is trivial. It is always possible to find arbitrarily large (small) upper (lower) bounds for the range of a real–world random variable, and if the range is bounded, then, of course, all moments exist.

(weakly) rational expectation of PR three months in advance can be computed and will be denoted PREX3, or, if expressed in logarithms[132], LNPREX3.

By a completely analogous procedure, a proxy for the rational expectations of PR nine months in advance, PREX9, and its logarithm, LNPREX9, can be constructed. Using

$$E[PR_{t+9}] = E[\ \exp\{LNPR_{t+9}\}\ ] = E[\ \sum_{i=0}^{\infty} \frac{(LNPR_{t+9})^i}{i!}\ ] \approx E[\ \sum_{i=0}^{12} \frac{(LNPR_{t+9})^i}{i!}\ ],$$

we can define

$$E_P := E[LNPR_{t+9}] = (\alpha_1^9 + 8\alpha_1^7\alpha_2 + 21\alpha_1^5\alpha_2^2 + 20\alpha_1^3\alpha_2^3 + 5\alpha_1\alpha_2^4)\ LNPR_t$$
$$+ (\alpha_1^8\alpha_2 + 7\alpha_1^6\alpha_2^2 + 15\alpha_1^4\alpha_2^3 + 10\alpha_1^2\alpha_2^4 + \alpha_2^5)\ LNPR_{t-1}$$

and

$$u := \epsilon_{t+9} + \alpha_1\ \epsilon_{t+8} + (\alpha_1^2 + \alpha_2)\ \epsilon_{t+7} + (\alpha_1^3 + 2\alpha_1\alpha_2)\ \epsilon_{t+6}$$
$$+ (\alpha_1^4 + 3\alpha_1^2\alpha_2 + \alpha_2^2)\ \epsilon_{t+5} + (\alpha_1^5 + 4\alpha_1^3\alpha_2 + 3\alpha_1\alpha_2^2)\ \epsilon_{t+4}$$
$$+ (\alpha_1^6 + 5\alpha_1^4\alpha_2 + 6\alpha_1^2\alpha_2^2 + \alpha_2^3)\ \epsilon_{t+3}$$
$$+ (\alpha_1^7 + 6\alpha_1^5\alpha_2 + 10\alpha_1^3\alpha_2^2 + 4\alpha_1\alpha_2^3)\ \epsilon_{t+2}$$
$$+ (\alpha_1^8 + 7\alpha_1^6\alpha_2 + 15\alpha_1^4\alpha_2^2 + 10\alpha_1^2\alpha_2^3 + \alpha_2^4)\ \epsilon_{t+1}.$$

With these redefinitions the expressions for $E[(LNPR_{t+9})^i]$, $i = 2, ..., 12$, are precisely the same as those given above for $E[(LNPR_{t+3})^i]$. After estimating the moments of u, the expectation can be computed as before.

As I noted earlier, PREX9 can be thought of as being influential to farmers determining which crop to plant on their area. Suppose that alternative crops require also roughly nine months until they can be harvested. There is then no need for PREX9 to be discounted. This, however, is different for stockholders, who, rather than carrying stocks for three months, could hold interest bearing certificates. Thus I

---

132 We thus take the logarithm of the price's expected value, $\ln(E_t[PR_{t+3}])$, which is in general different from the expected value of the price's logarithm, $E_t[\ln(PR_{t+3})] = E_t[LNPR_{t+3}]$.

Table 14

Tests for Unit Roots

Model: $y_t = \mu\ \mathrm{CNST} + \alpha\ y_{t-1} + \beta\ \mathrm{TREND} + u_t$

<u>Note:</u> $Z_1(\cdot)$ tests (μ, α, β) as H_0: $(\mu, 1, 0)$ against H_1: (μ, α, β)
$Z_2(\cdot)$ tests (μ, α, β) as H_0: $(0, 1, 0)$ against H_1: (μ, α, β)
$Z_3(\cdot)$ tests (μ, α, β) as H_0: $(0, 1, 0)$ against H_1: $(\mu, \alpha, 0)$

Variable	Trunc. Param.	$Z_1(F)$	$Z_1(t)$	$Z_1(\alpha)$	$Z_2(F)$	$Z_3(F)$	$Z_3(t)$	$Z_3(\alpha)$	Null
PREX3	3	4.29	-2.89	-15.91	2.86	3.98	-2.82	-15.40*	rejected (?)
	5	4.15	-2.84	-15.33	2.77	3.84	-2.77	-14.84*	
	10	4.52	-2.98	-16.86	3.02	4.23	-2.91*	-16.38*	
LNPREX3	3	2.89	-2.19	-8.46	1.92	1.85	-1.92	-7.30	accepted
	5	2.86	-2.17	-8.29	1.90	1.82	-1.91	-7.18	
	10	2.86	-2.17	-8.32	1.91	1.85	-1.92	-7.31	
PREX9	3	4.35	-2.91	-16.11	2.90	4.03	-2.84	-15.59*	rejected (?)
	5	4.19	-2.86	-15.47	2.80	3.88	-2.79	-14.98*	
	10	4.57	-2.99	-17.02	3.05	4.27	-2.92*	-16.54*	
LNPREX9	3	2.90	-2.20	-8.53	1.93	1.86	-1.93	-7.38	accepted
	5	2.86	-2.17	-8.33	1.91	1.83	-1.91	-7.22	
	10	2.86	-2.17	-8.35	1.91	1.86	-1.93	-7.34	
PREX3D	3	4.62	-2.98	-16.42	3.08	4.20	-2.90*	-15.85*	rejected (?)
	5	4.49	-2.94	-15.86	2.99	4.07	-2.85	-15.31*	
	10	4.85	-3.06	-17.37	3.23	4.45	-2.98*	-16.85*	
LNPREX3D	3	2.90	-2.20	-8.54	1.93	1.86	-1.93	-7.35	accepted
	5	2.87	-2.18	-8.36	1.91	1.82	-1.91	-7.21	
	10	2.87	-2.18	-8.38	1.91	1.85	-1.93	-7.33	

denote by PREX3D the discounted rational price expectation three months ahead and LNPREX3D is the natural logarithm thereof[133].

While we know LNPR to be I(1), the stochastic nature of price expectations is unclear. This is due to the fact that non–linear transformations (exponential, logarithmic) are applied to a linear combination of $LNPR_t$ and $LNPR_{t-1}$ in order to derive the expectations on the levels or the logarithms of these expectations. Discounting may in some circumstances also influence stochastic properties such as stationarity. Thus we do need to test the unit root hypothesis.

As can be inferred from Table 14, this hypothesis cannot be rejected for LNPREX3, LNPREX3D, and LNPREX9. It appears, however, that rejection is possible for PREX3, PREX3D, and PREX9 at the 5% level of significance. Yet the residuals of autoregressions for these variables display extremely strong heteroskedasticity and hence an important condition for the validity of the Phillips–Perron tests is not met[134]. The robustness of the Phillips–Perron tests against this violation has to my knowledge not yet been studied; thus the seemingly significant test statistics deserve a cautious reception. The only conclusion that can safely be drawn is that while PREX3, PREX3D, and PREX9 may indeed not display a unit root, these variables will certainly be nonstationary since their error processes are heteroskedastic.

5.7 World Systematic Excess Production

Turning to world systematic excess production WOREXC, we first note that the unit root hypothesis is unambiguously rejected (Table 15). This gives rise to a very interesting problem: We would expect WOREXC to respond positively to increases in domestic prices and production incentives as well as to favorable long run price expectations PREX9. I have argued earlier that the former may in turn depend on lagged world market prices. From our analysis in Section 5.4 (see in particular

[133] I use three–months–Euro–Dollar interest rates for discounting. The rates are taken from Deutsche Bundesbank, *Monatsberichte*, and the *OECD Financial Statistics*.

[134] I have argued earlier that the Phillips–Perron tests should be preferred to the Said–Dickey procedures since the former are compatible with mildly heteroskedastic error processes. But the degree of heteroskedasticity encountered in the autoregressions of PREX3, PREX9, or PREX3D is far stronger than one might possibly tolerate in applying the Phillips–Perron tests. This does not really invalidate my argument since e. g. many of the stock data we will use in Section 5.8 display weaker notions of heteroskedasticity.

Table 15

Tests for Unit Roots

Model: $y_t = \mu$ CNST $+ \alpha y_{t-1} + \beta$ TREND $+ u_t$

Note: $Z_1(t)$ tests (μ, α, β) as H_0: $(\mu, 1, 0)$ against H_1: (μ, α, β)

Variable	Truncat. Param. l	$Z_1(F)$	$Z_1(t)$	$Z_1(\alpha)$	Null
WOREXC	3	15.54**	-5.6**	-56.2**	rejected
	5	16.15**	-5.7**	-58.6**	rejected
	10	15.53**	-5.6**	-56.2**	rejected

* = significant at the 5%-level
** = significant at the 1%-level

Table 10) we could infer that a lag of as much as twenty–seven months might be appropriate. Economic intuition would thus suggest to include PREX9(–9) and PR(–27) among the explanatory variables for WOREXC. But while WOREXC is stationary, PREX9 aimposrestriction that the right–hand–side variables be cointegrated by the vector of coefficients.

We know PREX9 and PR to be strongly heteroskedastic processes but it is not clear whether the heteroskedasticity is due to unit roots or to heteroskedastic innovations driving these processes. In any case, while cointegration of, say, I(1)–processes is a familiar issue, researchers have, to my knowledge, not yet extended the notion of cointegration to cover stationary linear combinations of, for instance, random walks and non–unit–root hetero– skedastic processes. To illustrate the issue, consider the following simple

Example:

Let x_0 be the (fixed) initial value for the conventional random walk

$$\begin{aligned} x_t &= x_{t-1} + \epsilon_t \\ &= x_0 + \sum_{\tau=1}^{t} \epsilon_\tau \end{aligned}$$

driven by a white noise process $(\epsilon_t)_{t=1}^{\infty}$ with variance σ_ε^2. Let further $(\eta_t)_{t=1}^{\infty}$ be a zero–mean random process with constant variance σ_η^2 and suppose the covariance between ϵ_t and η_t to decay in absolute terms with rising t:

$$E[\epsilon_\tau \ \eta_t] = -\frac{\sigma_\varepsilon \ \sigma_\eta}{\sqrt{t}} \qquad \forall\ t,\ \tau = 1 \ldots \infty$$

Defining $(u_t)_{t=1}^{\infty}$ by

$$u_t := (\sqrt{t} - 1)\ \eta_t, \qquad \forall\ t = 1 \ldots \infty$$

we clearly see that both (x_t) and (u_t) are instationary, but only the former is I(1). Moreover, there exists a unique (non–trivial) linear combination of these processes, which is (weakly) stationary[135]. This combination is given by

$$z_t := x_t + \frac{\sigma_\varepsilon}{\sigma_\eta} u_t,$$

for then we have

$$E[z_t] = x_0 \qquad \forall\ t = 1 \ldots \infty$$

and

[135] Uniqueness is, of course, subject to normalization. With slightly stronger assumptions strict stationarity may be obtained.

$$\mathrm{var}(z_t) = \mathrm{var}(x_t) + \frac{\sigma_\varepsilon^2}{\sigma_\eta^2}\,\mathrm{var}(u_t) + 2\,\frac{\sigma_\varepsilon}{\sigma_\eta}\,\mathrm{cov}(x_t, u_t)$$

$$= t\ \sigma_\varepsilon^2 + (\sqrt{t} - 1)^2\ \sigma_\varepsilon^2 - 2\ \sqrt{t}\,(\sqrt{t} - 1)\ \sigma_\varepsilon^2$$

$$= \sigma_\varepsilon^2 \qquad \forall\, t = 1 \ldots \infty.$$

Note that this example is constructed such that

$$\rho(x_t, u_t) = -1 \qquad \forall\, t = 1 \ldots \infty,$$

i. e. (x_t) and (u_t) are perfectly correlated. By adding independent white noise to (u_t), any degree of (negative) correlation can be obtained without affecting the possibility of cointegration.

Now recall that the unit root hypothesis could not be rejected for PR, while in testing PREX9 some seemingly significant statistics were found. While – as I have noted earlier – the validity of these latter tests remains dubious due to apparently strongly heteroskedastic error processes, the above example clearly shows that the variables PREX9(–9) and PR(–27) might be cointegrated[136] even if only one of them is actually I(1).

With this in mind, we may turn to equation (51), which shows the specification of WOREXC together with estimation results. We find lagged systematic excess production to be the sole regressor of satisfactory significance. However, the coefficients of PREX9(–9) and PR(–27) do display the expected positive sign and the estimated probabilities for their true coefficients to be positive indeed (0.915 and 0.838, respectively) make it seem inappropriate to

$$\begin{aligned} \text{WOREXC} = {} & \underset{(-1.93)}{-126}\ \text{CNST} + \underset{(15.07)}{0.73^{**}}\ \text{WOREXC}(-1) + \underset{(1.72)}{3.29}\ \text{PREX9}(-9) \\ & + \underset{(1.40)}{5.07}\ \text{PR}(-27) + E_{51} \end{aligned}$$

$$\bar{R}^2 = 0.612 \qquad \text{DW} = 1.879 \qquad (51)$$

---

[136]I will henceforth extend the conventional meaning of cointegration to include any stationary linear combination of non–stationary time series.

delete these rather natural explanatory variables. As far as the regression test statistics are concerned, the normality hypothesis cannot be rejected, despite an estimate for the kurtosis which is fairly close to its upper 5% critical value (see Table A2.3 in the Appendix). Further, all specification tests yield satisfactory P–values (Table A2.4).

But does this apparently quite appealing specification fulfill the requirement of cointegration among its explanatory variables? In order to answer this question, we have to investigate whether the linear combination β_2 PREX9(–9) + β_3 PR(–27) in equation (51) is in fact a stationary process[137]. Testing this hypothesis is complicated by our ignorance of the true coefficients β_2 and β_3 and exact testing procedures are not yet available. As we will encounter the same problem more than only once in this study, I will briefly mention two approaches which are readily at hand and should, on intuitive reasons, perform fairly well: *Either* the linear combination of nonstationary regressors and respective regression coefficients is treated as if it were one time series and tested by the conventional unit root tests. *Or* the regression equation (i. e. equation (51) in our context) is interpreted as a cointegrating regression (including a couple of stationary variables), and the residuals of this regression are tested for the presence of unit roots using the critical values for cointegration tests[138].

It is not clear to me which of these procedures has superior properties. For the sake of completeness, I give the results of both testing strategies. Testing 3.29 PREX9 + 5.07 PR(–18) as a proxy for β_2 PREX9 + β_3 PR(–18) yields only insignificant test statistics (Table 16); the unit root hypothesis cannot be rejected. However, apart from the problem that we use regression coefficients rather than the true β_2 and β_3, we once again observe strongly heteroskedastic innovations driving the sequence to be tested and this may possibly affect the power of the tests. This suspicion is reinforced if we compare the above results with those we obtain by interpreting the residuals E_{51} as the residuals of a cointegrating regression. Tests for cointegration then clearly indicate that the null of no cointegration is absolutely inappropriate (Table 17); all test statistics are far beyond their 1% level of significance. Even if minor objections regarding the testing procedure were legitimate, the residuals E_{51} are undisputably not I(1). Hence specification and estimation of

---

[137]Here β_2 and β_3 denote the "true" coefficients whose OLS–estimates are given by 3.29 and 5.07, respectively.

[138]For if β_2 PREX9(–9) + β_3 PR(–27) were instationary, then so would be the residuals of equation (51). In particular, if these residuals displayed a unit root, then this should be detected by the cointegtation tests, while any sort of non–unit–root heteroskedasticity in the errors would supposedly be indicated by the Goldfeld–Quandt test.

Table 16

Tests for Unit Roots

Null Hypothesis: β_2 PREX9 + β_3 PR(−18) is I(1)

Trunc. Param.	$Z_1(F)$	$Z_1(t)$	$Z_1(\alpha)$	$Z_2(F)$	$Z_3(F)$	$Z_3(t)$	$Z_3(\alpha)$	Null
3	3.19	-2.37	-10.5	2.13	2.46	-2.22	-9.8	
5	3.27	-2.37	-10.9	2.18	2.57	-2.27	-10.2	accepted
10	3.31	-2.41	-11.1	2.21	2.65	-2.30	-10.5	

* = significant at the 5%-level
** = significant at the 1%-level

Table 17

Test for Cointegration

Null Hypothesis: Absence of Cointegration

Equation #	Variables	Dickey-Fuller	Augmen. Dickey-Fuller	Truncation Parameter l	Z(t)	Z(α)
(51)	WOREXC WOREXC(-1) PREX9(-9) PR(-27)	-13.97**	-7.59**	3	-13.99**	-204.10**
				5	-14.00**	-207.23**
				10	-13.98**	-197.92**
1% Critical Values		-4.70	-4.72	—	-4.30	-36.16

* = significant at the 5%-level
** = significant at the 1%-level

equation (51) are justified.

It would be interesting to estimate analogous equations for country–specific systematic excess production. However, it is basically area planted which responds to price incentives and while in the world aggregate area planted changes virtually every month, it changes only once a year countrywise. Thus the 240 monthly observations shrink to effectively 20 annual values and – as I have already noted in Section 5.3 – for any kind of unit root or cointegration test this is very little. Preliminary investigations on the country level did not seem to render reliable results and hence I have not pursued this matter any further.

5.8 Stock Demand by Countries

A country–specific analysis will thus be reserved for stock demand, to which we now turn. A first conceptual problem arises if we recall from Part I that even in an unregulated market situations may arise, in which agents hold involuntary stocks. Hence we cannot necessarily identify observed stock levels with stock demand. However, Part I also showed that involuntary stocks can be both positive and negative, hence I will assume its *a priori* expected value to be zero. Provided involuntary stocks are not subject to any other kind of systematic effects, they do thus simply become a part of the error process. True stock demand can then be estimated by regressing observed stock levels on the explanatory variables.

I have specified and estimated stock demand equations for those countries which participated as exporting members in the ISAs of 1968 or 1977, i. e. the importing members Canada, Japan, and the United States or non–members such as the EEC were excluded from the analysis. This is motivated by the fact that tests for structural change (the focal point in the analysis of stock demand) are obsolete for countries without quota or stock obligations under the Agreements. Also excluded is the aggregate "rest of the world", since ROW comprises only very few and very tiny exporting members amidst lots of non–members or importing member–countries. The Soviet Union, finally, was an importing member with certain export allowances (Articles 39 and 32 of the 1968 and 1977 ISA, respectively), but only in 1970 and 1971 did her actual exports come close to the prespecified limits. Apart from that, the reliability of monthly Soviet stock data is very low (recall they had to be constructed from annual figures), such that abstention from further analysis seems both advisable and not too costly.

For the remaining sixteen countries and the world aggregate the endogenous variable is used either in levels or in logarithms, depending on the best fit in the stock demand regression[139]. Table 18 displays the results of the unit root tests for the stock variables in their respective transformation, i. e. stock data are tested in levels (logarithms) if the subsequent stock demand equations are specified in levels (loga–

Table 18

<u>*Tests for Unit Roots*</u>

Model: $y_t = \mu\ \mathrm{CNST} + \alpha\ y_{t-1} + \beta\ \mathrm{TREND} + u_t$

<u>Note:</u> $Z_1(\cdot)$ tests (μ, α, β) as H_0: $(\mu, 1, 0)$ against H_1: (μ, α, β)
$Z_2(\cdot)$ tests (μ, α, β) as H_0: $(0, 1, 0)$ against H_1: (μ, α, β)
$Z_3(\cdot)$ tests (μ, α, β) as H_0: $(0, 1, 0)$ against H_1: $(\mu, \alpha, 0)$

Variable	Trunc. Param.	$Z_1(F)$	$Z_1(t)$	$Z_1(\alpha)$	$Z_2(F)$	$Z_3(F)$	$Z_3(t)$	$Z_3(\alpha)$	Null
LNARGSTO	3	18.51**	-6.08**	-63.0**	-	-	-	-	rejected
	5	18.29**	-6.05**	-62.1**	-	-	-	-	
	10	18.66**	-6.11**	-63.6**	-	-	-	-	
AUSSTO	3	9.74**	-4.38**	-36.8**	-	-	-	-	rejected
	5	10.48**	-4.55**	-39.8**	-	-	-	-	
	10	9.56**	-4.34**	-36.0**	-	-	-	-	
LNBRASTO	3	3.49	-2.63	-14.34	2.33	2.54	-2.25	-9.93	accepted
	5	3.97	-2.81	-16.28	2.65	2.84	-2.38	-11.16	
	10	3.41	-2.60	-14.01	2.27	2.44	-2.20	-9.53	

* = significant at the 5%-level
** = significant at the 1%-level

[139]Various rivaling specifications were estimated. As I have explained in Section 5.3, I eventually chose the specification with the most satisfactory test statistics for the specification tests (see Table A.6 in the Appendix). However, I refrained from using Box–Cox transformations other than logarithms, since the abundancy of possible transformations would seriously distort the level of the tests.

Table 18
(cont'd)

Tests for Unit Roots

Variable	Trunc. Param.	$Z_1(F)$	$Z_1(t)$	$Z_1(\alpha)$	$Z_2(F)$	$Z_3(F)$	$Z_3(t)$	$Z_3(\alpha)$	Null
LNCOLSTO	3	8.70**	-4.16**	-31.4**	-	-	-	-	rejected
	5	8.14*	-4.02**	-29.2*	-	-	-	-	
	10	7.54*	-3.87*	-26.7*	-	-	-	-	
CUBSTO	3	12.74**	-5.03**	-48.1**	-	-	-	-	rejected
	5	13.74**	-5.23**	-52.1**	-	-	-	-	
	10	12.22**	-4.93**	-46.0**	-	-	-	-	
LNDOMSTO	3	9.93**	-4.45**	-39.0**	-	-	-	-	rejected
	5	11.10**	-4.71**	-43.7**	-	-	-	-	
	10	9.49**	-4.35**	-37.3**	-	-	-	-	
LNFIJSTO	3	17.48**	-5.89**	-60.9**	-	-	-	-	rejected
	5	17.18**	-5.84**	-59.7**	-	-	-	-	
	10	18.15**	-6.00**	-63.6**	-	-	-	-	
LNGUYSTO	3	54.48**	-10.4**	-148.**	-	-	-	-	rejected
	5	55.08**	-10.5**	-151.**	-	-	-	-	
	10	59.59**	-10.9**	-173.**	-	-	-	-	
LNINDSTO	3	3.20	-2.52	-13.20	2.19	2.12	-2.02	-7.75	accepted
	5	3.94	-2.80	-15.98	2.67	2.50	-2.21	-9.34	
	10	4.33	-2.94	-17.54	2.92	2.69	-2.29	-10.09	
LNMAUSTO	3	21.89**	-6.61**	-74.1**	-	-	-	-	rejected
	5	21.41**	-6.54**	-72.1**	-	-	-	-	
	10	19.46**	-6.23**	-63.9**	-	-	-	-	

* = significant at the 5%-level
** = significant at the 1%-level

Table 18
(cont'd)

Tests for Unit Roots

Variable	Trunc. Param.	$Z_1(F)$	$Z_1(t)$	$Z_1(\alpha)$	$Z_2(F)$	$Z_3(F)$	$Z_3(t)$	$Z_3(\alpha)$	Null
LNMEXSTO	3	3.89	-2.54	-14.85	2.80	0.81	-1.00	-4.23	accepted
	5	4.47	-2.79	-17.58	3.16	1.03	-1.23	-5.59	
	10	3.73	-2.46	-14.08	2.70	0.72	-0.88	-3.59	
LNPHISTO	3	3.81	-2.76	-15.19	2.58	3.06	-2.45	-11.76	?
	5	4.72	-3.07	-18.83	3.18	3.73	-2.72	-14.51*	
	10	4.31	-2.94	-17.19	2.91	3.41	-2.59	-13.19	
LNSAFSTO	3	11.25**	-4.74**	-41.9**	-	-	-	-	rejected
	5	11.20**	-4.73**	-41.7**	-	-	-	-	
	10	10.59**	-4.60**	-39.2**	-	-	-	-	
LNSWASTO	3	16.97**	-5.82**	-62.4**	-	-	-	-	rejected
	5	16.81**	-5.80**	-61.7**	-	-	-	-	
	10	14.57**	-5.40**	-52.7**	-	-	-	-	
TAISTO	3	8.21*	-4.02**	-33.8**	-	-	-	-	rejected
	5	8.84**	-4.17**	-36.3**	-	-	-	-	
	10	8.06*	-3.98**	-33.2**	-	-	-	-	
LNTHASTO	3	16.75**	-5.79**	-61.2**	-	-	-	-	rejected
	5	16.80**	-5.80**	-61.5**	-	-	-	-	
	10	14.73**	-5.43**	-53.1**	-	-	-	-	
LNWORSTO	3	2.11	-2.03	-7.81	1.63	0.84	-1.01	-2.38	accepted
	5	2.62	-2.28	-9.91	1.92	0.96	-1.19	-3.17	
	10	2.61	-2.27	-9.87	1.91	0.96	-1.18	-3.14	

* = significant at the 5%-level
** = significant at the 1%-level

rithms). Cf. equations (57) – (59) and Tables 22 below. In most cases the null of a unit root is strongly rejected already by those tests which allow for a trend term in the alternative. For Brazil, India, Mexico, and the world total no rejection is possible and the null hence accepted[140]. The evidence for LNPHISTO, finally, is very weak, with only one significant statistic ($Z_3(\alpha)$ with l=5 rejects at the 5% level). However, in the case of LNPHISTO the null should presumably be tested against a stationary alternative with a one–time structural change with effect of January 1975. For with the expiration of the Philippino–American Sugar Agreement in 1974, President Marcos completely restructured the marketing of the domestic sugar economy by establishing the Philippine Sugar Commission (Philsucom). A structural change in stock demand patterns is thus very well conceivable.

Applying Perron's (1989) unit root test against a stationary alternative with a one–time parameter shift in 1975, yields high t–values for the dummies employed (cf. Section 5.1). Equation (52) gives the results of the OLS–regression. If this were the efficient method of estimation (which is – note the low Durbin–Watson statistic – apparently not the case), then both dummies would be significant at the 1%–level. But even in the presence of serially correlated errors these t–values are large enough to suspect a structural change in January 1975:

$$\underset{}{\text{LNPHISTO}} = \underset{(44.8)}{5.76\ \text{CNST}} + \underset{(7.50)}{1.88\ \text{CDM}} + \underset{(1.53)}{0.36\ \text{TREND}} - \underset{(-3.33)}{0.88\ \text{TRENDDM}} + E_{52}$$

$$\bar{R}^2 = 0.334 \qquad \text{DW} = 0.212 \tag{52}$$

Here CDM is zero prior to 1975 and one subsequently. Correspondingly, TRENDDUM is zero prior to 1975 and a linear trend thereafter. I will hence use Perron's (1989) model C. The corresponding test statistics unambiguously reject the null (see Table 19).

Consequently, LNPHISTO should be treated as two time series, the first stretching from 1967 to 1974, the second from 1975 to 1986. But it turns out that for the analysis of export restrictions under the International Sugar Agreements we need only deal with this second series, since the Philippines did not export to the free market from 1969 to 1972 anyway, and quotas under the 1968 ISA were inoperative

---

[140]If logarithms are used, the world total is, of course, not the sum of the country data. Hence LNWORSTO could well be stationary, even though LNBRASTO or LNMEXSTO are not.

Table 19

Perron's (1989) Unit Root Test

Null Hypothesis: LNPHISTO is I(1)

Variable	truncation parameter l	$Z_C(t)$	$Z_C(\alpha)$
LNPHISTO	3	-4.85**	-45.47**
	5	-5.51**	-59.26**
	10	-5.05**	-49.50**

* = significant at the 5%-level
** = significant at the 1%-level

afterwards[141]. Thus from now on I will only make use of Philippine stock data from 1975 to 1986 (144 observations) and will, for simplicity, denote them by LNPHISTO as before.

In the specification of stock demand equations I will primarily use the real price (current or lagged[142]) and discounted price expectations three months ahead of the real price as explanatory variables for the speculative component of stock demand. (Their partial derivatives should, of course, be negative and positive, respectively). Transactionary and precautionary stock demand may be explained by either a trend term or the consumption data. In fact, a simple linear trend does in most regressions appear to reflect this component of stock demand better than consumption. However, the latter is useful in cointegrating regressions (i. e. in those cases in which the dependent variable is I(1)), even though sugar consumption data are in general stationary. Table 20 displays the results of the unit root tests for LNBRACON, LNINDCON, LNMEXCON, and LNWORCON. For Brazil, Mexico, and the world total the test statistics are significant at the 1% level, while for India we obtain only

[141]In fact, quotas had already been lifted in January 1972.

[142]From the theoretical point of view, only unlagged prices (and price expectations) should be used, since only they determine stock demand. However, in reporting stock data, the simultaneity of prices and stock demand may be distorted. For instance, one or two months might easily pass until sugar purchased for storage is shipped to the stockholder and recorded as physical stocks in his accounts. Depending on where and when stockholders buy and sell, such lags may vary considerably.

Table 20

Tests for Unit Roots

Model: $y_t = \mu$ CNST $+ \alpha y_{t-1} + \beta$ TREND $+ u_t$

Note: $Z_1(\cdot)$ tests (μ, α, β) as H_0: $(\mu, 1, 0)$ against H_1: (μ, α, β)

Variable	Truncation Parameter l	$Z_1(F)$	$Z_1(t)$	$Z_1(\alpha)$	Null
LNBRACON	3	20.92**	-6.45**	-66.0**	rejected
	5	21.11**	-6.48**	-66.8**	
	10	19.69**	-6.26**	-60.6**	
LNINDCON	3	5.85	-3.42*	-23.2*	rejected
	5	6.43*	-3.59*	-25.5*	
	10	5.18	-3.22	-20.5	
LNMEXCON	3	15.52**	-5.52**	-63.0**	rejected
	5	15.73**	-5.56**	-63.8**	
	10	11.90**	-4.81**	-48.2**	
LNWORCON	3	9.77**	-4.39**	-33.0**	rejected
	5	9.89**	-4.42**	-33.5**	
	10	8.74**	-4.14**	-28.6**	

* = significant at the 5%-level
** = significant at the 1%-level

Table 21

Tests for Cointegration

Null Hypothesis: Absence of Cointegration

		Results of Cointegrating Regressions					Test Statistics					
Equation-#	Dep. Var. (# of observ.)					DW / $\bar{R}^2$	Dickey-Fuller	Augmen. Dickey-Fuller	Trunc. Param. l	Z(t)	Z(α)	Null
(53)	LNBRASTO (240)	variable	LNBRACON	LNPR	LNPREX3D	0.180 / 0.521	-3.00	-3.27	3	-3.63	-27.58	rejected
		coefficient	0.67	-0.71	0.42				5	-3.83*	-30.55*	
		t-value OLS	10.03	-2.43	1.45				10	-3.45	-25.10	
(54)	LNINDSTO (240)	variable	LNINDCON	LNPR	LNPREX3D	0.125 / 0.604	-2.72	-3.07	3	-3.22	-20.63	accepted
		coefficient	1.04	0.67	-0.69				5	-3.39	-22.82	
		t-value OLS	17.64	1.69	-1.76				10	-3.30	-21.69	
(55)	LNMEXSTO (240)	variable	LNMEXCON	LNPR	—	0.207 / 0.636	-2.69	-4.07*	3	-3.55*	-29.43**	rejected
		coefficient	0.92	-0.34	—				5	-3.88**	-34.39**	
		t-value OLS	13.47	-13.94	—				10	-3.54*	-29.28**	
(56)	LNWORSTO (240)	variable	LNWORCON	LNPR	LNPREX3D	0.142 / 0.839	-2.79	-4.22*	3	-3.69	-27.71	rejected
		coefficient	1.01	-0.31	0.16				5	-4.10*	-34.10*	
		t-value OLS	25.23	-3.40	1.80				10	-3.83*	-29.79*	

* = significant at the 5%-level
** = significant at the 1%-level

5% significance. For all other countries with the exceptions of Cuba and the Soviet Union[143] the unit root hypothesis can also be rejected, but since I will not use consumption as a regressor in their stock demand equations, these results are not given.

Besides prices, price expectations, and consumption, lagged stock data appear as explanatory variables in the stock demand equations. Their presence is, of course, due to the intertemporal character of the stock identity, to which the agents' maximizing behavior is subject. Moreover, including one or at most two lagged endogenous variables in the stock demand equations allows for specifications with serially uncorrelated error terms.

Again, tests for cointegration are carried out for those stock data which are I(1). I include the (stationary) consumption variables in the cointegrating regression with the same reasoning as in the price equation (45): Since they are truely explanatory, exogenous variables, their effect on what is called the equilibrium error should be taken into account.

In the case of Mexico, the coefficient of the price expectation LNPREX3D was far from all reasonable significance levels[144]. Due to its apparent lack of explanatory power LNPREX3D has hence been omitted from the cointegrating regression of LNMEXSTO. The main results of the cointegrating regressions together with the corresponding tests statistics for LNBRASTO, LNINDSTO, LNMEXSTO, and LNWORSTO can be found in Table 21.

For Brazil, Mexico, and WOR all coefficients display the expected signs, while in the case of India the signs for LNPR and LNPREX3D are reversed. The significance levels (as estimated by OLS) are very high for consumption, but less convincing for the price and its expectation. This is probably due to the fact that LNPR and LNPREX3D are near collinear and thus their standard errors are fairly high. In the case of Mexico, where no collinearity exists, the price is also highly significant.

The null of no cointegration is rejected for Brazil, Mexico, and the world, but accepted for India (see Table 21). As far as the rejections are concerned, the evidence is weakest for Brazil and strongest for Mexico (with some statistics significant at the 1%–level). The residuals of the three successfully cointergrating regressions may be viewed as equilibrium errors and serve as regressors in error–correction specifications.

---

[143]Interestingly, Cuban and Soviet monthly consumption data are those which had to be constructed from quarterly or annual figures, respectively.

[144]The OLS–based estimate of the t–value was 0.87. The true value is probably even smaller, since OLS underestimates the true standard errors in the face of (positive) serial correlation of the residuals.

I denote these residuals (i. e. the error correction terms) ECBRA, ECMEX, and ECWOR, respectively. In the absence of cointegration for LNINDSTO, I chose an autoregressive specification for this variable.

Specifications and regression results for the three error–correction forms are given in equations (57) – (59) below[145]. We find relatively low values of $\overline{R}^2$, particularly in the case of Brazil, equation (57). This is not too surprising since the dependent variable is in first difference form. It is noteworthy that the coefficients of the error–

$$\Delta LNBRASTO = \underset{(1.70)}{0.04}\ ECBRA(-1) + \underset{(3.72)}{0.24^{**}}\ \Delta LNBRASTO(-1)$$

$$- \underset{(-1.81)}{0.14}\ \Delta LNBRACON(-1) + E_{57}$$

$$\overline{R}^2 = 0.095 \qquad DW = 1.889 \qquad (57)$$

$$\Delta LNMEXSTO = \underset{(2.77)}{0.07^{**}}\ ECMEX(-1) + \underset{(5.68)}{0.38^{**}}\ \Delta LNMEXSTO(-1)$$

$$- \underset{(-2.08)}{0.14^{*}}\ \Delta LNMEXSTO(-2) + \underset{(1.75)}{1.70}\ \Delta LNPREX3D$$

$$+ \underset{(1.70)}{0.49}\ \Delta LNPREX3D(-1) + \underset{(2.52)}{0.24^{*}}\ \Delta LNPREX3D(-2)$$

$$- \underset{(-1.72)}{2.38}\ \Delta LNPR + E_{58}$$

$$\overline{R}^2 = 0.203 \qquad DW = 1.906 \qquad (58)$$

[145]Here, as in all subsequent regressions, I estimate the equations by OLS. More sophisticated methods of estimation would strongly complicate, if not make intractable, tests for structural change and simulations procedures that are to follow in Part III. I will briefly elaborate this issue later in the text. Further, as Krämer (1980) points out, OLS may in fact be superior to alternative approaches if the regression to be estimated deviates from the classical regression model by more than only one of the standard properties. See also Krämer (1985).

$$\Delta LNWORSTO = \underset{(-3.27)}{-0.05^{**}} ECWOR(-1) + \underset{(13.77)}{0.69^{**}} \Delta LNWORSTO(-1)$$

$$- \underset{(-2.71)}{0.15^{**}} \Delta LNWORSTO(-3) + \underset{(2.02)}{0.39^{*}} \Delta LNPREX3D$$

$$+ \underset{(1.92)}{0.11} \Delta LNPREX3D(-1) + \underset{(2.19)}{0.04^{*}} \Delta LNPREX3D(-2) - \underset{(-2.06)}{0.56^{*}} \Delta LNPR$$

$$+ \underset{(2.32)}{0.21^{*}} \Delta LNWORCON - \underset{(-4.07)}{0.37^{**}} \Delta LNWORCON(-1) + E_{59}$$

$$\overline{R}^2 = 0.478 \qquad DW = 1.987 \qquad (59)$$

correction terms in equations (57) and (58) do not display the expected negative sign. This is to say that stockholders sometimes fail to correct deviations of actual stocks from their desired level within one period. Since there is no reason to suppose that stockholders would not do so if they could, we may infer that there are situations when they cannot. In other words, a positive sign for the coefficient of the error–correction term signals the persistence of involuntary stocks (positive or negative) in at least a subset of the sample period. This finding is precisely in line with the results of the theoretical analysis of Part I, Chapter 2.

For the world aggregate, on the other hand, we note a clearly negative coefficient of the error–correction term, i. e. we do not find periods of significant involuntary stockholding on the world level. We thus conclude that while some countries (e. g. Brazil and Mexico; possibly others for which no error–correction form has been specified) involuntarily hold stocks every once in a while, most countries do not, such that in the aggregate the level of involuntary stocks is of minor importance[146].

Coefficients of lagged endogenous variables are mostly highly significant, whereas the significance for the effects of changes in prices and price expectations is somewhat weaker. The latter phenomenon is probably due to the problem already encountered in the cointegrating regressions of Table 21, namely the near collinearity of prices and price expectations. The corresponding coefficients, however, display the expected

---

[146]It is, of course, premature to interpret the existence of involuntary stocks as evidence for quota–induced stockholding attributable to the ISAs, since, as we know, even the unregulated market does not necessarily clear.

Table 22

Specifications of Stock Demand Equations

Equ. #	Dependent Variable	Explanatory Variables							Meth. of est.
		β_0	β_1	β_2	β_3	β_4	β_5	β_6	
(60)	LNARGSTO	—	LNARGSTO(-1)	—	PR	PREX3D	—	ARGINFDUM	OLS
(61)	AUSSTO	CNST	AUSSTO(-1)	—	_LNPR	_LNPREX3D	—	TREND	OLS
(62)	LNCOLSTO	CNST	LNCOLSTO(-1)	—	LNPR(-1)	LNPREX3D(-1)	—	TREND	OLS
(63)	CUBSTO	CNST	CUBSTO(-1)	CUBSTO(-2)	—	—	—	TREND	OLS
(64)	LNDOMSTO	CNST	LNDOMSTO(-1)	LNDOMSTO(-2)	—	—	—	TREND	OLS
(65)	LNFIJSTO	—	LNFIJSTO(-1)	—	—	—	—	—	OLS
(66)	LNGUYSTO	CNST	LNGUYSTO(-1)	—	LNPR(-1)	LNPREX3D(-1)	—	—	OLS
(67)	LNINDSTO	—	LNINDSTO(-1)	LNINDSTO(-2)	—	—	—	—	OLS
(68)	LNMAUSTO	CNST	LNMAUSTO(-1)	LNMAUSTO(-2)	LNPR(-1)	LNPREX3D(-1)	—	TREND	OLS
(69)	LNPHISTO	CNST	LNPHISTO(-1)	LNPHISTO(-2)	LNPR(-1)	LNPREX3D(-1)	LNPREX3D(-2)	TREND	OLS
(70)	LNSAFSTO	—	LNSAFSTO(-1)	LNSAFSTO(-2)	LNPR(-2)	LNPREX3D(-2)	—	TREND	OLS
(71)	LNSWASTO	—	LNSWASTO(-1)	LNSWASTO(-2)	LNPR(-1)	LNPREX3D(-1)	LNPREX3D(-2)	TREND	OLS
(72)	TAISTO	CNST	TAISTO(-1)	TAISTO(-2)	PR(-1)	PREX3D(-1)	—	—	OLS
(73)	LNTHASTO	CNST	LNTHASTO(-1)	LNTHASTO(-2)	LNPR(-1)	LNPREX3D(-1)	LNPR(-2)	TREND	OLS

signs, i. e. positive for price expectations and negative for prices. Note that the coefficients of the price expectations in equations (58) and (59) add up to approximately the negative of the coefficient of the price term.

The null of normally distributed error terms is unequivocally rejected for all three equations, see Table A2.5 in the Appendix. The test statistics for the specification tests (Table A2.6) are mostly satisfactory. However, the composite null of a correct specification must be rejected for equation (58), where a significant degree of heteroskedasticity (see the P–value for the Goldfeld–Quandt test) is apparent[147]. For equation (57), the statistic of the Rainbow test just barely avoids rejection of the composite null, thus the estimated function is possibly merely a linear approximation to the true one.

The specifications of the other country–by–country stock demand equations are given in Table 22[148]. As I have already mentioned earlier, the specifications usually result from preliminary regressions and comparisons of the associated test statistics for the specification tests. I have always tried to find specifications involving "causal" regressors such as prices and price expectations. However, whenever the significance of these regressors was beyond the limits of reasonable inference (t–values smaller than 1), I confined myself to simple autoregressive specifications. Interestingly, most final specifications share approximately the same functional form in the sense that the regressor matrix consists of, among others, lagged values of the endogenous variable and, possibly, levels or logarithms of prices and price expectations[149]. As for the regressors intended to capture precautionary and transactionary motives of stockholding, a linear trend generally outperformed consumption; thus the former is included in the regressor matrix.

The regression results for equations (60) – (73) can be found in Table 23. Again, we usually find the significance levels to be high for the lagged endogenous variables, but not quite as high for prices and price expectations, presumably due to the near

---

[147]This deficiency could be corrected using either GLS estimates or modeling an ARCH specification (Engle (1982)). Yet, similar to my argument in the preceding footnote, both would entail severe problems for the intended analysis in Part III, and since OLS is a consistent method of estimation even in the presence of heteroskedastic error terms, I dispense with such efforts.

[148]ARGINFDUM is a dummy for Argentinian hyperinflation: It assumes the value two, when inflation is between 100% and 500%, three, when inflation exceeds 500% and one otherwise.

[149]The only exception is the Australian stock demand equation (61). Here a regressor matrix including *changes* in the logarithms of prices and price expectations led to a much more satisfactory specification than did alternatives expressed in terms of levels or logarithms.

collinearity of these regressors. All coefficients display the expected sign[150] and for all equations which involve prices, we verify that the cumulated coefficients of the price terms roughly equal the negative of the price expectations' cumulated coefficients – as we would expect. Thus these results very much resemble the results we obtained for the error–correction specifications (57) – (59).

Table A2.5 in the Appendix demonstrates that none of the regressions (60) – (73) displays normally distributed errors. As for the specification tests (Table A2.6), the Durbin–Watson and the Cumulated–Periodogram test indicate serially uncorrelated error terms and the Chow test does not signal a structural change (at the sample's midpoint). However, the composite null hypothesis cannot be maintained for equations (60) – (73), since quite a few (bootstrap–based) P–values for the Goldfeld–Quandt test suggest the presence of heteroskedasticity (equations (62), (66), (69), (72), and (73)) and the P–values for Rainbow and Reset hint at undetected nonlinearities in almost all equations.

To start with the latter, I have in vain tried to single out the presumed non–linearities. They are not discernible by eye in two–dimensional scatter plots, nor have I found alternative specifications with a better performance[151]. I have finally contented myself with interpreting equations (60) – (73) as first–order approximations to the true, possibly enhanced non–linear functions.

The apparent heteroskedasticity could have been easily taken care of by using GLS instead of OLS or by modeling an ARCH–type error process (Engle (1982)). However, as I have already pointed out in my earlier footnote, this would have raised serious problems for the validity of the tests for structural change and for the simulations that are to follow. To illustrate the issue, consider the case of GLS estimates: Any test for structural change could easily be applied to a model transformed by premultiplying with the square root of the inverse of its covariance matrix, so long as the true covariance matrix is known. Yet if the covariance matrix

[150]It may take the reader by surprise that in the Thai stock demand regression (equation (73)) the coefficient of LNPR(–2) is positive. Together with the regression estimate for LNPR(–1), however, we may rewrite –6.921 LNPR(–1) + 2.205 LNPR(–2) as –4.716 LNPR(–1) – 2.205 ΔLNPR(–1). By this reasoning, it is perfectly clear that the coefficients in equation (73) do indeed display the expected sign. Yet the regression results also show that we found another equation (besides equation (60)) in which the *change* in LNPR plays a role. See the preceding footnote.

[151]Using simulations, I have checked the robustness of the Rainbow and the Reset test with respect to lagged endogenous variables in the regressor matrix and found this to be very satisfactory. Strongly non–normal error terms seem also unable to jeopardize the validity of these tests, if P–values are computed as bootstrap estimates.

Table 23

Regression Results: Coefficients, t–values, $\bar{R}^2$

Equ. #	Dependent Variable (# of observ.)	Estimated Coefficients of Explanatory Variables (t-values)							$\bar{R}^2$
		b_0	b_1	b_2	b_3	b_4	b_5	b_6	
(60)	LNARGSTO	—	0.847**	—	-0.019*	0.016	—	0.024**	0.791
	(239)	—	(24.73)	—	(-2.10)	(1.86)	—	(2.08)	
(61)	AUSSTO	0.099**	0.848**	—	-0.681**	0.451**	—	0.0005**	0.851
	(238)	(3.47)	(24.17)	—	(-2.86)	(2.59)	—	(2.91)	
(62)	LNCOLSTO	0.110*	0.784**	—	-0.560*	0.484*	—	0.0005**	0.810
	(239)	(1.97)	(20.41)	—	(-2.41)	(2.11)	—	(2.64)	
(63)	CUBSTO	0.171**	1.078**	-0.285**	—	—	—	0.0004**	0.783
	(238)	(5.09)	(17.20)	(-4.52)	—	—	—	(2.55)	
(64)	LNDOMSTO	-0.070**	1.281**	-0.416**	—	—	—	0.0007**	0.910
	(238)	(-2.95)	(21.32)	(-6.92)	—	—	—	(3.55)	
(65)	LNFIJSTO	—	0.741**	—	—	—	—	—	0.542
	(239)	—	(16.79)	—	—	—	—	—	
(66)	LNGUYSTO	0.341**	0.299**	—	-1.057*	0.911	—	—	0.166
	(238)	(3.19)	(4.90)	—	(-2.00)	(1.74)	—	—	

* = significant at the 5%-level
** = significant at the 1%-level

Table 23
(cont'd)

Regression Results: Coefficients, t-values, $\bar{R}^2$

Equ. #	Dependent Variable (# of observ.)	Estimated Coefficients of Explanatory Variables (t-values)							$\bar{R}^2$
		b_0	b_1	b_2	b_3	b_4	b_5	b_6	
(67)	LNINDSTO	—	1.466**	-0.497**	—	—	—	—	0.970
	(238)	—	(25.39)	(-8.80)	—	—	—	—	
(68)	LNMAUSTO	-0.101**	0.790**	-0.147*	-0.634	0.589	—	0.0017**	0.711
	(238)	(-1.17)	(12.32)	(-2.32)	(-1.81)	(1.69)	—	(4.55)	
(69)	LNPHISTO	0.428*	1.468**	-0.581**	-1.217*	0.703*	0.443**	-0.0014**	0.959
	(144)	(3.35)	(22.04)	(-8.88)	(-2.42)	(1.96)	(2.90)	(-3.24)	
(70)	LNSAFSTO	—	0.939**	-0.127*	-0.274*	0.248*	—	0.0005**	0.813
	(238)	—	(14.62)	(-1.99)	(-2.48)	(2.26)	—	(3.37)	
(71)	LNSWASTO	—	0.856**	-0.234**	-3.903**	2.765**	1.004**	0.0023**	0.761
	(237)	—	(13.53)	(-3.73)	(-3.16)	(3.19)	(2.58)	(6.00)	
(72)	TAISTO	0.276**	1.100**	-0.347**	-0.015	0.014	—	—	0.700
	(238)	(5.80)	(17.70)	(-5.57)	(-1.72)	(1.63)	—	—	
(73)	LNTHASTO	-0.434**	0.957**	-0.257**	-6.921*	4.700*	2.205*	0.0035**	0.919
	(237)	(-3.77)	(14.84)	(-4.02)	(-2.08)	(2.02)	(2.17)	(5.91)	

needs to be estimated from the data, the distribution of the test statistic will generally depend on this estimate and on the true covariance matrix, such that the appropriate critical values are unknown. On the other hand, using OLS in the estimation of the stock demand equations may or may not involve a loss of efficiency as opposed to using GLS (recall Krämer's (1980, 1985) arguments), but does in any case yield a consistent estimate of the true parameters. Moreover, tests for structural change and simulations of different regimes are comparably easy if OLS–based regressions results are used.

There is one problem which remains: Prices and price expectations are instationary time series when given in levels or logarithms. Hence equations (60), (62), (66), and (68) – (73) involve a–priori–restrictions demanding that the instationary regressors be cointegrated and that their true coefficients be collinear to the cointegrating vector[152]. For instance, equation (60) requires β_4 PR + β_5 PREX3D to be stationary.

However, we have no knowledge of the cointegrating vectors. Thus two approaches for estimation are conceivable: Either we explicitly pay tribute to the restriction by estimating the desired cointegrating vector beforehand[153], replace the instationary regressors by the estimated residuals of the cointegrating regression and then apply OLS. Alternatively, we could utilize OLS to estimate the stock demand equations without the restriction and then test whether the regression coefficients ensure a stationary linear combination of the instationary regressors.

The latter strategy is clearly preferable for equations (69), (71), and (73), since there we have three instationary regressors, with the consequence that the cointegrating vector may not be unique. Hence the OLS–estimate in the cointegrating regression might pick the "wrong" cointegrating vector, i. e. a cointegrating vector which is not collinear to the coefficients of the instationary regressors, and the subsequent regression would be badly distorted[154]. With only two instationary regressors this problem vanishes; still I prefer the unrestricted estimate of the stock

[152]If there are more than two instationary regressors, as is the case in equations (69), (71), and (73), then, of course, the cointegrating vector may not be unique. In this case the restrictions postulate that the true coefficients of the instationary regressors be collinear to one of the cointegrating vectors.

[153]Cointegration between these variables is clearly fulfilled. See Table 24 below for the cointegrating regressions and associated tests.

[154]Johansen (1988) derives test statistics to test for the number of cointegrating vectors. He is also able to estimate the cointegrating vectors by means of maximum likelihood methods. The underlying assumption of Gaussian error terms, is, however, not fulfilled in our context. Even if it were, Johansen's procedure would imply quite some extra effort which we can circumvene by using unrestricted OLS and proceed as described above.

Table 24

Tests for Cointegration

Null Hypothesis: Absence of Cointegration

Results of Cointegrating Regressions						Test Statistics					
Equ. #	Dep. Var. (# obs.)			Durbin-Watson	$\bar{R}^2$	Dickey-Fuller	Augmen. Dickey-Fuller	Trunc. Param. l	Z(t)	Z(α)	Null
(74)	PREX3D (239)	Variable	PR	1.745	0.986	-13.6**	-6.92**	3	-13.54**	-207.65**	rejected
		Estim. Coeff.	1.010					5	-13.54**	-207.45**	
		t-value (OLS)	(131.8)					10	-13.55**	-209.23**	
(75)	LNPREX3D (239)	Variable	LNPR	1.316	0.994	-11.0**	-7.30**	3	-10.90**	-159.87**	rejected
		Estim. Coeff.	0.997					5	-10.82**	-155.72**	
		t-value (OLS)	(192.6)					10	-10.82**	-155.79**	

* = significant at the 5%-level
** = significant at the 1%-level

demand equations, since it leaves the possibility of finding the restriction violated *a posteriori*, which would hint at a serious misspecification.

Before testing the null of the restriction of cointegration among the regressors being violated, it is advisable to check whether the instationary regressors are cointegrated at all. Since testing strategies for non–unit–root heteroskedastic processes are not available, I will treat all processes as if they were I(1). The multivariate stock demand specifications display four different combinations of instationary regressors:

(i) (PR, PREX3D) in equations (60) and (72),
(ii) (LNPR, LNPREX3D) in equations (62), (66), (68), and (70),
(iii) (LNPR, LNPREX3D, LNPREX3D(–1)) in equations (69) and (71), and
(iv) (LNPR, LNPREX3D, LNPR(–1)) in equation (73).

We need only test (i) and (ii). For if we find cointegration for these, then (iii) and (iv) are also cointegrated. In fact, since LNPR and LNPREX3D are I(1), we know already one cointegrating vector for (iii) and one for (iv), namely $cv_3 := (0, 1, -1)'$ and $cv_4 := (1, 0, -1)'$, respectively. Thus if we find cointegration for (i) and (ii), then we also know the space spanned by the cointegrating vectors of (iii) and (iv).

The cointegrating regressions are specified with the price expectation as the dependent variable[155]. Regression results and the corresponding test statistics are given in Table 24. Rejections with extremely high significance levels are possible, such that no serious doubts about a cointegrating relationship should remain even though the testing procedure for (i) (equation (74)) may not be fully adequate in the face of a heteroskedastic error process.

We can now compare the estimated cointegrating vectors with the estimated coefficients of the instationary regressors in the stock demand equations. For this purpose, we will have to normalize these coefficients with the same normalizations we used in the cointegrating regressions above, i. e. the coefficient of LNPREX3D is set equal to one, while the coefficient of LNPR varies. For regressions (69), (71), and (73), the coefficient of the third instationary regressor is normalized to equal zero. This transformation is easily accomplished by using the known cointegrating vector cv_3 and cv_4.

[155]This is motivated by the idea that prices are causal for price expectations. The reverse is probably also true, but no qualitative changes would arise if the cointegrating regressions were specified the other way around.

Table 25

Comparison of Different Estimates for Cointegrating Vectors

Estimate from equation #	Normalized Coefficients of			
	PREX3D	PR	LNPREX3D	LNPR
(60)	1	-1.197	--	--
(72)	1	-1.096	--	--
(74)	1	-1.010	--	--
(62)	--	--	1	-1.159
(66)	--	--	1	-1.160
(68)	--	--	1	-1.077
(69)	--	--	1	-1.061
(70)	--	--	1	-1.101
(71)	--	--	1	-1.036
(73)	--	--	1	-1.004
(75)	--	--	1	-0.997

Table 25 shows the appropriately normalized estimates of the cointegrating vectors. The different estimates are fairly close, but it would be premature to conclude that the restriction of cointegration among the instationary regressors of the stock demand equations is met. For while the coefficient estimates from the cointegrating regressions are almost equal in absolute value, they lie generally farther apart if estimated from the stock demand equations. Thus formal tests are called for.

I proceed like I did in Section 5.7, where we encountered the same problem in the specification of the functional form of WOREXC, equation (51). I again give the results of both testing strategies: Table 26 refers to the standard unit root tests applied to a linear combination of the instationary regressors using their regression coefficients as weights and Table 27 gives the results of the standard tests for cointegration if the stock demand equations are treated as if they were cointegrating regressions. In the latter case I will use the critical values corresponding to the number of regressors in the stock demand equation.

With the exception of equations (71) (Swaziland) and (73) (Thailand), all statistics in Table 26 are significant far beyond the 1%.–level. For equation (73) rejection at the 5%–level is quite convincing, while in the case of Swaziland the evidence might be considered fairly weak. All ambiguities vanish immediately, however, as soon as Table 27 is taken into account: Here all statistics reject the null at the 1%–level. We may hence infer that the OLS–estimates of the multivariate stock demand equations do all approximately meet the restriction of cointegrating coefficients for the non–stationary regressors. This, in turn, indicates that we have chosen an at least roughly correct functional form.

Table 26

Tests for Cointegration in Stock Demand Equations

Null Hypothesis: Linear Combination is I(1)

Estim. from equ. #	Linear Combination b_3	b_4	b_5	Trunc. Param. l	$Z_1(F)$	$Z_1(t)$	$Z_1(\alpha)$	Null
				3	15.05**	-5.49**	-50.9**	
(60)	PR	PREX3D	---	5	14.46**	-5.38**	-48.5**	rejected
				10	18.02**	-6.00**	-63.1**	
				3	45.63**	-9.49**	-101.2**	
(62)	LNPR	LNPREX3D	---	5	47.60**	-9.71**	-117.3**	rejected
				10	54.83**	-10.44**	-156.2**	
				3	44.89**	-9.41**	-100.0**	
(66)	LNPR	LNPREX3D	---	5	46.86**	-9.63**	-115.7**	rejected
				10	53.99**	-10.36**	-154.0**	
				3	122.73**	-15.60**	-192.2**	
(68)	LNPR	LNPREX3D	---	5	117.43**	-15.27**	-220.4**	rejected
				10	120.85**	-15.52**	-285.0**	
				3	12.95**	-5.02**	-39.0**	
(69)	LNPR	LNPREX3D	LNPREX3D(-1)	5	12.38**	-4.91**	-36.4**	rejected
				10	16.70**	-5.74**	-55.4**	
				3	12.85**	-5.03**	-42.2**	
(70)	LNPR	LNPREX3D	---	5	11.74**	-4.80**	-37.4**	rejected
				10	12.64**	-4.99**	-41.2**	
				3	6.26*	-3.40	-20.7	
(71)	LNPR	LNPREX3D	LNPREX3D(-1)	5	5.61	-3.18	-17.7	rejected
				10	5.37	-3.09	-16.5	

Table 26

(cont'd)

Tests for Cointegration in Stock Demand Equations

Estim. from equ. #	Linear Combination b_3	b_4	b_5	Trunc. Param. l	$Z_1(F)$	$Z_1(t)$	$Z_1(\alpha)$	Null
(72)	PR	PREX3D	---	3	31.69**	-7.96**	-95.5**	rejected
				5	32.05**	-8.00**	-97.1**	
				10	39.32**	-8.87**	-128.4**	
(73)	LNPR	LNPREX3D	LNPR(-1)	3	7.12*	-3.74*	-27.0*	rejected
				5	6.20	-3.49*	-23.3*	
				10	6.41*	-3.55*	-24.1*	

Table 27

Tests for Cointegration in Stock Demand Equations

Null Hypothesis: Residuals of Stock Demand Regressions are I(1)

Residuals from regression	Dickey-Fuller	Augmen. Dickey-Fuller	Trunc. Param. l	Z(t)	Z(α)	Null
(60)	-14.30**	-8.97**	3	-14.31**	-221.28**	rejected
			5	-14.31**	-221.56**	
			10	-14.26**	-204.69**	
(62)	-14.86**	-9.77**	3	-14.87**	-229.32**	rejected
			5	-14.86**	-220.97**	
			10	-14.90**	-205.40**	
(66)	-15.77**	-8.91**	3	-15.77**	-243.99**	rejected
			5	-15.77**	-244.34**	
			10	-15.77**	-251.61**	

* = significant at the 5%-level
** = significant at the 1%-level

Table 27
(cont'd)

Tests for Cointegration in Stock Demand Equations

Null Hypothesis: Residuals of Stock Demand regressions are I(1)

Residuals from regression	Dickey-Fuller	Augmen. Dickey-Fuller	Trunc. Param. l	Z(t)	Z(α)	Null
(68)	-15.45**	-8.79**	3	-15.39**	-236.48**	rejected
			5	-15.40**	-232.50**	
			10	-15.42**	-224.43**	
(69)	-12.90**	-6.33**	3	-12.89**	-157.52**	rejected
			5	-12.87**	-165.00**	
			10	-12.87**	-164.96**	
(70)	-15.74**	-8.29**	3	-15.74**	-240.95**	rejected
			5	-15.75**	-235.74**	
			10	-15.76**	-235.26**	
(71)	-15.39**	-9.15**	3	-15.37**	-238.61**	rejected
			5	-15.37**	-238.59**	
			10	-15.37**	-236.31**	
(72)	-14.48**	-8.67**	3	-14.48**	-221.79**	rejected
			5	-14.46**	-212.75**	
			10	-14.46**	-213.07**	
(73)	-15.08**	-8.62**	3	-15.18**	-233.66**	rejected
			5	-15.18**	-231.65**	
			10	-15.18**	-232.37**	

* = significant at the 5%-level
** = significant at the 1%-level

PART III

PRICE STABILIZATION ON THE WORLD SUGAR MARKET

Chapter 6: The International Sugar Agreements

In the preceding section I described specification and estimation of the basic three behavioral determinants of the world sugar economy – world systematic excess production, stock demand, and price determination. Of key importance to the analysis was the implicit assumption of *parameter constancy* during the sample period 1967 to 1986. While this is a standard assumption in time series econometrics, its appropriateness is obscure in our context since the International Sugar Agreements of 1968 and 1977 exhibited economic provisions aimed at stabilizing prices. As should be clear from the theoretical part of this study, the nature of our model is such that only a parameter shift can achieve price stabilization. Thus the assumption of parameter constancy is tantamount to asserting the ineffectiveness of the International Sugar Agreements. In other words: In order to assess the effects of the allegedly price stabilizing mechanisms of the ISAs, we need to test for structural change. The results of the preceding section then serve as estimates under the null of parameter constancy.

In the following we will *inter alia* have to deal with the problem of how to formulate the appropriate alternative. To this end, a closer look at the economic provisions of the International Sugar Agreements and their actual performance seems advisable.

6.1 Design of the International Sugar Agreements of 1968 and 1977

The ISA of 1968 and the ISA of 1977 were signed and ratified by both sugar importing and sugar exporting countries, the so–called members of the Agreements. Thus, far from being a mere exporter cartel, the objectives of the Agreements (as stipulated in almost identical wording in their respective Article 1) tried to reconcile the diverging views of importing and exporting, developing and developed nations. In particular, the Agreements aimed at

- increased export earnings of developing countries,
- stable prices, remunerative and just to producers, but not encouraging expanded production in developed countries,
- increased sugar consumption,
- adequate supplies of sugar meeting the requirements of importing countries at fair and reasonable prices.

Qualifications like "remunerative", "just", "fair", and "reasonable" obviously demand further elaboration. Therefore the signatories agreed on a (fairly technical) definition of what they called the "prevailing price"[156] and specified a target zone for this prevailing price. For instance, the desired price range for the 1968 ISA was 3.50 – 5.25 cts/lb, while the 1977 Agreement initially aimed at 11 – 21 cts/lb; after readjustments in 1980 this was set at 13 – 23 cts/lb.

There were several measures designed to help defend these price floors. Most importantly, exporting member countries had agreed on "basic export tonnages" (BET), the main determinant of the country–specific export quotas (cf. Article 40, ISA 1968, as well as Article 34 and Annex I, ISA 1977)[157]. The export quotas restricte exports to the free world market within one calendar year (so–called quota–

[156]See Article 33 of the 1968 ISA. See also Article 2, Paragraph (21), and Article 61 of the 1977 ISA. The definitions are not precisely the same, but the difference does hardly matter for our purposes.

[157]The 29 largest exporting nations that joined the 1977 ISA were listed in Annex I of the Agreemnent. These are countries such as Cuba, Australia, Brazil, the Philippines, Thailand,South Africa, India, etc. They are sometimes briefly referred to as Annex–I–members. Analogously, 21 exporters of minor importance (export entitlements of 70,000 tons each) are called Annex–II–members.

quota–year) and were – with few exceptions – defined as percentages of the respective country's BET.

In the following I give a relatively detailed description of the (supposedly) price–stabilizing mechanisms of the 1968 ISA. The 1977 ISA was in many respects similar to its predecessor; hence I will subsequently confine myself to noting the most distinct differences between the two Agreements.

Article 48 of the 1968 ISA authorized the International Sugar Council to establish the initial level of export quotas in each quota year and to increase or reduce the level of quotas in effect subject to the following provisions:

- If the prevailing price is above 4 cts/lb, then quotas shall not be restrained below 100% BET, unless the Council, by *special vote*[158], decides otherwise.

- If the prevailing price rises above 4.50 cts/lb, then quotas shall not be restrained below 110% BET.

- If the prevailing price exceeds 5.25 cts/lb, then all quotas shall be inoperative.

- If the prevailing price, having been above 5.25 cts/lb, falls below 5 cts/lb, then quotas shall not exceed 115% BET, unless the Council decides otherwise.

- If the prevailing price falls below 4.50 cts/lb, then quotas shall be reduced by 5% of BET, unless the Council decides otherwise.

- If the prevailing price falls below 4 cts/lb, then quotas in effect shall be reduced by another 5% of BET, unless the Council decides otherwise.

- If the prevailing price is at or below 3.50 cts/lb, then quotas in effect shall be at a level of 90% BET, unless the Council, by *special vote*, decides on a higher level.

- If the prevailing price falls to a level of 3.25 cts/lb or below, then the Council may, *by special vote*, establish quotas not lower than 85% BET.

---

[158]A *special vote* was defined to be a vote supported by a two–thirds majority of the exporting members and by a two–thirds majority of the importing members.

It is important to note that quotas were treated as both an export allowance and an export obligation. Exporting members had to notify the Council if they expected to export less than their quota in effect would allow them to do. The Council could, but did not have to, reallocate the announced quota shortfalls. If a country did not fulfill its quota obligations in one year, then potential quota reallocations to this country in the next year were lessened by the amount of the preceding shortfall[159] (Articles 46 and 47, 1968 ISA).

If a member country's exports exceeded its quota in effect within a certain tolerance (10,000 tons or 5% BET, whichever is less), then this quantity was subtracted from the country's quota in the following year. If a member country exceeded its quota beyond this tolerance for the first time, then again the excess was deducted from next year's quota. If a member country, for the second or subsequent time, exceeded its quota in effect, then twice the excess was subtracted from this country's quota in the next year (cf. Article 32).

In addition to these quota–based mechanisms, Articles 52 and 43 of the 1968 ISA payed tribute to the influence stocks exert on world market prices. Exporting members were required to adjust their production such that prior to the new harvest stocks would either not exceed 20% of their production in the immediately preceding calendar year or not exceed 20% of their BET *after* deduction of stocks held for domestic consumption purposes.

This "maximum stock provision" was complemented by a "minimum stock provision": Not counting any stocks required to meet the needs of domestic consumers and obligations under special arrangements, minimum stocks requirements were set at 15% and 10% BET for developed and developing exporting members, respectively. Article 30 then demanded that 50% of the minimum stocks held by exporting members should be released for prompt sale and shipment if the prevailing price rose about 4.75 cts/lb, and the remaining quantity was to be shipped when the prevailing price exceeded 5 cts/lb.

In both cases the quantities of sugar released were supposed to be offered to importing members of the Agreement. Should the prevailing price exceed 5.25 cts/lb, exporting members had to give priority to importing members in all sales to the free market. Should it even exceed 6.50 cts/lb, any importing member enjoyed the option to purchase a well–defined quantity[160] of sugar from its traditional exporting members

[159]Unless the Council accepted *force majeure* as a reason for this shortfall.

[160]This well–defined quantity roughly equalled the two–year average of the free market exports of the exporting member to the importing member concerned, less any such exports in the relevant quota year already traded at a lower price.

at the "supply commitment price" of 6.50 cts/lb (see Article 30, Paragraph 4).

Importing members had their obligations, too. So long as export quotas were in force, importing members were not allowed to permit the import of sugar from non–members exceeding the average quantity imported from these non–members over the three–year period 1966 to 1968. Further, if the prevailing price was lower than 3.25 cts/lb, then all imports from non–members were prohibited. Did an importing member in one quota year not satisfactorily comply with these regulations, then exporting members were relieved from their supply commitments towards this particular country in the next quota year (Article 28, Paragraph 8).

Apart from these fairly precise economic provisions, the signatories also agreed on general formulations demanding a cautious handling of production subsidies (Article 50) and an increased stimulus of sugar consumption (Article 55). However, these articles constituted hardly more than mere declarations of goodwill. Their actual enforcement was impossible due to their contourless wording.

Comparing the 1968 ISA with its 1977 counterpart, a much broader price range in the latter is the most apparent difference: World market prices were now desired to stay within a band of 11 to 21 cts/lb (later changed to 13 to 23 cts/lb). However, while this was but a quantitative change, some qualitative deviations from the 1968 Agreement can be noted. In my opinion the three most important ones are:

a) The introduction of a (misleadingly) so–called "global quota".

The global quota was derived by the Sugar Council as next year's presumed free market import requirements minus estimated exports to the free market by non–members and by member countries not listed in Annex I. It thus essentially described world residual demand after allowing for non–member trade and exports of small member countries. Consequently, the global quota was supposed to be distributed as effective import quotas to the Annex–I–exporters pro rata to their BETs (Article 40(4), ISA 1977). Thus, the new feature (as opposed to the 1968 ISA) was given by the explicit incorporation of demand conditions in the quota mechanism. However, the strength of the global quota was considerably weakened by the restriction that quotas in effect should not be less than 85% BET (in some rare cases not less than 82.5% BET) (see Article 41).

b) The dual role of stocks.

Stocks were viewed in the dual role of ensuring a smooth pattern of domestic trade and consumption (transactionary motive) and of serving as a reserve in times of crisis (precautionary motive). Hence the ISA 1977 demanded that stocks held for domestic needs were separated from the (newly introduced) "special stocks" (Article 46 of the Agreement). The latter – all of which were to be held by Annex–I–members – were clearly intended to serve as precautionary stocks with an aspired level of 2.5 million tons in the aggregate. Their release was prescribed when the world market price exceeded specific thresholds (Article 44 B).

This mechanism replaced the minimum stock provision of the 1968 ISA and was considered to be more effective, since in contrast to the setup of the earlier Agreement the released special stocks were definitely available for immediate shipment and prompt sale was mandatory. The maximum stock provision (Article 48) was virtually identical to its 1968 analog, and referred, of course, to total stocks held, i. e. it included both transactionary and special stocks.

c) Automatic adjustments of BETs.

BETs for the third and subsequent years of the Agreement were not fixed in advance. If, as was likely, efforts to renegotiate BETs lacked success, then BETs were supposed to be calculated according to a fall–back formula. This formula attempted to adjust BETs with respect to the exporters' actual performances[161]. Its basic idea was to set the new BET at the average of the two highest relative export performances in the preceding three years[162]. For developing exporters which had registered expansion projects before the entry into force of the Agreement, the formula also granted the possibility of adding 80% of any unexportable surplus production to their BETs. More details of the fall–back formula are given in Article 34, ISA 1977.

Figure 5 depicts the main price stabilizing mechanisms of the 1977 ISA. It is easily seen that unlike its 1968 predecessor the 1977 Agreement confined quota–based measures to the defense of the lower part of the price range, while special stocks were

---

[161]Certain safeguards to cover cases of *force majeure* in production were included.

[162]The relative export performance was defined to be a country's free market net exports (less any quantity in excess of the quota in effect, less any deficit in stock accumulation) divided by the aggregate of all such net exports of Annex–I–members and multiplied by the sum of all BETs in the previous year.

Figure 5

Price Stabilizing Mechanisms of the 1977 ISA

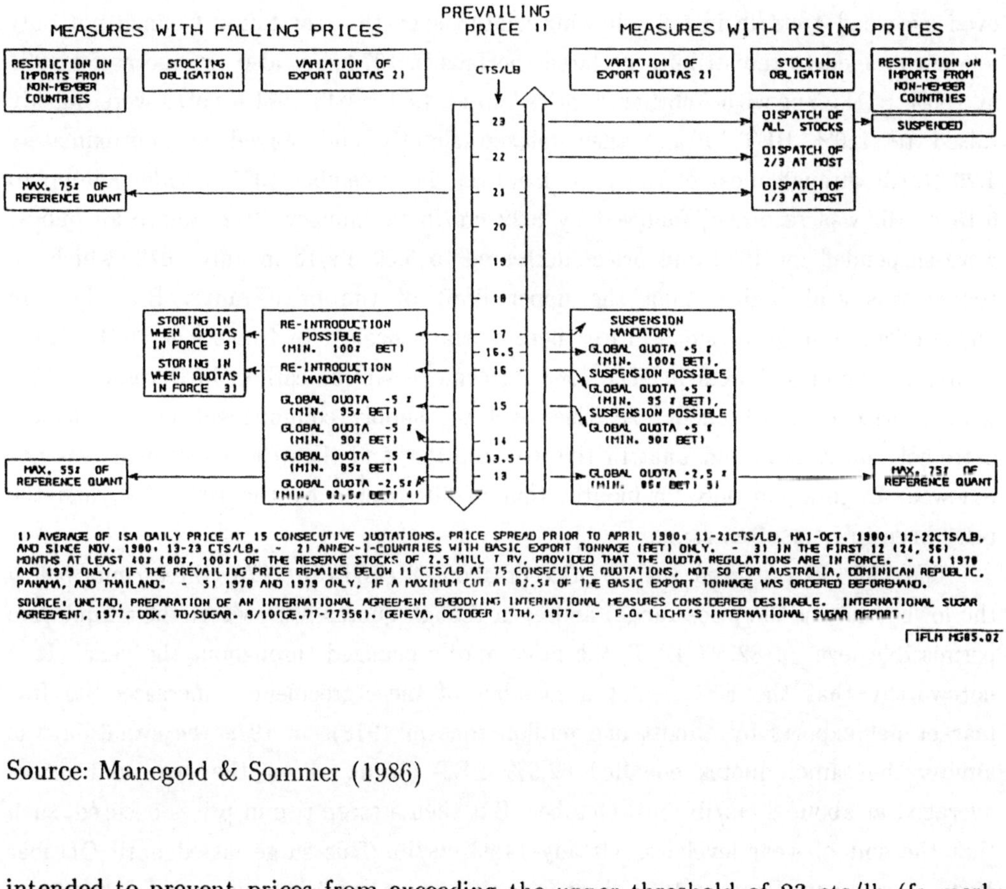

Source: Manegold & Sommer (1986)

intended to prevent prices from exceeding the upper threshold of 23 cts/lb (formerly 21 cts/lb). Apart from that the adjustment mechanisms were very similar. For a very careful ex–ante analysis of the 1977 ISA see Schmidt (1978).

6.2 The Agreements in Practice

When the 1968 ISA came into effect in January 1969, the nominal world market price was at 2.96 cts/lb, well below the lower limit of the price range of 3.50 cts/lb. Quotas were hence set at 90% BET and declared shortfalls were not redistributed. The price rose by almost 1 ct/lb until June 1969, but then fell again to a level of 2.86 cts/lb at the end of the year. Consequently, initial quotas for 1970 still equalled 90% BET. Rising slowly, the price moved into the price range in March 1970 and even exceeded 4 cts/lb in the following winter, such that the Sugar Council not only felt encouraged to redistribute declared shorfalls in 1970, but also set quotas for 1971 at 100% BET. Yet with February's prices up at 4.83 cts/lb 1971–quotas were quickly raised to 110% BET. Prices then relaxed slightly and stayed at approximately 4.20 cts/lb through most of the year. However, in December 1971 a sudden jump to 6.15 cts/lb was recorded, followed by 8.29 cts/lb in January 1972. Hence all quotas were suspended for 1972 and prices decreased to 5.60 cts/lb in July 1972, which, of course was still higher than the upper limit of the price range. But then an unprecedented surge of sugar prices began, which peaked in November 1974 with a *nominal* price of 57.58 cts/lb. The 1968 Agreement expired earlier, in December 1973, with a price of 11.81 cts/lb. At this level the supply commitment price[163] looked extremely unrealistic and unattractive to exporters and thus the Agreement was not renewed. In total, in only 25 months (out of 60 covered by the 1968 ISA) had the price been in its aspired range.

The 1977 ISA started with a price of about 8 cts/lb in 1978 (three cents below the lower limit of the price range) and even though quotas were set at their minimum permissible level of 82.5% BET, the price hardly changed throughout the year. (It is noteworthy that the EEC – not a member of the Agreement – increased its free market net exports by almost one million tons in 1978). In 1979 the situation was almost the same; quotas equalled 82.5% BET during all of the year and prices averaged at about 8 cts/lb until October. But then a steep rise in prices occured, such that the end–of–year level was already 14.93 cts/lb. This surge lasted until October 1980. Already in January 1980, however, all quotas had been suspended and special stocks had been released in three equal installments in February. Two million tons had so far been accumulated, but the effect of their release was so insignificant, that the missing 500,000 tons would almost certainly not have made any difference. Not

[163]The supply commitment price equalled 7.60 cts/lb in 1973. It had been set at this higher level after changes in the gold parity of the dollar.

even increased EEC exports (an additional 800,000 tons as opposed to 1978 and 1979) were able to reverse the trend.

With the turn of the year 1980/81, prices suddenly fell (and rapidly so), such that quotas were reintroduced in May 1981 at 100% BET. This, however, hardly restricted the supply side, since exports attributable to sales prior to the reestablishment of quotas were exempted from a country's yearly total of free market net exports if this total exceeded the quota in effect (Article 45 (6), ISA 1977). Thus from June to December 1981 Annex–I– members could actually export as much sugar as would usually have been their allowance for the whole year. Consequently, the ISA was widely regarded as ineffective in 1981 and, possibly also in response to EEC exports of 5.3 million tons (up 1.1 million tons from 1980), prices more than halved: From 27.93 cts/lb in January down to 12.98 cts/lb in December.

The BETs for 1981 were the first to be determined by the fall–back formula. As a result of using the two best export performances out of the last three years in the calcualtion, the total of BETs increased by 9%. In 1982 the same procedure applied, and this time BETs were inflated by 12%. Even though quotas for 1982 were set at the minimum level of 85% BET, the control of the market was not tight enough to prevent the price from falling to 6.31 cts/lb in December 1982. This of course, was an embarrassing situation for the ISA, since not only had sugar prices halved once again within a single year, but also had the *lower* bound of the desired price range just been redefined at 13 cts/lb.

Despite this apparent failure, a special Council session in November 1982 decided to extend the Agreement for two more years until the end of 1984. BETs were frozen at their 1982 level and quotas for both 1983 and 1984 remained at 85% BET. Yet prices stayed well below 13 cts/lb throughout these years, and despite a mild recovery until June 1983 (10.74 cts/lb) a price as low as 3.55 cts/lb had to be recorded in December 1984. Disenchanted by these experiences, the members of the 1977 ISA decided not to prolong the Agreement any further and replaced it by the 1984 ISA, a purely administrative accord renouncing measures of market control.

It is finally of interest to review the actual exports of Annex–I–members to the free market in years in which quotas have been operative. Since it is not clear when precisely a quota for a specific country has been binding, I prefer to identify those periods, in which either quotas have definitely *not* been binding, or in which countries have apparently ignored their restrictions and exported in excess of quotas.

As for the first, it is natural to suppose that a quota has not been binding if the country in question exported less than 95% of its quota in effect, since that, under Articles 46 and 42 of the ISA 1968 and 1977, respectively, constituted a violation of

Table 28

Quota–Related Export Performance of Selected ISA–Members[164]

	69	70	71	78	79	81	82	83	84
ARG			–		–	+	–	+	–
AUS						–		–	–
BRA						–		+	+
COL	–	–	–	/	/	–	–	+	–
CUB			–				–	–	–
DOM	–					–	–		–
FIJ			–			–		–	–
GUY	–	–				–	–	–	–
IND	–		–			–	–	+	–
MAU			–			–		–	–
MEX	–	–	–		–	–	–	–	–
PHI						–	–	–	–
SAF						–		–	–
SWA									+
TAI	–	–	–	/	/	/	/	/	/
THA	/		/		+	–	+	+	+

– = Exports less than 95% of quota in effect.

\+ = Exports in excess of quota in effect plus tolerance specified in Article 32, ISA 1968, or Article 45, ISA 1977.

/ = Not an ISA-member in the respective year.

[164]For years in which quotas have been in force. Entries for Guyana under the 1968 ISA actually refer to the West Indies.

export commitments. Analogously, if actual exports exceeded the basic export tonnage by more than 5% (or 10,000 tons, whichever was less), then, in accordance with Article 32, ISA 1968, and Article 45, ISA 1977, I consider this to be in breach with quota restrictions.

Table 28 gives a quick survey of member countries' export performances in quota–governed years. Apparently, two countries (Colombia and Taiwan) never complied with their quota obligations and two others (Mexico and Thailand) closely followed their footprints. For the 1968 ISA, no exports in excess of quotas had to be recorded, but there have been quite a few quota shortfalls. For the 1977 ISA, member countries were well disciplined during 1978 and 1979. As I have noted above, quotas in 1981 have been largely ineffective due to their delayed reestablishment; only two countries (Cuba and Swaziland) may nevertheless have felt restricted. The situation improved slightly in 1982, but, probably attributable to inflated BETs, significantly more shortfalls occurred than in 1978 and 1979. Finally, in 1983 and 1984 the Agreement was hardly respected any more; in fact, not a single country fulfilled its quota obligations in 1984, and in 1983 only two (the Dominican Republic and Swaziland) did. Despite the considerably inflated BETs, eight cases of excessive exports had to be noted in these years.

The decay of an ISA's authority in its last year (or years) of existence has often been deplored by analysts. Most likely it is due to the fact that enforcement mechanisms of an ISA are usually defined with respect to next year's quotas, BETs, voting rights, etc., such that these are unimpressive if the Agreement is known to expire in the next year. We will come back to this issue in the next chapter.

Chapter 7: Structural Change on the World Sugar Market

7.1 Tests and Monte Carlo Results

While the ISAs of 1968 and 1977 undisputably failed to meet their self–defined objectives[165], this does not necessarily imply that they did not have any effect at all. A evaluation of what the ISAs accomplished and an analysis of the causes for their failure is hence desirable.

To this end, I will assume that the world sugar market has been subject to two distinct regimes, which I will call the free–trade– and the ISA–regime. Such an assumption greatly simplifies the analysis since most tests for structural change specify an alternative of precisely two regimes. It is, however, indeed a simplification, for the price–stabilizing mechanisms of the two ISAs concerned were, as illustrated above, only similar, but not really identical.

On the other hand, a more appropriate way of modeling switching regimes is not readily at hand. This is due to the fact, that even the ISAs taken separately did not display a constant structure. Rather, BETs have often been renegotiated or recalculated, hardship funds have been allocated to particular countries and thus distorted BETs, some countries have been exempted from their obligations for various reasons, a couple of countries acceded to the Agreements later than 1969 or 1978, respectively, and others withdrew prematurely[166]. Most (if not all) of these issues were presumably of minor importance, but so, I believe, were the discrepancies between the price stabilizing mechanisms of the 1968 and the 1977 ISA.

---

[165]For the 1977 ISA the price stayed in the desired price range during 24 out of 72 months, even though the price range was much broader than in the 1968 ISA.

[166]During the 1977 ISA, even the desired price range changed.

Modeling the world sugar market with three or more regimes could thus also be subject to legitimate criticism. Moreover, testing strategies would be fairly complicated since the true shift points are often unknown[167] and the power of the tests is likely to suffer if the alternative specifies more regimes than necessary.

Tests for structural change are quite abundant in the literature, and hence we have to select some of them. The most well–known example is the Chow–test[168]. This is a parametric F–test and thus not particularly appropriate for our problem, where most disturbances are non–normal. However, using bootstrap estimates, the Chow–test can still sensibly be applied.

The Wilcoxon–, the van–der–Waerden–, and the Median–test are nonparametric in nature, i. e. they are valid for any (continuous) i.i.d. distribution of the error terms[169]. All of these tests take the residuals obtained under the null of structural constancy, group them into two subsamples corresponding to the alternative's different regimes, and then check whether the errors in the subsamples stem from the same distribution. Specifically, the Wilcoxon test compares the sum of the ranks in the subsamples, the van–der–Waerden test sums ranks transformed by the inverse of a normal distribution function, and the Median test simply compares the medians of the subsamples. The results of these tests are often very similar; my motivation for using them simultaneously lies in the fact that their power properties vary with different distributions. For instance, the Wilcoxon test is locally most powerful if the distribution of the error terms is logistic, while the van–der–Waerden test has asymptotically optimal properties for normal distributions.

The CUSUM– and the CUSUM–of–Squares–test rely on test statistics using standardized sums of recursive residuals, or squares thereof, respectively, (see e. g. Krämer & Sonnberger (1986)). They display the interesting property that the shift point between the two regimes need not be known a priori, but can (in principle) be inferred from the time path of the recursive residuals. (The shift point is usually presumed to be approximately where recursive residuals start wandering off their expected value under the null hypothesis). Empirically, however, this point is still extremely difficult to identify.

---

[167]This is due to the fact that subperiods of the ISAs may have been ineffective – a difficulty already prevalent with only two regimes.

[168]I use this test also as a regression subroutine. A brief discussion can therefore be found in the Appendix.

[169]Strictly speaking, these tests do not even require serial independence of the errors. A slightly weaker notion called "interchangeability" is already sufficient, see McCabe (1989).

The apparent disadvantage of the CUSUM–of–Squares is its need for normally distributed error terms. Since this condition is hardly ever fulfilled in the world sugar economy, I will not use this test. The CUSUM, on the other hand, is distribution–free and should therefore give a valid test statistic, even though the critical values can only approximately be determined whenever the shift point does not split the sample into equally large parts.

Recently, Ploberger et al. (1989) suggested to use a test statistic based on recursive standardized parameter estimates rather than recursive residuals. This so–called fluctuation test can be viewed as a backward CUSUM–procedure; it is distribution–free and does not require knowledge of the true shift point. Ploberger et al. show that it compares favorably with both the CUSUM and the CUSUM–of–Squares in the classical linear set–up. I have hence considered to use this test alongside the above mentioned ones.

However, all of these tests are constructed for a model with an exogenous regressor matrix. Yet the equations to be tested in this application also display lagged *endogenous* variables as regressors. This casts some doubts on the validity of the tests, especially in finite samples. For knowledge on the tests' distributions under dynamic specifications is – as far as I know – limited to asymptotic results, see e. g. Dufour (1982), Krämer & Sonnberger (1986), and Krämer et al. (1988). I thus tried to assess the seriousness of the problem by running a small simulation study.

I first constructed a zero–mean first order autoregressive process with autoregressive parameter α:

$$y_t = \alpha\, y_{t-1} + \epsilon_t$$

Errors (ϵ_t) were obtained from independent drawings of a standard normal distribution using the GAUSS random number generator. I picked hundred observations for each realization of the process. For a given value of α, the Chow–, the Wilcoxon–, the van–der–Waerden–, the Median–, the CUSUM–, and the Fluctuation–test were applied to a total of thousand realized processes. For all tests the alternative postulated a structural change at the sample's midpoint, i. e. after fifty observations. Table 29 shows the actual rejection rates at the 10%–, the 5%–, and the 1%–level of significance for selected values of α.

It is immediately seen that the Fluctuation test is totally inacceptable in the presence of lagged endogenous variables in the regressor matrix. The test is extremely liberal in this case and its performance deteriorates with $|\alpha|$ approaching 1. As for the other tests, we note that in the random walk case of $|\alpha| = 1$ almost all of the

Table 29

Monte Carlo Results: The Null of Structural Constancy is True

α	Nominal Signif. Level	Rejection Rates (1000 Realizations)					
		Chow	Wilcoxon	v.d.Waer.	Median	CUSUM	Fluctuat.
1	10%	0.120	0.132	0.132	0.180	0.122	0.838
	5%	0.064	0.061	0.062	0.095	0.066	0.804
	1%	0.010	0.004	0.006	0.013	0.009	0.738
0.9	10%	0.091	0.090	0.086	0.159	0.074	0.415
	5%	0.050	0.034	0.030	0.074	0.032	0.356
	1%	0.006	0.002	0.001	0.009	0.008	0.258
0.7	10%	0.090	0.089	0.091	0.152	0.065	0.280
	5%	0.038	0.039	0.041	0.051	0.029	0.215
	1%	0.008	0.005	0.006	0.004	0.006	0.140
0.3	10%	0.085	0.089	0.094	0.150	0.068	0.140
	5%	0.043	0.045	0.047	0.054	0.029	0.096
	1%	0.005	0.004	0.004	0.008	0.002	0.062
-0.3	10%	0.093	0.091	0.096	0.143	0.064	0.162
	5%	0.052	0.051	0.052	0.064	0.030	0.113
	1%	0.009	0.007	0.006	0.007	0.003	0.066
-0.7	10%	0.090	0.101	0.095	0.154	0.067	0.259
	5%	0.048	0.051	0.045	0.074	0.028	0.201
	1%	0.001	0.011	0.008	0.011	0.009	0.140
-0.9	10%	0.099	0.084	0.083	0.160	0.057	0.455
	5%	0.047	0.039	0.045	0.061	0.028	0.400
	1%	0.013	0.007	0.008	0.005	0.005	0.298
-1	10%	0.120	0.107	0.115	0.166	0.062	0.827
	5%	0.058	0.059	0.057	0.070	0.027	0.789
	1%	0.016	0.007	0.009	0.008	0.005	0.708

tests are liberal at the 10%– and 5%–level of significance. (The exception is the CUSUM, which is conservative for $\alpha = -1$). The Median–test is generally liberal at the 10%– and at the 5%–level. In all other cases the simulated rejection rates are either close to their expected values or suggest mildly conservative tests. Out of these it appears that the CUSUM is the most conservative test.

I have run an analogous simulation with a regressor matrix in which the lagged endogenous variable is complemented by an exogenous regressor and a constant. Here the performance of the Fluctuation test was even worse; for instance in the case of $\alpha = 1$ *all* statistics for this test rejected even at the 1%–level. Otherwise the results were similar to those displayed in Table 29; however, in some constellations tests which looked conservative in the purely autoregressive case did now appear slightly liberal (the CUSUM, most notably, but also the Wilcoxon– and the van–der–Waerden–test). Thus the actual level of the tests in application with lagged endogenous variables as regressors cannot easily be inferred from Table 29. All that can definitely be said relates to the inappropriateness of the Fluctuation test.

7.2 Formulating Alternatives

In testing for structural change on the world market for sugar I will hence use the Chow–, the Wilcoxon–, the van–der–Waerden–, the Median– and the CUSUM–test. Since there are various equally plausible alternative hypotheses, I will run the tests against those alternatives, which appear most appealing from what we know about the performance of the ISAs. In general, the following alternatives will be used:

(1) There was a structural change for the ISA 1968 but not for the ISA 1977, i. e. the ISA–regime is confined to the years 1969 to 1973.

(2) There was a structural change for the ISA 1977, but not for the ISA 1968, i. e. the ISA–regime is confined to the years 1978 to 1984.

(3) There was a structural change for both the ISA 1968 and the ISA 1977, i. e. the ISA–regime consists of the years 1969 to 1973 and 1978 to 1984.

As we have seen, the ISAs eroded considerably already one or two years before actual expiration (cf. Table 28). It is in particular the last year which is cumbersome, since for this year the enforcement mechanisms of the Agreements lacked strength.

Also, Table 28 strongly suggests that the ISA 1977 suffered from a severe loss of authority already in 1983. Therefore I modify the above alternatives by omitting 1973 (last year of the 1968 ISA) as well as 1983 and 1984 (last two years of the 1977 ISA). I will call this the "narrow" definition of the ISAs:

(4) There was a structural change for the ISA 1968 in its narrow definition, but not for the ISA 1977, i. e. the ISA–regime is confined to the years 1969 to 1972.

(5) There was a structural change for the ISA 1977 in its narrow definition, but not for the ISA 1968, i. e. the ISA–regime is confined to the years 1978 to 1982.

(6) There was a structural change for both the ISA 1968 and the ISA 1977 in their narrow definitions, i. e. the ISA–regime consists of the years 1969 to 1972 and 1978 to 1982.

Apart from stockholding, the provisions of the ISAs may also have influenced systematic excess production. For instance, systematic excess production might have decreased in, say, the first one or two years of an Agreement (as a result of expected quota restrictions), such that quotas were basically not binding any more after this adjustment process took place. Stock demand equations should then be tested against alternatives specifying a structural change for the first one or two years of the Agreement. This is even more appropriate as Table 28 suggests that quota discipline has been particularly good in the beginning of the ISAs. For these reasons not only the stock, but (consequently) also the price equations should be tested against the following alternatives:

(7) There was a structural change for the first two years of each Agreement, i. e. the ISA–regime consists of the years 1969 to 1970 and 1978 to 1979.

(8) There was a structural change for the very first year of each Agreement, i. e. the ISA–regime consists of the years 1969 and 1978.

In testing the equation for world systematic excess production WOREXC, the analog to alternatives (7) and (8) will be formulated in terms of the narrow definitions of the ISAs:

(7*) There was a structural change for the third and following years of the ISAs in their narrow definition, i. e. the ISA–regime comprises the years 1971 to 1972 and 1980 to 1982.

(8*) There was a structural change for the second and following years of the ISAs in their narrow definition, i. e. the ISA–regime comprises the years 1970 to 1972 and 1979 to 1982.

For stock demand equations we should also test the following alternative:

(9) There was a structural change for those years, in which the quota for the country in question may have been binding (as indicated by Table 28).

The motivation for such an alternative is the idea that if actual exports were close to the quantity allowed under the quota, the country may temporarily have felt confined in its export policies even though there was no involuntary stockholding at the end of the year. Of course, specifying an alternative like (9) basically asserts that the ISAs were (sometimes, at least) successful in preventing *lower* prices, while they were unable to counteract price booms. (Note that under alternative (9) years with high world market prices do not belong to the ISA–regime).

For all of these alternatives the observations have to be regrouped if the CUSUM–test is to be applied. I do always group observations from the ISA–regime first and observations from the free–trade regime last[170]. The reason for not choosing the reverse order is the following: By letting the ISA–observations precede the free–trade observations, the last years of the ISA–regime are next to the beginning of the free–trade regime. Since the last years of the ISAs may actually have been ineffective, this ordering is preferable with respect to the power of the tests. The order of the observations within the two supposed subsamples is chronological.

However, by the nature of the CUSUM–test, no particular alternative needs to be specified. Applying the CUSUM to all observations in proper chronological order yields a test with the most general alternative:

(10) There was at least one structural change during the sample period.

---

[170]I also used the data in the neighborhood of the shift point. Thus, for instance, the first observation of a new regime will in general partly be explained by the last observation of the old regime.

Unfortunately, since regimes may have been switching back and forth, the power of this test may be pretty poor. Still, this is the most natural way to use the CUSUM–test and it is desirable to have at least one test testing against alternative (10). As should be plain, the Chow–test and the non–parametric tests[171] cannot be used together with alternative (10).

It is somewhat arbitrary to specify the above alternatives and omit others, which might also be legitimate. However, the more alternatives we test, the stronger does this distort the level of the tests, since the likelihood for finding at least one significant statistic naturally increases with the number of alternatives specified. For the ten above alternatives applied to the five different tests, we get already a total of 46 test statistics[172] for country–specific stock equations and 41 test statistics for equations without exploitable information on potentially binding quota years.

Obviously, some of these test statistics will be strongly correlated. For instance, suppose the true ISA–regime to be confined to the first two years of each Agreement. Then it may well be that the test statistics for *all* alternatives suggest rejection of the null even though all but one are specified with the *wrong* alternative. Since we do not have any a–priori– knowledge on the degree of correlation between test statistics from different tests and different alternatives, the level of the tests taken on a comprehensive basis is also unknown.

Due to this problem, I have arbitrarily decided to reject the null of structural constancy whenever at least one out of the total of all test statistics rejects at the 1%–level of significance or whenever at least three statistics are 5%–significant. In case of rejection, the alternative to be accepted has to be selected with regard to the P–values of the test statistics, the CUSUM–plots, and possible external information.

---

[171]Henceforth I will summarize the Wilcoxon–, the van–der–Waerden–, and the Median–test by speaking of the "nonparametric" tests. The CUSUM–test, although also distribution– free, shall not be covered by this terminology.

[172]Recall alternative (10) can only be used with the CUSUM.

7.3 Testing in Practice: Stock Demand Equations

I will start with applying the above tests to the stock demand equations (57) – (73):

a) Argentina (Table 30)

We get six test statistics with P–values smaller than 5%, out of which one corresponds to a probability of precisely 1%. All other P–values are fairly high. The rejections occur for alternatives (1) and (4), i. e. for the 1968 ISA in its wide and in its narrow definition. The P–values for the narrow definition are slightly smaller than for the wide definition, thus accepting a structural change for the narrow definition

Table 30

Tests for Structural Change: LNARGSTO (Equ. (60))

Alter-native #	Under alterna-tive ISA-re-gime comprises	P-values				
		Chow	Wilcoxon	v.d.Waer.	Median	CUSUM
1	69-73	0.256	0.023*	0.036*	0.017*	> 0.10
2	78-84	0.214	0.313	0.389	0.279	> 0.10
3	69-73, 78-84	0.297	0.306	0.309	0.292	> 0.10
4	69-72	0.087	0.016*	0.027*	0.010**	> 0.10
5	78-82	0.233	0.379	0.376	0.551	> 0.10
6	69-72, 78-82	0.235	0.245	0.313	0.119	> 0.10
7	69-70, 78-79	0.474	0.226	0.311	0.150	> 0.10
8	69, 78	0.574	0.867	0.907	0.667	> 0.10
9	69, 70, 78	0.494	0.690	0.719	0.718	> 0.10

* = significant at the 5%-level
** = significant at the 1%-level

might be preferable. However, the chronological CUSUM–plot[173], although not significant, strongly suggests that if a structural change took place for the 1968 ISA, then the ISA–regime ended with the beginning of 1972 (Figure 6). I thus accept the alternative of having an ISA–regime from 1969 to 1971 and a free–trade regime elsewhere.

Figure 6

CUSUM–Plot for LNARGSTO (Alternative 10)

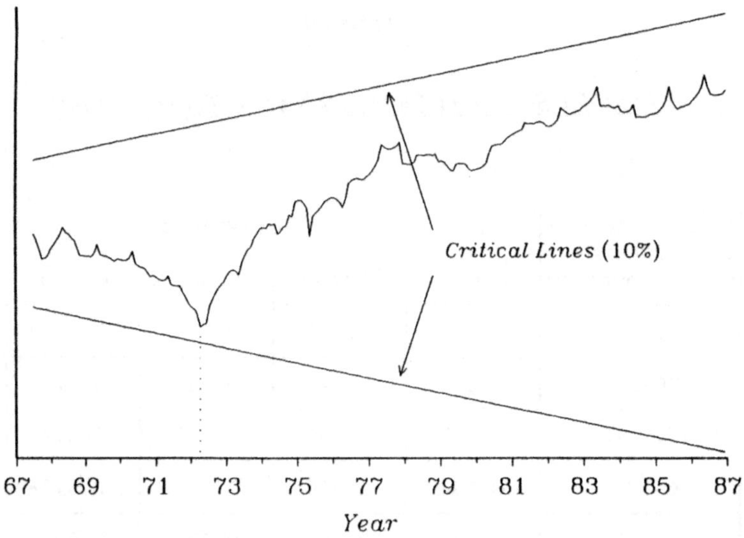

[173]Many of the CUSUM–plots I obtain are insignificant even at the 10%–level. However, it may occur that insignificant CUSUM–plots nevertheless hint at the location of a possible break point. I will thus sometimes give figures of insignificant CUSUM–plots instead of significant ones if the former allow an apparently easier inference on the alternative to be accepted.

b) Australia (Table 31)

We find solely test statistics with P–values much higher than 5%, thus we will suppose structural constancy.

Table 31

Tests for Structural Change: AUSSTO (Equ. (61))

Alter-native #	Under alterna-tive ISA-re-gime comprises	P-values				
		Chow	Wilcoxon	v.d.Waer.	Median	CUSUM
1	69-73	0.470	0.736	0.842	0.371	> 0.10
2	78-84	0.471	0.945	0.938	0.588	> 0.10
3	69-73, 78-84	0.934	0.817	0.801	0.792	> 0.10
4	69-72	0.481	0.659	0.525	0.999	> 0.10
5	78-82	0.248	0.440	0.354	0.765	> 0.10
6	69-72, 78-82	0.336	0.751	0.768	0.795	> 0.10
7	69-70, 78-79	0.745	0.702	0.726	0.423	> 0.10
8	69, 78	0.517	0.478	0.446	0.999	> 0.10
9	69-71,78-79,82	0.194	0.676	0.604	0.259	> 0.10
10	not specified	-	-	-	-	> 0.10

* = significant at the 5%-level
** = significant at the 1%-level

c) Brazil (Table 32)

There is not a single significant test statistic, hence the null will be accepted.

Table 32

Tests for Structural Change: ΔLNBRASTO (Equ. (57))

Alter-native #	Under alternative ISA-regime comprises	P-values				
		Chow	Wilcoxon	v.d.Waer.	Median	CUSUM
1	69-73	0.171	0.544	0.874	0.073	> 0.10
2	78-84	0.185	0.103	0.180	0.104	> 0.10
3	69-73, 78-84	0.169	0.292	0.242	0.999	> 0.10
4	69-72	0.195	0.498	0.866	0.053	> 0.10
5	78-82	0.205	0.072	0.132	0.073	> 0.10
6	69-72, 78-82	0.199	0.305	0.239	0.999	> 0.10
7	69-70, 78-79	0.240	0.936	0.800	0.423	> 0.10
8	69, 78	0.824	0.745	0.989	0.196	> 0.10
9	69-71,78-79,82	0.813	0.643	0.927	0.259	> 0.10
10	not specified	-	-	-	-	> 0.10

* = significant at the 5%-level
** = significant at the 1%-level

d) Colombia (Table 33)

Colombia acceeded to the 1977 ISA with more than two years delay in the middle of 1980, thus the years 1978 to 1980 belong to the free–trade regime[174]. In particular, alternatives (7) and (8) refer to 1981, 1982, and 1981, respectively. Alternative (9) could not be specified since there are no possibly binding quota years discernable (Table 28).

All test statistics are insignificant, with the exception of the CUSUM–test which rejects twice at the 5%–level. According to our prespecified rule this is not sufficient for rejection of the null of structural constancy, but since this rule has been arbitrarily set, the matter deserves further analysis.

Both rejections refer to an alternative in which solely the 1968 ISA is assumed to cause a structural change. These two CUSUM–plots are very similar; I depict the plot for alternative (4) (ISA 1968 in its narrow definition) in Figure 7. It is easy to see that the point where the CUSUM–plot starts moving in the direction of the critical region is far off the 1968 ISA. In fact, it almost coincides with the year 1978, the beginning of the 1977 ISA, and the plot behaves normally again following Colombia's accession to the ISA in 1980. The same phenomenon can be observed in the chronological CUSUM–plot (Figure 8), which, however, does not move into the critical region (the graphic shows the critical 10%–lines).

It thus appears that Colombia built up unusually high stocks in 1978 and 1979, and one reason for that might have been a distortion of traditional trading patterns by the ISA. For instance, the USA have formerly been one of Colombia's main trading partners (in 1975 US imports from Colombia were close to 150,000 mt). But in 1978 and 1979 Colombia exported only 45,000 mt and 13,000 mt, respectively, to the United States. Now note that in these years the United States as a member of the 1977 ISA was granted only few free market imports from non–members like Colombia (such import allowances totalled 50,000 tons in 1978 and no imports at all in 1979). In fact, the US actually exceeded their import allotments in both years, and would thus have had great difficulties in importing even more sugar from Colombia. The way out of this dilemma was Colombia's accession to the Agreement, which resulted in Colombian exports to the US being up again at 175,000 tons already in 1980.

The two significant CUSUM–statistics can thus plausibly be viewed as being due to a temporary distortion of trading patterns. This distortion is attributable to the

---

[174] I include 1980, the year of accession, in the free–trade regime since quotas have been inoperative in this year. As Colombia had not yet accumulated special stocks to be released, the country was essentially unrestricted in its export policies in 1980.

Figure 7
CUSUM–Plot for LNCOLSTO (Alternative 4)

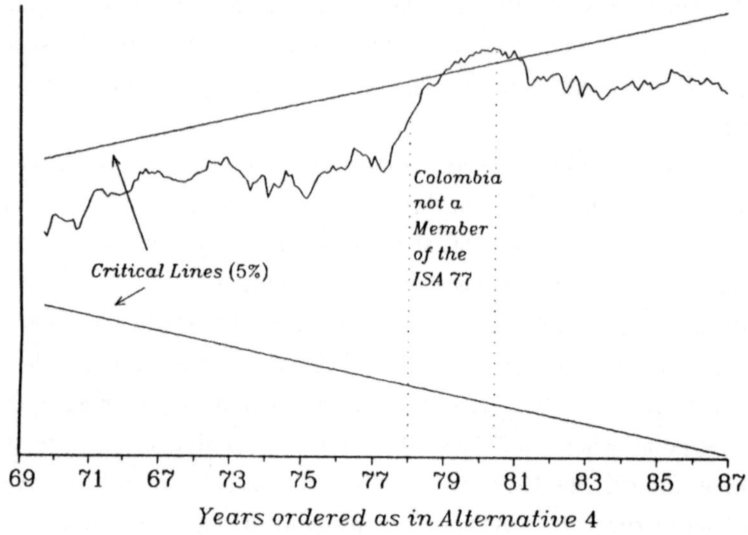

Figure 8
CUSUM–Plot for LNCOLSTO (Alternative 10)

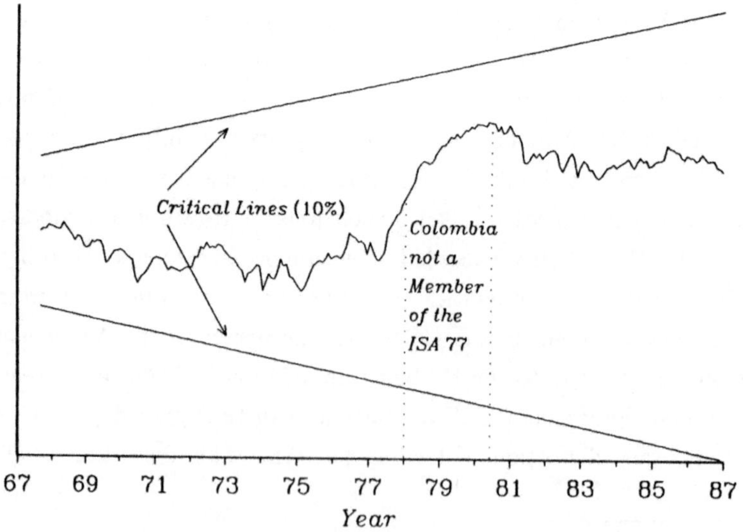

1977 ISA, but it should not be viewed as evidence for a structural change in our model. For we suppose regimes which are stable and thus admit an equilibrium interpretation. Colombia, however, had she stayed outside of the ISA, would probably sooner or later have found new trading partners and would then have disposed of her surplus production. The increased stock levels in 1978 and 1979 can hence only be viewed as the result of an adjustment process; they would not have persisted in equilibrium. With this reasoning I decide to accept the null of structural constancy.

Table 33

Tests for Structural Change: LNCOLSTO (Equ. (62))

Alter-native #	Under alterna-tive ISA-re-gime comprises	P-values				
		Chow	Wilcoxon	v.d.Waer.	Median	CUSUM
1	69-73	0.670	0.417	0.523	0.232	< 0.05*
2	81-84	0.468	0.656	0.388	0.332	> 0.10
3	69-73, 81-84	0.473	0.286	0.210	0.795	> 0.10
4	69-72	0.610	0.868	0.929	0.518	< 0.05*
5	81-82	0.163	0.495	0.287	0.999	> 0.10
6	69-72, 81-82	0.239	0.554	0.438	0.572	> 0.10
7	69-70, 81-82	0.130	0.853	0.752	0.747	> 0.10
8	69, 81	0.207	0.856	0.878	0.999	> 0.10
10	not specified	-	-	-	-	> 0.10

* = significant at the 5%-level
** = significant at the 1%-level

e) Cuba (Table 34)

No significant test statistics are found and therefore the null will be accepted.

Table 34

Tests for Structural Change: CUBSTO (Equ. (63))

Alter-native #	Under alternative ISA-regime comprises	P-values				
		Chow	Wilcoxon	v.d.Waer.	Median	CUSUM
1	69-73	0.749	0.810	0.775	0.766	> 0.10
2	78-84	0.909	0.581	0.633	0.279	> 0.10
3	69-73, 78-84	0.853	0.453	0.473	0.188	> 0.10
4	69-72	0.550	0.726	0.898	0.747	> 0.10
5	78-82	0.389	0.515	0.597	0.551	> 0.10
6	69-72, 78-82	0.197	0.776	0.721	0.795	> 0.10
7	69-70, 78-79	0.675	0.756	0.974	0.631	> 0.10
8	69, 78	0.245	0.305	0.378	0.389	> 0.10
9	69-70,78-79,81	0.287	0.190	0.317	0.136	> 0.10
10	not specified	-	-	-	-	> 0.10

* = significant at the 5%-level
** = significant at the 1%-level

f) The Dominican Republic (Table 35)

A couple of significant CUSUM–statistics make it easy to reject the null. It is, however, less clear which alternative should be accepted. The CUSUM–plots significant at the 1%–level do not reveal a possible point of parameter shift, although both relate to the ISA of 1968. For the narrow definition of this Agreement, the other tests display P–values between 25% and 36%, while in the wide definition some P–values are much higher. This may indicate that the narrow definition is more appropriate. The chronological CUSUM–plot, though insignificant, supports this view insofar as it suggests that possible effects of the 1968 ISA on Dominican stockholding faded prior to the expiration of the Agreement (cf. Figure 9).

On the other hand, the CUSUM–statistics for alternative (7) (first two years of each Agreement) and (9) (binding quota years) suggest that the years 1978 and 1979 might also have caused a structural change. Combining these, I will adopt the alternative hypothesis of an ISA–regime comprising years 1969 to 1972 and 1978 to 1979).

Figure 9

CUSUM–Plot for LNDOMSTO (Alternative 10)

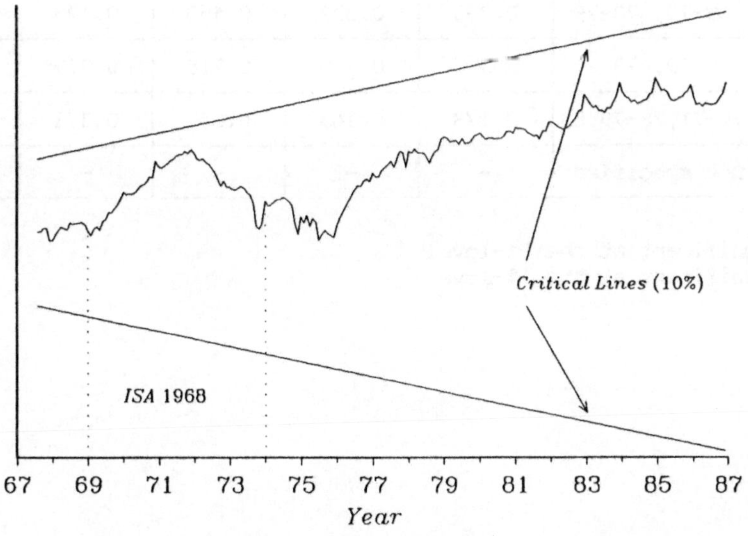

Table 35

Tests for Structural Change: LNDOMSTO (Equ. (64))

Alter-native #	Under alterna-tive ISA-re-gime comprises	P-values				
		Chow	Wilcoxon	v.d.Waer.	Median	CUSUM
1	69-73	0.129	0.837	0.695	0.999	< 0.01**
2	78-84	0.267	0.619	0.979	0.176	> 0.10
3	69-73, 78-84	0.462	0.505	0.749	0.188	< 0.05*
4	69-72	0.253	0.313	0.355	0.333	< 0.01**
5	78-82	0.646	0.664	0.998	0.136	> 0.10
6	69-72, 78-82	0.236	0.665	0.456	0.604	< 0.05*
7	69-70, 78-79	0.263	0.522	0.450	0.423	< 0.05*
8	69, 78	0.306	0.785	0.718	0.999	> 0.10
9	70-71,78-79,83	0.178	0.163	0.143	0.371	< 0.05*
10	not specified	-	-	-	-	> 0.10

* = significant at the 5%-level
** = significant at the 1%-level

g) Fiji (Table 36)

All test statistics are insignificant and hence the null is accepted.

Table 36

Tests for Structural Change: LNFIJSTO (Equ. (65))

Alter-native #	Under alterna-tive ISA-re-gime comprises	P-values				
		Chow	Wilcoxon	v.d.Waer.	Median	CUSUM
1	69-73	0.497	0.118	0.085	0.551	> 0.10
2	78-84	0.348	0.138	0.149	0.278	> 0.10
3	69-73, 78-84	0.745	0.951	0.905	0.597	> 0.10
4	69-72	0.651	0.690	0.581	0.747	> 0.10
5	78-82	0.227	0.336	0.338	0.551	> 0.10
6	69-72, 78-82	0.647	0.605	0.695	0.435	> 0.10
7	69-70, 78-79	0.650	0.110	0.149	0.149	> 0.10
8	69, 78	0.258	0.089	0.128	0.197	> 0.10
9	69-70,78.79 82	0.715	0.085	0.110	0.136	> 0.10
10	not specified	-	-	-	-	> 0.10

* = significant at the 5%-level
** = significant at the 1%-level

h) Guyana (Table 37)

Four statistics are significant, out of which one has a probability of less than 1% under the null. The CUSUM–test rejects in favor of alternative (4) (narrow definition of the 1968 ISA), but the plot does not indicate the point of structural shift; it actually crosses the critical 5%–line far off where the alternative supposed the shift to take place (Figure 10). As far as the other tests are concerned, most P–values for alternative (7) are much lower than for alternative (4). For that reason I accept alternative (7) (first two years of each Agreement)[175].

Table 37

Tests for Structural Change: LNGUYSTO (Equ. (66))

Alter-native #	Under alterna-tive ISA-re-gime comprises	P-values				
		Chow	Wilcoxon	v.d.Waer.	Median	CUSUM
1	69-73	0.701	0.484	0.564	0.233	> 0.05
2	78-84	0.424	0.668	0.566	0.417	> 0.10
3	69-73, 78-84	0.437	0.841	0.961	0.792	> 0.10
4	69-72	0.653	0.399	0.516	0.107	< 0.05*
5	78-82	0.557	0.603	0.858	0.551	> 0.10
6	69-72, 78-82	0.355	0.258	0.497	0.069	> 0.10
7	69-70, 78-79	0.182	0.013*	0.046*	0.002**	> 0.10
8	69, 78	0.575	0.199	0.329	0.197	> 0.10
9	71, 78-79	0.247	0.315	0.357	0.470	> 0.10
10	not specified	-	-	-	-	> 0.10

* = significant at the 5%-level
** = significant at the 1%-level

[175]The significant CUSUM–statistic with alternative (4) may in fact well be attributable to a structural change in accordance with alternative (7). The analysis of the other CUSUM–plots is not very fruitful in determining the appropriate alternative.

Figure 10

CUSUM–Plot for LNGUYSTO (Alternative 4)

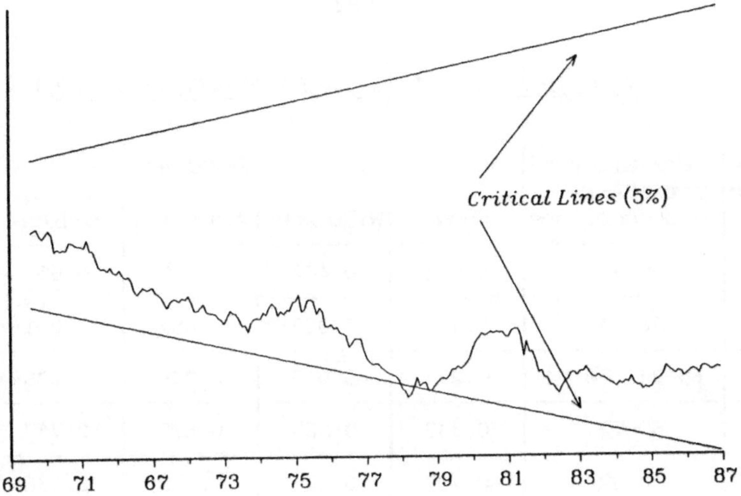

i) India (Table 38)

Rejection of the null is obvious here, but the correct alternative is unclear. The CUSUM–plots do not give any clue to finding the correct ISA–regime. P–values for alternative (7) are lower than for the related alternatives (8) and (9), hence (7) should be preferred to (8) and (9). Moreover, tests statistics rejecting in favor of alternative (2) look more convincing than those in favor of alternative (3). Thus either alternative (2) or alternative (7) should be accepted.

What is puzzling about accepting alternative (2) (ISA 1977 in its wide definition) is the fact that no rejection is possible for alternative (5) (ISA in its narrow definition). The years 1983 and 1984 thus appear to be quite influential with respect to the resulting test statistics. From what we know about the performance of the 1977 ISA, we may consider it very unlikely that the final impetus for rejecting the null should be attributable to the effects of the ISA exerted in 1983 and 1984.

But recall that the United States cut its import quotas under the US Sugar Act by roughly 50% in May 1982, thereby causing a major shock to the world sugar economy. We may hence hypothesize that the rejecting statistics for alternative (2) reflect the effects of US sugar import policies rather than the effects of the 1977 ISA. We should therefore not interpret the significant statistics of alternative (2) as evidence for an ISA–induced structural change[176]. With this reasoning I accept alternative (7).

Table 38

Tests for Structural Change: LNINDSTO (Equ. (67))

Alter-native #	Under alterna-tive ISA-re-gime comprises	P-values				
		Chow	Wilcoxon	v.d.Waer.	Median	CUSUM
1	69-73	0.504	0.402	0.373	0.551	> 0.10
2	78-84	0.419	0.008**	0.052	0.001**	> 0.10
3	69-73, 78-84	0.277	0.065	0.269	0.008**	> 0.10
4	69-72	0.342	0.823	0.673	0.747	> 0.10
5	78-82	0.407	0.226	0.389	0.136	> 0.10
6	69-72, 78-82	0.140	0.382	0.681	0.119	> 0.10
7	69-70, 78-79	0.276	0.005**	0.048*	0.001**	> 0.10
8	69, 78	0.298	0.055	0.131	0.031*	> 0.10
9	70, 78-79	0.442	0.010**	0.084	0.001**	> 0.10
10	not specified	-	-	-	-	> 0.10

j) Mauritius (Table 39)

There is only one significant statistic: The CUSUM–plot for alternative (3) (both Agreements in their wide definition) rejects at the 5%–level. The location of a possible break point can, however, not be inferred from the plot, see Figure 11. For the analogous alternative with the narrow definition of the ISAs (alternative (6)) no rejection is possible, although the probability for the behavior of the CUSUM–plot is smaller than 10%. In view of what I said above, the null of structural constancy cannot be rejected.

[176]In face of the enormous importance of US sugar imports for the free world market, we may quite generally state that significant statistics for the ISA 1977 in its wide definition should be cautiously received whenever there is no sufficient evidence for rejection in the narrow definition.

Table 39

Tests for Structural Change: LNMAUSTO (Equ. (68))

Alter-native #	Under alternative ISA-regime comprises	P-values Chow	Wilcoxon	v.d.Waer.	Median	CUSUM
1	69-73	0.111	0.746	0.779	0.371	> 0.10
2	78-84	0.272	0.969	0.936	0.787	> 0.10
3	69-73, 78-84	0.562	0.746	0.864	0.598	< 0.05*
4	69-72	0.087	0.800	0.880	0.333	> 0.10
5	78-82	0.258	0.938	0.906	0.999	> 0.10
6	69-72, 78-82	0.327	0.786	0.986	0.436	> 0.05
7	69-70, 78-79	0.659	0.460	0.542	0.423	> 0.10
8	69, 78	0.843	0.771	0.747	0.667	> 0.10
9	70, 78-79	0.897	0.835	0.994	0.551	> 0.10
10	not specified	-	-	-	-	> 0.10

Figure 11

CUSUM-Plot for LNMAUSTO (Alternative 3)

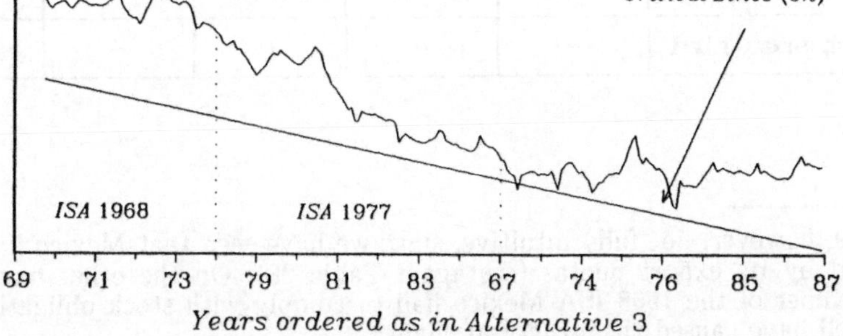

k) Mexico (Table 40)

There is but one possibly binding quota year for Mexico (cf. Table 28), thus testing against alternative (9) is not advisable due to problems with degrees of freedom. Convincing rejections are found for alternatives (1) and (4) (ISA 1968 in both the wide and the narrow definition; most P–values are even smaller for the wide definition). The null is also rejected when testing against the ISA 1977 in its wide definition, but not so in the narrow one. Also, the null is not rejected against the alternative of combining both ISAs (in either definition). Reiterating the argument of drastically reduced US import quotas in the middle of 1982, I thus refrain from supposing an ISA–induced structural change for the 1977 ISA. Instead, alternative (1) will be accepted[177].

Table 40

Tests for Structural Change: ΔLNMEXSTO (Equ. (58))

Alter-native #	Under alterna-tive ISA-re-gime comprises	P-values				
		Chow	Wilcoxon	v.d.Waer.	Median	CUSUM
1	69–73	0.073	0.004**	0.014*	0.003**	> 0.10
2	78–84	0.581	0.019*	0.050*	0.007**	> 0.10
3	69–73, 78–84	0.484	0.793	0.785	0.999	> 0.10
4	69–72	0.046*	0.011*	0.033*	0.004**	> 0.10
5	78–82	0.581	0.416	0.495	0.135	> 0.10
6	69–72, 78–82	0.119	0.182	0.260	0.297	> 0.10
7	69–70, 78–79	0.066	0.397	0.640	0.078	> 0.10
8	69, 78	0.383	0.622	0.588	0.667	> 0.10
10	not specified	-	-	-	-	> 0.10

[177]Doing so is, however, not fully intuitive, since we have seen that Mexico has hardly been bounded by its export quotas (see again Table 28). On the other hand, as an exporting member of the 1968 ISA Mexico had to comply with stock obligations, and these may well have caused the structural change.

l) Philippines (Table 41)

For Philippine stock data I noted earlier that there is evidence for a non–ISA–induced structural change in the mid–seventies. This would, in principle, require the specification and estimation of two distinct stock demand functions, to which the tests for structural change would separately have to be applied. However, while being a traditional exporter of sugar, the Philippines did not have a BET under the 1968 ISA, since almost all of their exports were covered by the US Sugar Act and were thus not a part of the free market. Hence I may confine my attention to the stock demand equation (69) and pursue only tests against alternatives referring to the 1977 ISA. Further, due to a lack of degrees of freedom, I omit alternative (8). Note that alternatives (7) and (9) coincide.

We find only one statistic which is significant at the 5%–level. Even though there are fewer tests here than we have for the other countries, this can hardly be considered sufficient for rejecting the null.

Table 41

Tests for Structural Change: LNPHISTO (Equ. (69))

Alter-native #	Under alterna-tive ISA-re-gime comprises	P-values				
		Chow	Wilcoxon	v.d.Waer.	Median	CUSUM
2	78-84	0.073	0.080	0.573	0.303	> 0.10
5	78-82	0.032*	0.299	0.490	0.733	> 0.10
7, 9	78-79	0.544	0.800	0.934	0.825	> 0.10
10	not specified	-	-	-	-	> 0.10

m) South Africa (Table 42)

The CUSUM rejects for most of the alternatives tested, including the very general alternative (10). The CUSUM–plots are difficult to interpret; in most cases they cross the critical lines very quickly (see, e. g. Figure 12). In this situation it seems reasonable to use the external information on (possibly) binding quota years and accept the respective alternative, i. e. alternative (9).

Table 42

Tests for Structural Change: LNSAFSTO (Equ. (70))

Alter-native #	Under alterna-tive ISA-re-gime comprises	P-values				
		Chow	Wilcoxon	v.d.Waer.	Median	CUSUM
1	69-73	0.272	0.291	0.360	0.550	< 0.01**
2	78-84	0.188	0.460	0.579	0.416	> 0.10
3	69-73, 78-84	0.281	0.829	0.787	0.791	< 0.01**
4	69-72	0.206	0.380	0.473	0.518	< 0.01**
5	78-82	0.304	0.332	0.256	0.370	> 0.10
6	69-72, 78-82	0.481	0.121	0.117	0.193	< 0.01**
7	69-70, 78-79	0.165	0.086	0.099	0.016*	< 0.05*
8	69, 78	0.144	0.928	0.974	0.389	> 0.10
9	69-71,78-79,82	0.349	0.174	0.187	0.090	< 0.01**
10	not specified	-	-	-	-	< 0.01**

Figure 12

CUSUM-Plot for LNSAFSTO (Alternative 10)

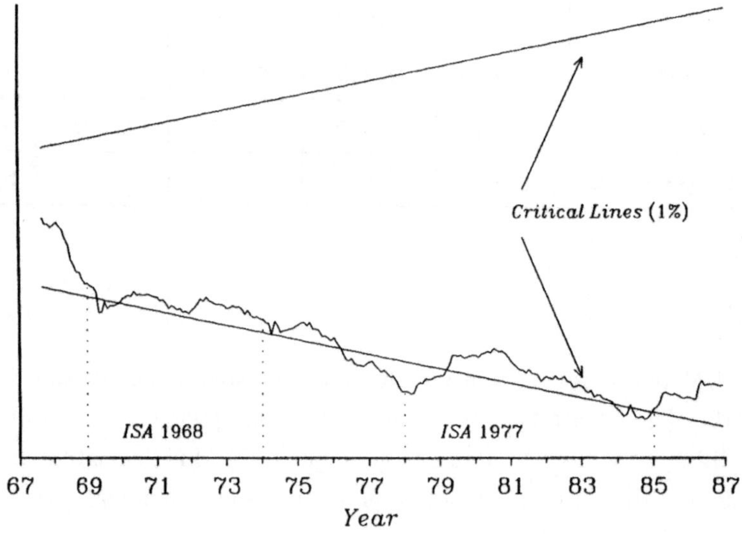

n) Swaziland (Table 43)

There are no significant statistics, hence the null will be accepted.

Table 43

Tests for Structural Change: LNSWASTO (Equ. (71))

Alter-native #	Under alterna-tive ISA-regime comprises	P-values				
		Chow	Wilcoxon	v.d.Waer.	Median	CUSUM
1	69-73	0.541	0.655	0.760	0.551	> 0.10
2	78-84	0.416	0.989	0.970	0.787	> 0.10
3	69-73, 78-84	0.405	0.703	0.759	0.792	> 0.10
4	69-72	0.543	0.212	0.335	0.107	> 0.10
5	78-82	0.405	0.247	0.264	0.136	> 0.10
6	69-72, 78-82	0.326	0.997	0.844	0.999	> 0.10
7	69-70, 78-79	0.728	0.938	0.943	0.631	> 0.10
8	69, 78	0.936	0.428	0.480	0.999	> 0.10
9	69-71,78-79,81-83	0.744	0.726	0.615	0.999	> 0.10
10	not specified	-	-	-	-	> 0.10

* = significant at the 5%-level
** = significant at the 1%-level

o) Taiwan (Table 44)

Taiwan was a member of the 1968 ISA, but it could not become a member of the 1977 ISA since it had been expelled from the United Nations in 1971[178]. Hence tests for structural change are applied solely against alternatives with reference to the 1968 ISA. Alternative (8) has not been used due to problems with degrees of freedom. During the 1968 ISA there have been no binding quota years for Taiwan (see Table 28), such that alternative (9) is obsolete. For the remaining tests no significant test statistic is found, therefore the null is not rejected.

Table 44

Tests for Structural Change: TAISTO (Equ. (72))

Alter-native #	Under alterna-tive ISA-re-gime comprises	P-values				
		Chow	Wilcoxon	v.d.Waer.	Median	CUSUM
1	69-73	0.221	0.470	0.379	0.550	> 0.10
4	69-72	0.204	0.831	0.930	0.518	> 0.10
7	69-70	0.100	0.886	0.762	0.999	> 0.10
10	not specified	-	-	-	-	> 0.10

* = significant at the 5%-level
** = significant at the 1%-level

[178]Without explicit reference to Taiwan, Article 57(2) of the 1977 ISA basically exempted this state from being treated as a non-member by importing member countries so long as Taiwan did not interfere with the objectives of the Agreement.

p) Thailand (Table 45)

Thailand participated for only one full year (1970) in the 1968 ISA, hence I omit tests where the alternative postulates a structural change solely for the 1968 ISA. All other alternatives are altered accordingly. Note that alternatives (8) and (9) coincide. Since no significant test statistics are found, I accept the null of structural constancy.

Table 45

Tests for Structural Change: LNTHASTO (Equ. (73))

Alter-native #	Under alterna-tive ISA-re-gime comprises	P-values				
		Chow	Wilcoxon	v.d.Waer.	Median	CUSUM
2	78-84	0.476	0.787	0.877	0.587	> 0.10
3	70, 78-84	0.571	0.772	0.863	0.792	> 0.10
5	78-82	0.426	0.277	0.434	0.135	> 0.10
6	70, 78-82	0.486	0.291	0.446	0.259	> 0.10
7	70, 78-79	0.560	0.145	0.156	0.210	> 0.10
8, 9	70, 78	0.738	0.733	0.863	0.667	> 0.10
10	not specified	-	-	-	-	> 0.10

* = significant at the 5%-level
** = significant at the 1%-level

□

We thus find evidence for a structural change in the stock data of six countries, namely Argentina, the Dominican Republic, Guyana, India, Mexico, and South Africa. It is noteworthy that the five dominant exporters Australia, Brazil, Cuba, Thailand, and the Philippines do not seem to have been severely affected by the ISAs. We will come back to this issue later.

Applying the tests for structural change to ΔLNWORSTO (equation (59)), yields the results displayed in Table 46. We obtain rejecting statistics for alternatives (1) and (2) (the ISAs of 1968 and 1977 in their wide definitions), but not for alternative (3) (both ISAs taken together) and not for the analogous alternatives (4) to (6) (the ISAs in their narrow definition). Since this picture is not too convincing, I prefer to accept alternative (7) (first two years of each ISA), where the non–parametric tests reject with P–values even slightly smaller than under alternatives (1) and (2).

Table 46

Tests for Structural Change: ΔLNWORSTO (Equ. (59))

Alternative #	Under alternative ISA-regime comprises	P-values				
		Chow	Wilcoxon	v.d.Waer.	Median	CUSUM
1	69-73	0.478	0.044*	0.057	0.135	> 0.10
2	78-84	0.623	0.024*	0.037*	0.057	> 0.10
3	69-73, 78-84	0.426	0.681	0.726	0.593	> 0.10
4	69-72	0.291	0.275	0.331	0.518	> 0.10
5	78-82	0.820	0.054	0.050*	0.232	> 0.10
6	69-72, 78-82	0.373	0.423	0.354	0.601	> 0.10
7	69-70, 78-79	0.468	0.016*	0.022*	0.016*	> 0.10
8	69, 78	0.276	0.057	0.040*	0.085	> 0.10
10	not specified	-	-	-	-	> 0.10

* = significant at the 5%-level
** = significant at the 1%-level

7.4 Testing in Practice: Systematic Excess Production and Price Equations

Testing world systematic excess supply (equation (51)) for a structural change, we find overwhelming evidence (see Table 47) for hypothesizing an ISA–regime in line with alternatives (7*) or (8*), i. e. for the ISAs in their narrow definition without the first two years or merely without the first year[179]. In both cases P–values for the non–parametric tests strongly reject the null and for alternative (7*) the CUSUM–plot is significant at the 10%–level. Some fairly low P–values for the slightly wider alternatives (3) and (6) make the evidence even stronger.

Table 47

Tests for Structural Change: WOREXC (Equ.(51))

Alter-native #	Under alterna-tive ISA-re-gime comprises	P-values				
		Chow	Wilcoxon	v.d.Waer.	Median	CUSUM
1	69-73	0.324	0.164	0.157	0.642	> 0.10
2	78-84	0.241	0.691	0.764	0.161	> 0.10
3	69-73, 78-84	0.098	0.087	0.102	0.060	> 0.10
4	69-72	0.752	0.472	0.418	0.867	> 0.10
5	78-82	0.310	0.227	0.202	0.128	> 0.10
6	69-72, 78-82	0.328	0.094	0.070	0.132	> 0.10
7*	71-72, 80-82	0.724	0.000**	0.000**	0.128	> 0.05
8*	70-72, 79-82	0.337	0.000**	0.000**	0.002**	> 0.10
10	not specified	-	-	-	-	> 0.10

* = significant at the 5%-level
** = significant at the 1%-level

[179]Recall that this formulation of the alternatives results from the possibility that farmers adjust their production in accordance with expected quota restrictions within one or two years after an ISA has been set into effect.

Whether to accept alternative (7*) or (8*) is difficult to decide and the analysis of the CUSUM–plots remains inconclusive. Somewhat arbitrarily I accept (8*), since this complements nicely with accepting alternative (8) for LNWORSTO: The analysis then suggests that the ISAs led to involuntary stockholding (due to production in excess of quotas) for the first two years of the Agreements, while adjustments of systematic excess production became effective in the third and subsequent years of the ISAs, apparently diminishing involuntary stocks.

Bearing this in mind, we may apply the tests for structural change to the price equations (equations (46) and (49)). From what we learnt so far, there should be two possibilities for a structural change to occur: *Either* it is the existence of involuntary stocks in the beginning of the Agreements plus the subsequent adjustment in production which causes a structural shift (i. e. the ISA–regime basically persists throughout the duration of the ISA)[180]. *Or* it is only while involuntary stocks are present (i. e. in the Agreements' first two years or so) that the price is determined under a different regime[181].

The latter possibility deserves elaboration. As we have just found evidence for a structural change in WOREXC, how is it possible that this does not induce a structural change for the price equations, which do, explicitly or implicitly, depend on WOREXC? To answer this question, think first of the multivariate specification (46). Here WOREXC is one component of one of LNPR's functional arguments, namely WORM. An adjustment in systematic excess production hence results in a change *in the value of an argument* of the function, (the value of WORM), but not in a change of its parametric form[182].

[180]This possibility might even require to specify three instead of two regimes, namely a free–trade–regime, an ISA–regime which accounts for the existence of involuntary stocks, and a subsequent ISA–regime which accounts for the structural change in world systematic excess production. Fortunately, we will see that we need not go into this trouble.

[181]From the point of formal logic there remains the third possibility of solely the adjustment in excess production causing a structural change. This, however, would neglect the fact that under a free–trade regime all sugar stored is in principle exportable, while under an ISA–regime ISA–induced involuntary stocks are not. These two types of stocks can hence not be identified. Yet since the functional forms of the free–trade regime do not provide for the possibility of unexportable stocks, the existence of such stocks does necessarily cause a structural change if these are to have an influence on the price at all.

[182]A short glance at problem (MIN) in Section 2.1 makes it plain that only changes in the parametric form of stock demand should be able to induce changes in the parametric form of the price function. Thus, if the ISAs' stock effects are indeed limited to approximately the first two years of the Agreements, then price equation (46) should not display a structural shift for an in some way extended subperiod. Conversely, if a structural shift for equation (46) were to persist for longer than these

For the autoregressive specification (49) the situation is slightly different: Equation (49) can be viewed as a reduced form approach to modeling the process of price formation and insofar we must expect a structural change in one of the structural equations of the system (i. e. equation (51) in our context) to induce a structural change in LNPR's autoregressive form. But LNPR is, as we know, I(1). Hence if, for instance, the ISAs induce a decrease in the constant term of WOREXC, then this would, given a linear system, cancel[183] in the *functional form* of (49). For such a reduction in WOREXC would, via WORM, result in not more than a one–time increase in the *functional argument* ΔLNPR. The ISA–effect would thus again be a change in the value of a functional argument rather than a change of the functional orm. This distinction is quite important and should carefully be observed. More

Table 48

Tests for Structural Change: ΔLNPR (Equ. (46))

Alter-native #	Under alterna-tive ISA-re-gime comprises	P-values				
		Chow	Wilcoxon	v.d.Waer.	Median	CUSUM
1	69-73	0.128	0.470	0.481	0.370	> 0.10
2	78-84	0.139	0.847	0.963	0.786	> 0.10
3	69-73, 78-84	0.041*	0.651	0.561	0.596	> 0.10
4	69-72	0.494	0.169	0.152	0.106	> 0.10
5	78-82	0.356	0.488	0.447	0.370	> 0.10
6	69-72, 78-82	0.203	0.087	0.069	0.037*	> 0.10
7	69-70, 78-79	0.776	0.014*	0.041*	0.000**	> 0.10
8	69, 78	0.999	0.470	0.550	0.389	> 0.10
10	not specified	-	-	-	-	> 0.10

* = significant at the 5%-level
** = significant at the 1%-level

---

two initial ISA–governed years, then this must be taken as evidence for having accepted the wrong alternative in the analysis of stock demand.

[183]The only exception is, of course, the very period in which the change in WOREXC becomes effective for the first time.

complicated changes in the functional form of WOREXC, however, might well induce a new functional form for the autoregressive specification of LNPR.

Testing the multivariate specification (equation (46)) against different alternatives of a shift in regime, yields the results given in Table 48: There are five significant statistics, out of which three reject in favor of alternative (7), i. e. the first two years of the ISAs may have been dominated by a distinct regime. Since we obtain only two single statistics with P–values smaller than 5% with alternatives (3) and (6), and since the lowest P–values are clearly assumed while testing against alternative (7), I accept the latter hypothesis.

This choice is reinforced by looking at the same tests applied to equation (49), the autoregressive specification of LNPR (Table 49). There is only one rejecting statistic, but this one is significant at the 1%–level. Therefore the null cannot be

Table 49

Tests for Structural Change: LNPR (Equ. (49))

Alter-native #	Under alterna-tive ISA-re-gime comprises	P-values				
		Chow	Wilcoxon	v.d.Waer.	Median	CUSUM
1	69-73	0.441	0.393	0.313	0.232	> 0.10
2	78-84	0.778	0.376	0.369	0.587	> 0.10
3	69-73, 78-84	0.871	0.916	0.986	0.596	> 0.10
4	69-72	0.444	0.416	0.305	0.332	> 0.10
5	78-82	0.851	0.849	0.752	0.550	> 0.10
6	69-72, 78-82	0.745	0.624	0.581	0.193	> 0.10
7	69-70, 78-79	0.650	0.150	0.246	0.006**	> 0.10
8	69, 78	0.999	0.925	0.965	0.667	> 0.10
10	not specified	-	-	-	-	> 0.10

* = significant at the 5%-level
** = significant at the 1%-level

upheld, and the respective alternative is precisely alternative (7). Besides, all other P–values are very high under this specification, such that they do not lend support to the rivalring alternatives (3) and (6).

While inference can never be beyond any doubt in empirical work, I believe to have presented relatively strong evidence in favor of alternative (7) for the price equations. We would thus conclude that the corresponding change of regimes is likely to be attributable to significant amounts of involuntary stocks held in the years 1969, 1970, 1978, and 1979. The hypothesized structural change in systematic excess demand in the subsequent years 1971, 1972, and 1980 to 1982 does, on the contrary, appear to have resulted in a change of the value of the price functions' arguments rather than in a change of their parametric form.

Chapter 8: Quantifying the Effects of the International Sugar Agreements

8.1 The Basic Idea: Using Simulations

By virtue of the results of the preceding section, we have drawn inference on whether or not the existence of an International Sugar Agreement affected stocks or systematic excess production in certain periods. It is the objective of this section to give a rough impression on how strong these effects might have been.

The basic approach will be the following: Whenever there is evidence for a structural change, I will specify two functions relating to the two hypothesized regimes. By means of simulations[184], we then obtain an estimate of the effects of the ISAs: Starting at the point where a structural change occurs, I successively calculate the optimal forecasts for the endogenous variable in the periods governed by the ISA–regime, one time using the free–trade–function, the other time using the ISA–related function.

To elucidate this idea, let y_t be an endogenous variable. Suppose its specification under the free–trade regime is given by

$$y_t = \alpha_0 + \alpha_1 y_{t-1} + \alpha_3 t + \epsilon_{1t}$$

and the specification under the ISA–regime has the form

$$y_t = \beta_1 y_{t-1} + \beta_2 y_{t-2} + \beta_3 t + \epsilon_{2t},$$

where the disturbances ϵ_{1t} and ϵ_{2t} are white noise. I have deliberately specified this

[184]For the terminology, see Pindyck & Rubinfeld (1976, pp. 312–313).

example such that the order of the AR–processes is different under the two regimes, since I will provide for this possibility in my subsequent estimations. Note that the distributions of the error terms ϵ_{1t} and ϵ_{2t} may – and, as we will later see, will – also be quite different under the two regimes.

Now assume there is a structural shift from the free–trade to the ISA–regime after period t (i. e. t+1 is the first period under the ISA–regime). This shift is to last for τ periods. We then get the following simulated values under the free trade regime:

$$\hat{y}_{t+1} := a_0 + a_1 y_t + a_3 \ (t+1)$$

$$\hat{y}_{t+2} := a_0 + a_1 \hat{y}_{t+1} + a_3 \ (t+2)$$

$$\vdots$$

$$\hat{y}_{t+\tau} := a_0 + a_1 \hat{y}_{t+\tau-1} + a_3 \ (t+\tau)$$

Analogously, the optimal forecasts under the ISA–regime are:

$$\tilde{y}_{t+1} := b_1 y_t + b_2 \ y_{t-1} + b_3 \ (t+1)$$

$$\tilde{y}_{t+2} := b_1 \tilde{y}_{t+1} + b_2 \ y_t + b_3 \ (t+2)$$

$$\tilde{y}_{t+3} := b_1 \tilde{y}_{t+2} + b_2 \ \tilde{y}_{t+1} + b_3 \ (t+3)$$

$$\vdots$$

$$\tilde{y}_{t+\tau} := b_1 \tilde{y}_{t+\tau-1} + b_2 \tilde{y}_{t+\tau-2} + b_3 \ (t+\tau)$$

Again, the a's and b's denote the OLS estimates of the α's and β's, respectively. The differences $\tilde{y}_{t+1} - \hat{y}_{t+1}, \ldots, \tilde{y}_{t+\tau} - \hat{y}_{t+\tau}$ then give us an estimate of the effects of the International Sugar Agreements, more precisely an estimate of the ex–ante expectations of these effects.

The above example assumes autoregressive specifications (including truely exogenous regressors) for the dependent variable. From the economist's point of view it would also be interesting to work with multivariate specifications. This would, in the cases of stock demand and systematic excess production, include regressors such as prices or price expectations. Simulation in an ISA–governed subperiod using the free-trade–function would require knowledge of how prices and price expectations would have behaved in this subperiod, had there been no ISA. Yet this knowledge is not available. Therefore, the multivariate approach is not too fruitful, so long as simulation is the objective[185]. Further, using autoregressive specifications[186] yields consistent estimates under fairly general conditions, even if the dependent variable and some of the regressors are I(1). Hence we do not need to bother about unit root tests, cointegration, or error correction forms (Park & Phillips (1988), Park & Phillips (1989)).

Most of the specifications will be in logarithmic form and thus require nonlinear transformations to give estimates of the ISA–effects in the levels. These estimates are, of course, no longer the optimal forecasts mentioned earlier. An optimal forecast in the levels could in principle be approximated by the same method we used to derive the optimal price expectation. There is, however, one big obstacle. Approximating the true expected values of the levels by a polynomial expansion of the logarithms involves estimating high–order moments of the disturbances. The distribution of the disturbances will, in general, not be the same for the two regimes[187], i. e. the moments must be estimated separately for the ISA– and for the free–trade–regime. Due to the much smaller number of observations during the ISA–regime, estimates of the high–order–moments for these subperiods are extremely instable and small changes in the estimated residuals strongly affect the results of the simulations. For this reason, I prefer to simulate the logarithms and take the exponential thereof.

---

[185]By contrast, while testing for structural change, multivariate specifications are clearly preferable. First, misspecifications of the functions to be tested are more easily detected since a priori restrictions on the signs of the regression coefficients exist. Second, the source of a structural change can be located, whereas autoregressive specifications (viewed as reduced forms) admit only inference on the existence of a structural change, but not on its cause.

[186]Prior to regression I checked all time series on moving average structures in the error terms, using the method recommended by Schlittgen & Streitberg (1989, pp. 227–235). Surprisingly, I almost never found any evidence for the need of an MA–representation, and the autoregressive lag structures indicated were rather short (three lags at most).

[187]Tests for equality of the distributions mostly reject the null at high levels of significance.

8.2 Effects of the ISAs on Stock Levels: A Conservative Approach

The tests for structural change performed in the preceding chapter indicate the presence of distinct free–trade– and ISA–regimes in the stock data of six sugar exporting countries. For others such a change may have gone undetected due to the power of the tests. In the following I will neglect this latter possibility and confine my attention to the six countries whose evidence was strong enough to reject the null of structural constancy. For all other countries the ISAs are implicitly assumed to have been ineffective as far as stock demand is concerned. I baptize this the "conservative approach" in order to remind the reader of the fact that there may well be more countries which experienced different free–trade– and ISA–regimes.

Table 50 contains the autoregressive specifications for the six countries' stock demand functions under the free–trade regime. The temporal definitions of free–trade– and ISA–regime precisely follow the alternatives accepted while testing for structural change. Five out of the six autoregressive stock demand functions display a trend term; the one exception refers to Guyana. In the case of Mexico, the trend is clearly U–shaped such that a quadratic trend term has to be employed; the squared trend regressor is denoted TRENDSQ. For all countries preliminary investigations showed

Table 50

Specifications of Stock Demand Equations for the Free–Trade–Regime: Conservative Approach

Equ. #	Dependent Variable	Explanatory Variables β_0	β_1	β_2	β_3	β_4	Meth. of est.
(76)	LNARGSTO	CNST	LNARGSTO(-1)	LNARGSTO(-2)	TREND	—	OLS
(77)	LNDOMSTO	CNST	LNDOMSTO(-1)	LNDOMSTO(-2)	TREND	—	OLS
(78)	LNGUYSTO	—	LNGUYSTO(-1)	LNGUYSTO(-2)	—	—	OLS
(79)	LNINDSTO	CNST	LNINDSTO(-1)	LNINDSTO(-2)	TREND	—	OLS
(80)	LNMEXSTO	—	LNMEXSTO(-1)	LNMEXSTO(-2)	TREND	TRENDSQ	OLS
(81)	LNSAFSTO	CNST	LNSAFSTO(-1)	—	TREND	—	OLS

the logarithmic stock data to be more appropriate than the levels. The most apparent problem in the levels was once again a fairly extreme degree of heteroskedasticity; the computed F–values for the Goldfeld–Quandt test were generally much higher in levels than in logarithms and the same held for the estimated kurtosis.

Regression results in Table 51 show satisfactory $\bar{R}^2$'s with the exception of Guyana. The estimated coefficients are mostly significant; however, equation (76) (Argentina) displays some rather inconclusive t–values. The null of normality is

Table 51

Regression Results: Coefficients, t–values, $\bar{R}^2$

Equ. #	Dependent Variable (# of observ.)	Estimated Coefficients of Explanatory Variables (t-values) b_0	b_1	b_2	b_3	b_4	$\bar{R}^2$
(76)	LNARGSTO	-0.059	0.952**	-0.104	0.0005	---	0.797
	(202)	(-1.64)	(13.46)	(-1.47)	(1.94)	---	
(77)	LNDOMSTO	-0.111**	1.343**	-0.496**	0.0009**	---	0.921
	(166)	(-3.12)	(18.94)	(-6.96)	(3.57)	---	
(78)	LNGUYSTO	---	0.288**	0.114	---	---	0.111
	(190)	---	(4.01)	(1.59)	---	---	
(79)	LNINDSTO	-0.058**	1.392**	-0.459**	0.0004**	---	0.972
	(190)	(-2.74)	(21.16)	(-7.07)	(2.89)	---	
(80)	LNMEXSTO	---	1.340**	-0.563**	-0.021**	0.00001**	0.968
	(177)	---	(20.60)	(-8.73)	(-5.57)	(5.89)	
(81)	LNSAFSTO	-0.067*	0.841**	---	0.0005*	---	0.802
	(166)	(-1.98)	(19.28)	---	(2.12)	---	

* = significant at the 5%-level
** = significant at the 1%-level

unanimously rejected for all equations, see Table A2.7 in the Appendix. The specification tests (Table A2.8) indicate a white noise structure for the disturbances and accept, see the results of the Chow–test, the null of structural constancy. (In the latter test, the P–value for Guyana is not too convincing, though). The test statistics for the Rainbow– and the Reset–test suggest the presence of nonlinearities; a problen I encountered here as well as in most of the other stock data specifications in this study. Unfortunately, I have not been able to find alternative specifications with a better fit, even if the AR–framework was complemented by squared and cubed regressors. The specified equations must thus be interpreted as first–order approximations to the true functions. Despite the logarithmic transformation, some degree of heteroskedasticity may have prevailed in equations (78), (79), and (81) (Guyana, India, and South Africa, respectively), for P–values are around 5% in these cases. In general I tolerate heteroskedasticity in the logarithms in order to not complicate simulations any further.

The specifications for the ISA–regime are given in Table 52, the regression results follow in Table 53. Significance of the estimated coefficients is very satisfactory, and

Table 52

Specifications of Stock Demand Equations for the ISA–Regime
Conservative Approach

Equ. #	Dependent Variable	Explanatory Variables					Meth. of est.
		β_0	β_1	β_2	β_3	β_4	
(82)	LNARGSTO	CNST	LNARGSTO(-1)	--	--	TREND	OLS
(83)	LNDOMSTO	--	LNDOMSTO(-1)	--	--	--	OLS
(84)	LNGUYSTO	CNST	LNGUYSTO(-1)	--	--	--	OLS
(85)	LNINDSTO	--	LNINDSTO(-1)	LNINDSTO(-2)	LNINDSTO(-3)	TREND	OLS
(86)	LNMEXSTO	--	LNMEXSTO(-1)	LNMEXSTO(-2)	--	TREND	OLS
(87)	LNSAFSTO	CNST	LNSAFSTO(-1)	LNSAFSTO(-2)	--	TREND	OLS

so are the $\overline{R}^2$'s with the exception of Guyana. Testing for normality leads to acceptance of the null in two cases, namely the stock equations for the Dominican Republic and India (Table A2.9). Due to the relatively small number of observations the specification tests do not include the Cumulative Periodogram Test. The Durbin-Watson statistics suggests accepting the absence of first-order autocorrelation among the residuals in all cases, even though the statistic for equation (83) is close to the inconclusive region. The Chow-test signals structural constancy throughout, and non-linearities (Rainbow/Reset) seem to be less significant under the ISA- than under the free-trade regime. Again, a moderate size of heteroskedasticity may be present in the error terms of equations (82), (83), and (85) (Argentina, the Dominican Republic, and India). See Table A2.10.

Table 53

Regression Results: Coefficients, t-values, $\overline{R}^2$

Equ. #	Dependent Variable (# of observ.)	Estimated Coefficients of Explanatory Variables (t-values)					$\overline{R}^2$
		b_0	b_1	b_2	b_3	b_4	
(82)	LNARGSTO	-0.350**	0.461**	--	--	-0.009**	0.643
	(36)	(2.92)	(3.05)	--	--	(-3.20)	
(83)	LNDOMSTO	--	0.923**	--	--	--	0.844
	(72)	--	(19.73)	--	--	--	
(84)	LNGUYSTO	0.118	0.402**	--	--	--	0.146
	(48)	(1.80)	(3.00)	--	--	--	
(85)	LNINDSTO	--	1.570**	-0.946**	0.259	0.0004*	0.948
	(48)	--	(10.78)	(-4.04)	(1.93)	(2.22)	
(86)	LNMEXSTO	--	1.015**	-0.248*	--	-0.001**	0.823
	(60)	--	(8.73)	(-2.02)	--	(-3.09)	
(87)	LNSAFSTO	-0.082	1.017**	-0.227*	--	0.0009*	0.827
	(72)	(-1.85)	(8.78)	(-2.02)	--	(2.38)	

* = significant at the 5%-level
** = significant at the 1%-level

Table 54

Average Simulated Effects of the ISAs on Stock Demand: Increase in Inventories per Country and Quota Year in 1000 mt; Conservative Approach

	69	70	71	72	73	78	79	83
ARG	166	80	-30	-	-	-	-	-
DOM	59	98	108	101	-	26	-50	-
GUY	4	4	-	-	-	4	4	-
IND	761	1306	-	-	-	823	1342	-
MEX	47	100	65	4	-77	-	-	-
SAF	11	27	34	-	-	93	110	128
Σ	1048	1615	177	105	-77	946	1406	128

With these results, we may turn our attention to simulation. Proceeding as described in the previous section and averaging the simulated monthly values for each year, we get an estimate for additional stockholding attributable to the ISAs (Table 54).

As was to be expected, the provisions of the ISAs generally led to increased stock levels. We can suspect that this was mostly due to exports being restricted by quotas, but it must be noted that minimum stock requirements may also have contributed to the pile–up. Additionally, we find three countries for which one year displays a ***negative*** simulated ISA–effect. While this is not completely impossible (recall maximum stock provisions), it is much more likely that in these cases the year in question did no longer belong to the ISA–regime (observe that all years with negative entries in Table 54 happen to be the last year of the ISA–regime for the respective country). In any case, the simulated negative effects are rather small and do not severely affect the picture presented in Table 54.

Summing the additional stocks over the six countries strongly supports an earlier hypothesis: Only in the first two years of each Agreement do we discern a substantial increase in world stock levels. This directly reinforces the results we obtained while testing for a structural change in the equations of LNPŔ and WOREXC (equations (46), (49), and (51)), where the corresponding alternatives (7) and (7*) were accepted.

A closer look at Table 54 shows that the significant increase in world stocks in 1969, 1970, 1978, and 1979 is almost exclusively attributable to extraordinarily huge stocks carried by India in these years: After two consecutive record harvests in 1969 and 1970, Indian stocks had risen from an average of 891,000 mt in 1968 to averages of 1,744,000 mt in 1969 and 2,623,000 mt in 1970. In 1978 and 1979 the situation was analogous: Another record harvest in 1978 and a fairly good harvest in 1979 made average stocks increase from 2,326,000 mt in 1977 to 3,919,000 mt in 1978 and 3,389,000 mt in 1979, before plunging to 1,835,000 mt in 1980.

Table 55

Average Simulated Effects of the ISAs on Stock Demand as a Percentage of Three–Year–Moving–Average Stock Levels; Conservative Approach

	69	70	71	72	73	78	79	83
ARG	29.3	16.0	-7.1	-	-	-	-	-
DOM	23.8	30.5	30.2	31.1	-	6.1	-12.1	-
GUY	16.6	17.2	-	-	-	20.2	18.3	-
IND	43.4	58.5	-	-	-	25.6	44.0	-
MEX	4.6	10.0	7.1	0.0	-9.2	-	-	-
SAF	3.1	7.9	8.6	-	-	18.9	20.0	31.4

This information might prematurely suggest that India bore the main burden imposed by the ISAs. For such a judgment, however, not absolute, but relative magnitudes should be considered: Table 55 depicts the simulated effects of the ISAs as a percentage of the three–year moving average stock level of each country[188]. We then see that while India's extraordinarily high burden is undisputable for both ISAs, some other countries have also suffered from severe shares of involuntary stocks: Most noteworthy are Argentina, the Dominican Republic, and Guyana for the 1968 ISA and

[188] I averaged the present, the preceding, and the following year. This seemed to be the most appropriate procedure in view of trended data.

Guyana and South Africa for the 1977 ISA. Of course, Argentina, the Dominican Republic, India, and South Africa are only medium–size exporters of sugar, and Guyana is even a very small one. The conservative approach thus results in the conclusion that the stock effects of the ISAs have essentially been confined to the first two years of each Agreement and may basically be attributed to a couple of small and medium–size exporting nations, while the big exporters Australia, Brazil, Cuba, the Philippines, and Thailand may have benefited from the ISAs without bearing their fair share of the Agreements' costs.

8.3 Effects of the ISAs on Stock Levels: A Liberal Approach

Since the last conclusion may be due to insufficient power of the tests for structural change, I will now work with an alternative approach. From Table 28 we have external knowledge about those years in which member countries' exports were close to their respective quotas in effect. We may thus simply hypothesize that the ISA–regimes coincided with these years.

I call this the "liberal" approach since the definition of the ISA–regime may well be too wide: Some countries' exports may in some years have been close to their quotas without really being restricted by them, i. e. those countries might not have exported any more sugar, even if there had been no quotas. Yet the approach is not truely liberal, since we may neglect some periods which actually belong to the ISA–regime: Imagine periods in which quotas have not been binding, but minimum or maximum stock provisions nevertheless made stocks deviate from their desired level under the free–trade regime.

Thus the "liberal" approach reduces to a rough approximation of the ISA–regimes based exclusively on scarce external knowledge. It is obviously less well founded than the conservative approach. Yet it is a valuable approach in the sense that it allows us to check the sensitivity of the conclusions drawn from the conservative approach to changes in the temporal definitions of the ISA–regimes.

There are thirteen countries with more than one potentially binding quota year listed in Table 28. (Countries with only one binding quota year (Mexico and Thailand) are excluded from this approach in order to circumvene problems with degrees of freedom). For South Africa the liberal and the conservative approach coincide, thus we need to analyze the stock demand functions of twelve countries. For each of these countries the liberal approach will hypothesize the ISA–regime to consist of the years with no entry in Table 28.

The autoregressive specifications for the free–trade regime are given in Table 56. There is only one specification in the levels, all others are logarithmic. Swaziland's stock data require a quadratic trend term, again denoted TRENDSQ. As for the four countries[189] whose stock demand functions have already been analysed under the conservative approach, specifications are identical under both approaches for the Dominican Republic and for India, but different for Argentina and Guyana.

Table 56

Specifications of Stock Demand Equations for the Free–Trade–Regime: Liberal Approach

Equ. #	Dependent Variable	Explanatory Variables					Meth. of est.
		β_0	β_1	β_2	β_3	β_4	
(88)	LNARGSTO	CNST	LNARGSTO(-1)	--	LNARGSTO(-3)	TREND	OLS
(89)	AUSSTO	CNST	AUSSTO(-1)	AUSSTO(-2)	--	TREND	OLS
(90)	LNBRASTO	--	LNBRASTO(-1)	LNBRASTO(-2)	--	--	OLS
(91)	LNCUBSTO	CNST	LNCUBSTO(-1)	LNCUBSTO(-2)	--	TREND	OLS
(92)	LNDOMSTO	CNST	LNDOMSTO(-1)	LNDOMSTO(-2)	--	TREND	OLS
(93)	LNFIJSTO	CNST	LNFIJSTO(-1)	--	--	TREND	OLS
(94)	LNGUYSTO	--	LNGUYSTO(-1)	--	--	--	OLS
(95)	LNINDSTO	CNST	LNINDSTO(-1)	LNINDSTO(-2)	--	TREND	OLS
(96)	LNMAUSTO	CNST	LNMAUSTO(-1)	LNMAUSTO(-2)	--	TREND	OLS
(97)	LNPHISTO	CNST	LNPHISTO(-1)	LNPHISTO(-2)	--	--	OLS
(98)	LNSWASTO	CNST	LNSWASTO(-1)	LNSWASTO(-2)	TREND	TRENDSQ	OLS
(99)	LNTHASTO	CNST	LNTHASTO(-1)	LNTHASTO(-2)	--	TREND	OLS

[189] There were six countries analysed under the conservative approach. Out of these, Mexico was excluded from the liberal approach due to too small a number of observations for the ISA–regime. For South Africa, on the other hand, the temporal definitions of the two regimes are identical under both approaches, thus so are the corresponding regression results.

Not surprisingly, regression results displayed in Table 57 show the conservative and the liberal point of view to result in similar coefficient estimates for the Dominican Republic and India (cf. Table 51). Even for Argentina and Guyana are equal regressors characterized by roughly equal coefficients under the two approaches. Significance levels for regressions (88) – (99) are mostly very satisfactory. However, a very low $\overline{R}^2$ is once more observed for Guyana and the $\overline{R}^2$ of Fiji is also not the most impressive.

Table 57

Regression Results: Coefficients, t–values, $\overline{R}^2$

Equ. #	Dependent Variable (# of observ.)	Estimated Coefficients of Explanatory Variables (t-values)					$\overline{R}^2$
		b_0	b_1	b_2	b_3	b_4	
(88)	LNARGSTO	-0.075*	0.920**	---	-0.083	0.0006*	0.801
	(201)	(-2.13)	(17.56)	---	(-1.59)	(2.33)	
(89)	AUSSTO	-72.18**	1.149**	-0.302**	---	0.565**	0.899
	(165)	(-3.25)	(14.05)	(-3.63)	---	(3.43)	
(90)	LNBRASTO	---	1.238**	-0.278**	---	---	0.942
	(165)	---	(16.49)	(-3.71)	---	---	
(91)	LNCUBSTO	-0.045*	1.152**	-0.366**	---	0.0004*	0.795
	(177)	(-1.98)	(15.92)	(-5.11)	---	(2.28)	
(92)	LNDOMSTO	-0.104**	1.320**	-0.469**	---	0.0008**	0.919
	(177)	(-3.45)	(19.07)	(-6.78)	---	(3.71)	
(93)	LNFIJSTO	-0.172	0.715**	---	---	0.011	0.545
	(177)	(-1.79)	(13.71)	---	---	(1.69)	
(94)	LNGUYSTO	---	0.373**	---	---	---	0.139
	(201)	---	(5.69)	---	---	---	

Table 57
(cont'd)

Regression Results: Coefficients, t-values, $\bar{R}^2$

Equ. #	Dependent Variable (# of observ.)	Estimated Coefficients of Explanatory Variables (t-values)					$\bar{R}^2$
		b_0	b_1	b_2	b_3	b_4	
(95)	LNINDSTO	-0.044*	1.427**	-0.491**	--	0.0003*	0.971
	(201)	(-2.35)	(23.29)	(-8.06)	--	(2.57)	
(96)	LNMAUSTO	-0.190**	0.806**	-0.154*	--	0.0016**	0.687
	(177)	(-3.15)	(10.75)	(-2.09)	--	(3.67)	
(97)	LNPHISTO	0.016	1.508**	-0.562**	--	--	0.954
	(120)	(1.32)	(20.12)	(-7.60)	--	--	
(98)	LNSWASTO	-0.142	0.853**	-0.254**	-0.002	0.00002**	0.797
	(141)	(-1.50)	(10.24)	(-3.03)	(-1.32)	(3.00)	
(99)	LNTHASTO	-0.363**	0.952**	-0.225**	--	0.003**	0.914
	(213)	(-5.11)	(13.98)	(-3.28)	--	(5.42)	

Tests for normality unanimously reject the null (see Table A2.11 in the Appendix). The specification tests confirm the hypothesis of white noise error terms and structural constancy, but do often suggest remaining heteroskedasticity despite the logarithmic transformation. The test statistics for Rainbow and Reset are mostly unsatisfactory, but I have again not been able to find superior specifications.

Let us now turn to the specifications of the stock demand functions under the ISA regime (Table 58). Here for none of the four countries already dealt with under the conservative approach do the functional forms coincide with their analogues in Table 52. Further, as the regression results in Table 59 reveal, coefficient estimates for equal regressors are mostly quite distinct under the two approaches.

It is most noteworthy to see that there is virtually no systematic structure in Guyana's stock demand during its hypothesized ISA–regime. Apart from that, Argentina and Fiji are also characterized by low values of $\bar{R}^2$. Tests for normality (Table A2.13) do not reject the null as strongly as was the case in the free trade

Table 58

Specifications of Stock Demand Equations for the ISA–Regime; Liberal Approach

Equa-tion #	Dependent Variable	Explanatory Variables β_0	β_1	β_2	β_3	β_4	Meth. of est.
(100)	LNARGSTO	--	LNARGSTO(-1)	--	--	--	OLS
(101)	AUSSTO	CNST	AUSSTO(-1)	--	--	TREND	OLS
(102)	LNBRASTO	--	LNBRASTO(-1)	LNBRASTO(-2)	--	TREND	OLS
(103)	LNCUBSTO	--	LNCUBSTO(-1)	--	--	--	OLS
(104)	LNDOMSTO	--	LNDOMSTO(-1)	--	LNDOMSTO(-3)	TREND	OLS
(105)	LNFIJSTO	--	LNFIJSTO(-1)	--	--	--	OLS
(106)	LNGUYSTO	--	LNGUYSTO(-1)	--	--	--	OLS
(107)	LNINDSTO	--	LNINDSTO(-1)	LNINDSTO(-2)	--	TREND	OLS
(108)	LNMAUSTO	CNST	LNMAUSTO(-1)	--	--	TREND	OLS
(109)	LNPHISTO	CNST	LNPHISTO(-1)	LNPHISTO(-2)	--	--	OLS
(110)	LNSWASTO	CNST	LNSWASTO(-1)	LNSWASTO(-2)	--	TREND	OLS
(111)	LNTHASTO	--	LNTHASTO(-1)	LNTHASTO(-2)	LNTHASTO(-3)	--	OLS

regime; in fact, for some equations the null is barely accepted[190]. As far as the specification tests (Table A2.14) are concerned, I note that only in the case of Swaziland there are enough observations for the Cumulated Periodogram Test. The Durbin–Watson, however, is mostly in the acceptance region; only for equation (104) it is inconclusive. We do not find rejecting statistics for the Chow–test and there are apparently less undetected nonlinearities than under the free–trade regime. Yet some of the equations still display heteroskedastic error terms.

---

[190]Recall my earlier warning about different residual distributions under the free–trade– and the ISA–regime.

Table 59

Regression Results: Coefficients, t–values, $\bar{R}^2$

Equation #	Dependent Variable (# of observ.)	Estimated Coefficients of Explanatory Variables (t-values)					$\bar{R}^2$
		b_0	b_1	b_2	b_3	b_4	
(100)	LNARGSTO	--	0.664**	--	--	--	0.406
	(36)	--	(5.27)	--	--	--	
(101)	AUSSTO	-52.04	0.803**	--	--	0.516*	0.814
	(72)	(-1.87)	(12.32)	--	--	(2.29)	
(102)	LNBRASTO	--	1.302**	-0.378**	--	0.0001	0.943
	(72)	--	(11.62)	(-3.39)	--	(1.45)	
(103)	LNCUBSTO	--	0.879**	--	--	--	0.753
	(60)	--	(13.55)	--	--	--	
(104)	LNDOMSTO	--	0.985**	--	-0.222**	0.0005**	0.822
	(60)	--	(11.79)	--	(-2.79)	(2.96)	
(105)	LNFIJSTO	--	0.713**	--	--	--	0.364
	(60)	--	(7.36)	--	--	--	
(106)	LNGUYSTO	--	0.284	--	--	--	0.005
	(36)	--	(1.74)	--	--	--	
(107)	LNINDSTO	--	1.514**	-0.738**	--	0.0008**	0.890
	(36)	--	(10.86)	(-5.01)	--	(2.77)	
(108)	LNMAUSTO	-0.198**	0.681**	--	--	0.0018**	0.727
	(60)	(-2.24)	(6.98)	--	--	(2.46)	
(109)	LNPHISTO	0.280**	1.129**	-0.592**	--	--	0.883
	(24)	(4.81)	(13.13)	(-5.52)	--	--	
(110)	LNSWASTO	-0.120	0.907**	-0.214*	--	0.0010	0.617
	(96)	(-1.49)	(8.96)	(-2.10)	--	(1.76)	
(111)	LNTHASTO	--	1.400**	-0.851**	0.398**	--	0.972
	(24)	--	(9.88)	(-4.33)	(3.30)	--	

Table 60

Average Simulated Effects of the ISAs on Stock Demand: Increase in Inventories per Country and Quota Year in 1000 mt; Liberal Approach

	69	70	71	78	79	81	82	83
ARG	127	153	–	29	–	–	–	–
AUS	185	163	152	92	44	–	–18	–
BRA	152	254	270	202	461	–	375	–
CUB	47	113	–	37	–15	–142	–	–
DOM	–	147	167	111	99	–	–	–56
FIJ	10	11	–	2	1	–	–4	–
GUY	–	–	0	0	0	–	–	–
IND	–	768	–	1177	1305	–	–	–
MAU	–3	–4	–	6	9	–	14	–
PHI	–	–	–	242	337	–	–	–
SAF	11	27	34	93	110	–	–	128
SWA	2	2	3	2	1	–2	–4	–7
THA	–	2	–	15	–	–	–	–
Σ	531	1636	626	2008	2352	–144	363	65

Turning to simulation, we get the average increases in stock levels as presented in Table 60. We again observe some negative effects in the last years of some of the hypothesized ISA–regimes, possibly indicating that a more confined definition of the ISA–regimes would have been superior. (In the case of Mauritius it may even have been inadequate to include any year covered by the 1968 ISA). Most simulated negative effects are small, however, the only exception is Cuba in 1981. By far the largest involuntary stocks (in absolute terms) are still found for India.

By summing over all countries, we get another estimate of the increase in world stocks attributable to the ISAs. This estimate is similar to its analogue under the conservative approach insofar as the years 1970, 1978, and 1979 are again characterized by huge amounts of involuntary stocks. The two estimates do not completely match, however, since the liberal approach finds two (roughly equal) medium–size pile–ups for 1969 and 1971, while in the conservative approach involuntary stocks in 1969 are large and more than five–fold the amount of 1971.

It is apparently India which is responsible for this effect. Recall that India had a record harvest in 1969, such that stocks more than doubled from 1968 to 1969 despite an increase in consumption of more than 60,000 mt. Still India declared a quota shortfall of 225,000 mt in 1969, which was, in fact, her total export allowance.

The reasons for this peculiar behavior I do not know. I can only speculate that political motives or problems with the infrastructure may have led to reduced exports. (There have been no exports to the free market in 1969, but about 93,000 mt of exports under special arrangements. This, too, was a relatively tiny amount). In any case, India had lots of sugar available, which, under normal circumstances, would have been subject to export.

This makes plain why the simulation results for the conservative and the liberal approach deviate as far as 1969 is concerned: The conservative approach implicitly assumes "normal circumstances" and takes it for granted that sugar stored is in principle exportable. The liberal approach uses the external information on quota deficits and thus concludes that no involuntary stocks were present.

To reconcile the diverging results, let us assume "normal circumstances". This would mean that we accept the conservative simulation result of 761,000 mt ISA–induced stocks, but subtract the 225,000 mt unused export allowance. This reduces Indian involuntary stocks for 1969 down to 536,000 mt. Inserting this in India's 1969 entries in Tables 54 and 60 we find world stocks increased by 723,000 mt under the conservative and 1,067,000 mt under the liberal approach.

With these considerations both approaches tell approximately the same story: The 1968 ISA increased 1969 world stocks by between 700,000 mt and 1,000,000 mt. The pile–up continued in 1970 to reach 1,600,000 mt. In 1971, most of these stocks were sold; only a small rest of between 200,000 and 400,000 mt remained. Finally, in 1972 and 1973 stocks were roughly back to normal.

The 1977 ISA caused involuntary stocks of between one and two million mt in 1978, and these rose to between 1.4 and 2.5 million mt in 1979. All stocks were released in 1980, and although there may have been ISA–induced extra stocks of at most 400,000 mt in 1982 and about 100,000 mt in 1983, no really significant pile–up of sugar was to be recorded in the early 1980's. Thus basically the simulations (in both approaches) confirm our supposition that stock provisions of the ISAs were effective instruments in the first two years of the Agreements but ineffective thereafter.

Table 61

Average Simulated Effects of the ISAs on Stock Demand as a Percentage of Three–Year–Moving–Average Stock Levels; Liberal Approach

	69	70	71	78	79	81	82	83
ARG	22.5	30.5	–	4.2	–	–	–	–
AUS	25.8	22.4	18.5	10.4	4.8	–	-1.8	–
BRA	7.4	12.4	12.9	6.3	14.2	–	12.6	–
CUB	4.6	8.8	–	2.6	-1.1	-9.5	–	–
DOM	–	45.6	46.7	25.9	23.7	–	–	-9.6
FIJ	28.7	29.4	–	3.9	1.6	–	-8.0	–
GUY	–	–	-1.0	0.0	0.0	–	–	–
IND	–	34.4	–	36.6	42.8	–	–	–
MAU	-3.2	-3.7	–	3.6	5.5	–	8.3	–
PHI	–	–	–	19.1	31.2	–	–	–
SAF	3.1	7.9	8.6	18.9	20.0	–	–	31.4
SWA	16.7	20.9	24.2	13.9	8.8	-15.0	-22.0	-23.3
THA	–	1.3	–	2.0	–	–	–	–

Table 61 displays the simulated effects of the ISAs (liberal approach) as percentages of three–year moving average stock levels[191]. We see that Argentina, Australia, the Dominican Republic, Fiji, India, and Swaziland seem to have borne the main burden of the 1968 ISA, for their stock levels were most strongly increased. Apart from Australia, all of these states are medium–size exporters of sugar. For the 1977 ISA, the Dominican Republic, India, the Philippines, and South Africa report relatively high levels of involuntary stocks. Again, only one of these states (the Philippines) is one of the world's main exporters. (In fact, the Philippines have been an important exporter to the free world market only if no US Sugar Act was in force). It thus appears that the big exporting countries Australia, Brazil, and Cuba (the so–called ABC–countries) quite successfully used their strong position to negotiate favorable BETs (and hence export quotas) for themselves[192]. In their place, smaller exporters may have contributed considerably to the effort of price stabilization. Recall that the same impression arose from the analysis of the conservative approach, Table 55.

In view of the theoretical results of Chapter 1, we may hence state: Provided the ISAs did indeed achieve price stabilization, then Brazil, Cuba, Thailand, and to a lesser extent Australia and the Philippines (as the countries with the largest market shares) benefited from this stabilization more strongly than did other member countries. However, they presumably bore a less than proportional share of the costs incurred by the mechanisms of the Agreements.

8.4 Effects of the ISAs on World Systematic Excess Production

We now need to quantify the effects of the ISAs on world systematic excess production. The tests for structural change suggested accepting alternative (7*), i. e. we hypothesize an ISA–induced structural change for the years 1971, 1972, and 1980 to 1982. Specification and regression results for WOREXC under the free–trade and under the ISA–regime are given in equations (112) and (113), respectively:

$$\text{WOREXC} = \underset{(16.39)}{0.784^{**}}\ \text{WOREXC}(-1) + E_{112}$$

$$\bar{R}^2 = 0.596 \qquad \text{DW} = 1.859 \qquad (112)$$

[191] Again, the figures of the present, the preceding, and the following year were averaged.

[192] Gordon–Ashworth (1984, p. 178) cites the sugar broker F. O. Licht with the assertion that quotas were distributed "not in accordance with the supply capabilities of the exporters but rather in recognition of negotiating strength and tactics".

$$\text{WOREXC} = -\underset{(-3.96)}{665^{**}} + \underset{(4.14)}{0.51^{**}}\ \text{WOREXC}(-1) + \underset{(1.83)}{0.23}\ \text{WOREXC}(-2)$$

$$-\underset{(-4.69)}{0.41^{**}}\ \text{WOREXC}(-5) + \underset{(3.13)}{3.28^{**}}\ \text{TREND} + E_{113}$$

$$\bar{R}^2 = 0.668 \qquad \text{DW} = 2.105 \qquad (113)$$

Both regressions have been estimated by OLS. Due to a substantial discrepancy in the residual distributions' kurtosises, the normality hypothesis is rejected for the free–trade–regime, but accepted for the ISA–regime (Table A2.15). Specification tests given in Table A2.16 do not reject the composite null of a correct specification despite a low P–value for the Chow–test in equation (113).

Still, the specification of WOREXC under the ISA–regime (equation (113)) is merely an approximation to the true function. More appropriate would an ARMA-representation have been, for there is an undeniable moving–average structure in the data. However, an MA–specification is not particularly advantageous for the purposes of simulation since the lagged errors to be inserted in the regressor matrix are not known. Hence, I prefer to approximate the true ARMA–process by an AR(5) (where two lags turn out to be highly insignificant). The endogenous variable with a lag of two periods is also not significant at the 5%–level, but with a t–statistic of 1.825 (corresponding to a P–value of 0.074), deletion did not deem reasonable. All other coefficient estimates are significant at the 1%–level.

By the now familiar approach of simulation, we get estimates of the ISAs' effects on world systematic excess production as shown in Table 62 (figures refer to 1000 mt). During both ISAs a substantial reduction of WOREXC seems to be apparent. This is not too surprising if we recall that the constant term is significantly negative in equation (113) but insignificant (i. e. zero) in equation (112). However, the discouragement of production was apparently stronger for the 1968 ISA than for its 1977 successor. This may either be attributable to the fact that the desired price floor for the 1977 ISA was much higher than in the 1968 Agreement, or to an anticipation of inflated quotas recalculated according to the rules set forth in Article 34(2) of the 1977 ISA.

While in the 1968 ISA an initial reduction of 2.9 million tons was succeeded by the quite tremendous amount of 7.7 million tons, the 1977 ISA recorded the largest reduction of world systematic excess production in 1980 (2.2 million tons). In subsequent years the ISA–effects faded away, possibly because production was again

Table 62

Average Simulated Effects of the ISAs on World Systematic Excess Production
(in 1000 mt)

		71	72	80	81	82
(A)	Reduction of systematic excess production attributable to the ISA's	2928	7732	2170	1085	652
(B)	Observed systematic excess production	-6787	-5571	-1587	973	-4768
(A)+(B)	Estimate of systematic excess production under a free-trade regime	-3859	2161	583	2058	-4116

fueled by the 1980 price boom.

Comparing the true (i. e. observed) WOREXC per year with what world systematic excess production would have been like had there been no ISAs, we find that the ISAs have mostly shifted WOREXC away from equilibrium. Solely in 1981 did the ISA–effect contribute to equilibrating the production–consumption balance, but precisely in this year its desirability is doubtful. For stocks had been drastically reduced during the 1980 price boom and positive excess production would have been likely to relax this situation. We have thus reason to conclude that the effects of the ISAs on systematic excess production have certainly not promoted stability on the world market for sugar.

8.5 Effects of the ISAs on the World Market Price for Sugar

The final investigations address the question of how changes in stock levels and systematic excess production affected world market prices. Since for both the multivariate and the autoregressive version of the price function (equations (46) and (49), respectively) a structural change was indicated for the first two years of each Agreement, I start with estimating these equations under the different regimes.

In order to establish multivariate specifications for LNPR, we will first have to examine the stationarity properties of the intended dependent and independent variables. I will use the same regressors as in Part II, i. e. WORM, WORZ, and LNPRWH. Nothing is changed for WORZ and LNPRWH as opposed to Part II, since they have not been subject to the mechanisms of the ISAs. WORM, however, is an aggregate including WORSTO and WOREXC among its components and thus experiences the same structural change as do these. Hence WORM and, of course, LNPR must be interpreted as consisting of two time series each and separate unit root tests must be applied[193].

Table 63

Tests for Unit Roots

Model: $y_t = \mu \text{ CNST} + \alpha\, y_{t-1} + \beta \text{ TREND} + u_t$

Note: $Z_1(\cdot)$ tests (μ, α, β) as H_0: $(\mu, 1, 0)$ against H_1: (μ, α, β)
$Z_2(\cdot)$ tests (μ, α, β) as H_0: $(0, 1, 0)$ against H_1: (μ, α, β)
$Z_3(\cdot)$ tests (μ, α, β) as H_0: $(0, 1, 0)$ against H_1: $(\mu, \alpha, 0)$

a) Free–Trade Regime: 1967–1968, 1971–1977, 1980–1986

Variable	Trunc. Param.	$Z_1(F)$	$Z_1(t)$	$Z_1(\alpha)$	$Z_2(F)$	$Z_3(F)$	$Z_3(t)$	$Z_3(\alpha)$	Null
LNPR	3	3.12	-2.15	-6.83	2.08	1.28	-1.60	-4.85	accepted
	5	3.17	-2.21	-7.46	2.11	1.43	-1.69	-5.46	
	10	3.20	-2.25	-7.79	2.14	1.54	-1.76	-5.91	
WORM	3	3.41	-2.43	-7.73	2.36	2.02	-1.94	-5.88	accepted
	5	3.48	-2.48	-8.41	2.40	2.16	-2.02	-6.52	
	10	3.44	-2.45	-8.08	2.38	2.12	-2.00	-6.35	

[193]Actually, things are not that easy for WORM. Observe that we found a structural change for WORSTO in the temporal definition given by alternative (7) and for WOREXC in the temporal definition of alternative (7*). This suggests already three different regimes for WORM. Two of them intersect for a single observation since WORSTO is lagged one period in the definition of WORM. All this could in principle be thoroughly dissolved and tested, but I doubt whether this would be very fruitful. For pragmatic reasons, I therefore prefer to split WORM into the same subseries as I do with LNPR and test for the presence of a unit root in these subseries.

Table 63
(cont'd)

b) ISA–Regime: 1969–1970, 1978–1979

Variable	Trunc. Param.	$Z_1(F)$	$Z_1(t)$	$Z_1(\alpha)$	$Z_2(F)$	$Z_3(F)$	$Z_3(t)$	$Z_3(\alpha)$	Null
LNPR	3	1.38	-1.35	-7.10	1.51	1.00	-0.51	-2.19	accepted
	5	1.72	-1.62	-9.08	1.66	1.05	-0.75	-3.41	
	10	1.64	-1.56	-8.65	1.63	1.03	-0.72	-3.22	
WORM	3	3.09	-2.46	-13.06	2.13	3.32	-2.54	-13.30	accepted
	5	3.22	-2.51	-13.56	2.21	3.44	-2.58	-13.80	
	10	2.65	-2.27	-11.24	1.85	2.89	-2.36	-11.53	

* = significant at the 5%-level
** = significant at the 1%-level

The results of these tests can be found in Table 63. Obviously, the time series preserve their unit root properties even if different regimes are taken into account.

We will thus have to test for cointegration between dependent and explanatory variables. The results of the cointegrating regressions are given in Table 64. Equations (114) and (115) refer to the free–trade regime, while equations (116) and (117) refer to the ISA–regime, i. e. to the years 1969, 1970, 1978, and 1979. Equations (114) and (116) combine the instationary variables LNPR, WORM, and LNPRWH; equations (115) and (117) also include the stationary regressor WORZ. If cointegration is confirmed, then I will, as I have explained earlier, use the residuals of equations (115) and (117) in the specifications of error correction forms since these equations incorporate all relevant explanatory variables. However, the power of the tests may suffer due to the stationarity of the regressor WORZ, thus I apply the tests also to equations (114) and (116).

Comparing the coefficient estimates of equations (114) and (115) we see that the coefficients of WORM and LNPRWH are a little more vulnerable to adding the regressor WORZ than in the analysis of Part II (equations (44) and (45)). Yet the observed changes in the coefficients do never even come close to one (OLS–based) standard error, thus in terms of the true (larger) standard errors the variability of the estimates is still small. Note that again the coefficient of WORZ is substantially larger (in absolute terms) than the coefficient of WORM.

Table 64

<u>*Tests for Cointegration*</u>

Null Hypothesis: Absence of Cointegration

Results of Cointegrating Regressions							Test Statistics					
Equation #	Dep. Var. (# of observ.)					DW / $\bar{R}^2$	Dickey-Fuller	Augmen. Dickey-Fuller	Trunc. Param. l	Z(t)	Z(α)	Null
(114)	LNPR (192)	variable	WORM	—	LNPRWH	0.178 / 0.733	-3.03	-3.52	3	-3.39*	-22.06*	rejected
		coefficient	-0.818	—	0.846				5	-3.55*	-24.25*	
		t-value OLS	-11.73	—	5.93				10	-3.54*	-24.14*	
(115)	LNPR (192)	variable	WORM	WORZ	LNPRWH	0.196 / 0.757	-3.16	-3.42	3	-3.54	-24.20	accepted
		coefficient	-0.841	-1.435	0.763				5	-3.69	-26.30	
		t-value OLS	-12.61	-4.49	5.56				10	-3.62	-25.37	
(116)	LNPR (48)	variable	WORM	—	LNPRWH	0.558 / 0.542	-2.29	-3.10	3	-2.66	-14.57	accepted
		coefficient	-0.497	—	0.638				5	-2.80	-16.17	
		t-value OLS	-4.19	—	6.52				10	-2.60	-14.01	
(117)	LNPR (48)	variable	WORM	WORZ	LNPRWH	0.557 / 0.532	-2.29	-3.09	3	-2.66	-14.58	accepted
		coefficient	-0.496	-0.022	0.638				5	-2.80	-16.18	
		t-value OLS	-3.96	-0.04	6.40				10	-2.60	-14.01	

* = significant at the 5%-level
** = significant at the 1%-level

In the case of equations (116) and (117) the coefficients of WORM and LNPRWH are virtually identical, which is not very surprising in the face of WORZ being completely insignificant. In fact, the insignificance of this regressor is to be expected, since in quota–governed periods stochastic shocks in production will often not be transmitted to the world market: Shocks, be they positive or negative, are likely to merely increase or decrease involuntary stocks if the quota in effect is binding.

The test statistics of the cointegration tests are also given in Table 64. All Phillips–Ouliaris test statistics for equation (114) reject the null of no cointegration at the 5%–level. All other test statistics are insignificant at the 5%–level, although the Phillips–Ouliaris statistics for equation (115) are very close to being 5%–significant. (They are, of course, significant at the 10%–level). We thus reject the null for the free–trade regime, but accept it for the ISA–regime. Actually, the lack of cointegration for the ISA–regime is not really surprising, since in a quota–governed market there should be no fundamental relationship between the world market price and the size of stocks (plus systematic excess production). To elucidate this point: If all countries participated in the ISAs and if all countries respected their quotas in effect, then it is not so much the size of stocks, but rather the amount of sugar covered by export quotas, which determines the world market price.

Since the null of no cointegration cannot be rejected for the ISA–regime, I will only specify an autoregressive price equation for the corresponding periods. For the free–trade regime both a multivariate and an autoregressive specification will be used. It will turn out that this is just sufficient for our purposes. Denoting the equilibrium error for LNPR under the free–trade–regime (i. e. the residuals of regression (115)) by ECLNPRFT and estimating by OLS, we obtain the following regression for the multivariate specification:

$$\Delta LNPR = -\ 0.082^{**}\ ECLNPRFT(-1) + 0.337^{**}\ \Delta LNPR(-1) + E_{118}$$
$$(-3.34) \qquad\qquad (4.95)$$
$$\overline{R}^2 = 0.138 \qquad DW = 1.945 \qquad (118)$$

Regression results for the autoregressive specifications of LNPR under the free–trade– and the ISA–regime are given in equations (119) and (120), respectively:

$$LNPR = 1.300^{**}\ LNPR(-1) - 0.303^{**}\ LNPR(-2) + E_{119}$$
$$(18.81) \qquad\qquad (-4.39)$$
$$\overline{R}^2 = 0.972 \qquad DW = 1.928 \qquad (119)$$

$$\text{LNPR} = \underset{(9.62)}{1.323^{**}}\ \text{LNPR}(-1) - \underset{(-2.29)}{0.318^{*}}\ \text{LNPR}(-2) + E_{120}$$

$$\overline{R}^2 = 0.978 \qquad \text{DW} = 2.054 \tag{120}$$

In all three regressions the estimates show satisfactory significance levels. The coefficient of the error correction term in (118) is negative as it should be. In the autoregressive specifications the coefficient estimates are remarkably close under the two regimes. Observe also that the unit root is clearly discernible in (119) and (120). The null of normality is rejected for the multivariate specification, but accepted for the two autoregressive forms (Table A2.15). However, the distributions of the residuals are probably not identical for the two autoregressive specifications, since the distribution under the free–trade regime is undeniably skewed to the right, while its ISA–counterpart is as strongly skewed to the left. (The distinctness of the distributions can, in fact, be verified by a Siegel–Tukey test). Given the observed similarity of the estimated coefficients, it is suggestive to suspect that it was the dissimilarity of the residual distributions, which made test statistics indicate a structural change for the autoregressive specification of LNPR in the earlier part of our analysis. The specification tests, finally, indicate correct functional forms in all three cases (Table A2.16).

To quantify the effects of the ISAs on world market prices, we now have to apply two different kinds of simulations. For the years 1969 to 1970 and 1978 to 1979 we pay tribute to the structural change in the price functions and simulate the effects of increased stockholding in the familiar manner by using the autoregressive functions (119) and (120). For the years 1971 to 1972 and 1980 to 1982, on the other hand, reduced systematic excess production resulted in a change in the *size* of WORM, an explanatory variable of equation (118), rather than in a change of the functional form of one of the price equations. I hence solve equation (118) for LNPR and compute simulated values for this variable, one time using the observed values of WORM, the other time adjusting WORM for the estimated effects of the ISA on systematic excess production, as given in the previous section.

After transforming logarithms to levels, we obtain estimates of how the ISAs affected the world market price (Table 65). We see that in both Agreements prices rose due to the "price–stabilizing" mechanisms. A dampening effect in periods with high sugar prices (particularly the years 1972, 1980, and 1981) is not conceivable. For both Agreements the price effects in the first ISA–governed year (1969 and 1978, respectively) are considerably smaller than in the second one (1970 and 1979, respectively). This is well in line with our earlier finding that total involuntary stocks in

Table 65

Effects of the ISAs on Real Prices
(yearly averages, in cts/lb)

	69	70	71	72	78	79	80	81	82	Mean
Price increase attributable to the ISAs	1.12	3.49	0.68	6.08	1.46	4.65	1.32	2.71	2.11	2.62
Observed real price	8.52	9.14	10.58	16.97	9.89	10.92	28.56	15.56	7.56	13.08
Estimate of real price under a free-trade regime	7.40	5.65	9.90	10.89	8.43	6.27	27.24	12.85	5.45	10.45

the second year of each Agreement were larger than in the first year. Depressed systematic excess production becoming effective in the third years causes only a minor additional price increase in 1971 and 1980, probably due to the fact that the reduction in systematic excess production gave room to disposing of previously accumulated involuntary stocks. The stock effect and the production effect thus counteracted each other in the third ISA–year.

For the 1968 ISA the year 1972 brought a very large reduction of systematic excess supply and thus the affiliated price increase was quite extraordinary (6.08 cts/lb in terms of *real* prices). In fact, it appears that this was both precondition and starting point of the 1972 – 1974 price boom on the world market. During the 1977 ISA, on the other hand, the ISA–induced reduction of systematic excess supply was of a more moderate size and so were the resulting price increases. The 1980 price boom for instance – its main determinant being presumably exceptionally bad harvests[194] – was only marginally reinforced by the decrease in systematic excess production. In the following years (1981 and 1982) we also find but a modest price increase. It is interesting to note an ISA–effect even for the depressed prices in 1982: According to the above estimates, the real world market price, averaging at 7.56 cts/lb, would have been down at 5.45 cts/lb had there been no ISA.

[194] In 1980, quota shortfalls in Cuba, the Dominican Republic, Mauritius, South Africa, and Thailand were accepted as attributable to *force majeure* by the International Sugar Council.

This is not at all unrealistic, since in subsequent periods without price support yearly real prices have assumed values as low as 3.54 cts/lb in 1985 and 5.43 cts/lb in 1986.

The ISAs thus appear to have resulted in an increase in the average world market price. If we confine our attention to the narrow definition of the ISAs and consider real prices, this increase averaged at 2.69 cts/lb. The standard deviation of the observed and simulated prices, however, is almost the same (6.22 cts/lb and 6.39 cts/lb, respectively). Stabilization in the sense of a reduction in the price's variance is hence not conceivable[195].

With these comments, we have completed our analysis on the effects of the International Sugar Agreements. What remains to be done, is a brief summary of the simulation results within a comprehensive survey of the findings of this study. This is left to the following Conclusions.

---

[195]These comments refer to the average *annual* values displayed in Table 65. They are not qualitatively altered by analysing the *monthly* data (observed and simulated); here we find standard deviations of 6.96 cts/lb for the simulated and 6.92 cts/lb for the observed prices, i. e. the standard deviations are virtually identical. The means are, of course, the same as for the annual averages.

CONCLUSIONS

Agricultural markets, though often cited as prime examples for competitiveness, are far from being accurately represented by the classical Walrasian model: Not only is production predetermined by the amount of area under cultivation, not only do stochastic shocks like weather or crop diseases distort the systematic effects of price expectations, but also – and most importantly – do government–imposed market regulations cause significant deviations from the conventional supply–demand structure.

An accout of such institutional constraints given for several *national* sugar markets clearly demonstrates their almost ubiquitous character. The effects of *world* market price stabilization should thus be evaluated under explicit consideration of regulative market interventions which define the *domestic* markets' status quo. Doing this in a theoretical model results in an undisputably benefitial effect of price stabilization. However, in the long run, i. e. with supply response, this gain may fade unless the governments properly adjust their intervention prices. The desirability of (world market) price stabilization for a single country will, in general, be the larger the larger this country's world market share (with reference to exports or imports) is.

Establishing domestic market regulations requires protective mechanisms in international trade. Thus consequences for the structure of the world market are imminent. It seems that most governments aspire fixed domestic prices for both farmers and consumers. Such policies result in price inelastic excess production on the world market. Corresponding tests applied to the data of 22 sugar trading countries do indeed not allow to reject the null of systematic excess production being statistically independent of the current world market price.

As stock demand is thus left to be the sole price elastic component of world agricultural markets, it is not too difficult to see that non–market–clearing may occur, particularly in the face of a substantial dispersion of stochastic production.

Prices can hence not completely clear the market. But they might be required to clear it as much as possible and simultaneously stay positive and finite. Such a postulate generalizes the traditional equilibrium concept. Under rational expectations, however, the two turn out to be equivalent. From this insight, it immediately follows that no rational expectations equilibria exist.

A linear approximation to this model allows us to derive a representation of the world market price in the frequency domain. Arguing that systematic production might be represented by a stationary process with an autoregressive coefficient close to unity, we find that prices will be trend–free but will display a cycle of at least four years' length, provided they respond to changes in systematic supply not more than eight times as sensitively as to stochastic shocks. It deems very unlikely that this latter condition is violated in real–world markets. The corresponding estimates for the sugar price function show that the coefficient for stochastic supply is in fact (in absolute terms) larger than its systematic counterpart by a factor of about 1.5. However, it remains unclear whether the two multipliers are indeed different at all, since the estimated discrepancy is not statistically significant.

The coefficient estimates for the sugar price function lead us to an interesting enigma concerning the International Sugar Agreements' inability to prevent sudden price booms: Sugar prices can apparently be represented by a semi–logarithmic price function, i. e. prices *in logarithms* are (inter alia) explained by systematic and stochastic supply *in levels.* This seems to suggest that it is easier to prevent high prices than to prevent low. For suppose that prices were low and quantity $\bar{q}$ were stored in order to raise them by 1 cts/lb. Suppose further that in a later period prices become high and quantity $\bar{q}$ is released. Should this, given the price function's semi–logarithmic form, not depress prices by significantly more than only 1 cts/lb? In other words: Should – in apparent contrast to the experience with the International Sugar Agreements – a relatively tiny quantity of stored sugar not be able to effectively prevent skyrocketing prices?

To answer this question note first that the argument works the other way, too: If prices are high, than a relatively small decrease in supply induces a strongly rising price. Further, it may well be that insufficient supplies are due to bad weather, i. e. we have a reduction in stochastic supply. The quantity stored, $\bar{q}$, however, is a component of systematic supply, since its release, by the rules set forth in the Agreements, is to be expected in the face of high prices. Now, if the coefficient of stochastic supply is (in absolute terms) larger than the coefficient of systematic supply (by a factor of 1.5, say), then the release of the stored quantity $\bar{q}$ can prevent a price increase only if the decrease in stochastic supply does not exceed 0.67 $\bar{q}$. In this sense quantity stored for the purpose of price stabilization is depreciated so long as marginal stochastic effects dominate marginal systematic ones.

There is little doubt that the ISAs did have a measurable effect on world sugar prices, particularly in their first two years of operation. Significant extra stocks have been accumulated in the years 1969–1970 and 1978–1979. However, it appears that subsequently farmers' production plans have been adjusted to the confined export possibilities that were to be expected under the established quota system. We find reduced systematic excess production in the years 1971–1972 and 1980–1982, such that quotas in effect leave room to dispose of accumulated involuntary stocks.

While these phenomena seem to be approximately equal for both Agreements, the following development is not. For in 1980 a series of disastrous harvests in major sugar producing countries hit the market, an event whose importance can equally well be discerned in the graphical representation of WORZ (Figure 4) as in the declarations of *force majeure* submitted to the International Sugar Council. Already characterized by a situation of tight systematic supplies, sugar prices quickly rose and marked the 1980 price boom.

In the years 1971–1973 no comparably bad harvest can be singled out. Instead, systematic supplies constantly deteriorated and prices – special stocks being unable to forcefully counteract this tendency – rose with accelerating speed. While the 1974 price peak occured after expiration of the 1968 Agreement, the simulations I present leave little doubt that the reduction in systematic excess production attributable to this Agreement was a major cause for the subsequent boom of sugar prices. The two sugar price booms of 1974 and 1980 thus turn out to have very different roots: In 1972 – 1974, prices did necessarily rise due to reduced systematic supplies, whereas in 1980 an unforeseeable shock drove prices upwards. In this view, the 1974 price boom is a direct consequence of the ISA, while its 1980 counterpart is not. However, this is not to say that the 1977 ISA did not contribute to the latter. For in 1980 prices might have responded less dramatically to the stochastic shock had not the ISA induced a situation of comparably tight systematic supplies.

Restrained exports and discouraging effects on production as a result of quota regulations are two features of the ISAs which are likely to push prices upwards. No equally forceful instruments seem to exist which might counteract price booms. Special stocks accumulated under the Agreements have been released in prespecified situations, but their effects were virtually nil. Thus it is not too surprising to find simulation results which suggest that the ISAs achieved an increase of the average world market price, but not a decrease of its variance. Such results would have fit an exporters' cartel well, but they are clearly not in accordance with the Agreements' self–defined objectives. Further, they do not make importer cooperation attractive if another ISA were to be negotiated.

There are a number of policy conclusions which may be drawn from this analysis. First, an ISA seems to be ill–fated if the negotiating strength of major exporting countries enables them to secure distinctively more generous export quotas for themselves than for other participants. Second, a quasi–automatic adjustment of BETs and corresponding quotas may easily inflate quotas in effect beyond any reasonable level. Third, it is important to secure quota discipline up to the end of the Agreement by suitable enforcement mechanisms.

But these are merely technical details to be taken care of in future negotiations. More important is the question whether a quota system can at all be recommended for price stabilization.

The answer I would like to give on the basis of my analysis is rather negative, although I note that under very special circumstances (as specified below) a more optimistic view is possible. In general, however, the following problem will be encountered: An effective quota system requires that quotas be fairly tight. Thus, as in the case of the first two years of the ISAs, involuntary stocks accumulate. Since storage of agricultural commodities is far from inexpensive, this initiates adjustment processes for stockholders and farmers which will eventually lead to reduced production. With (excess) production declining, the world market price rises and quotas cease to be binding. Momentarily, the Agreement may thus appear to be successful.

Unfortunately, this situation is highly instable, for it is not in the spirit of a Nash–equilibrium: Farmers now receive two signals, namely increased prices and inoperative quotas. Hence for a single farmer (who supposes all other farmers to keep their production at its present level) expanded production is very attractive. (In fact, as the price is now higher than it has been prior to stabilization, it is very well conceivable that farmers expand their production beyond its pre–stabilization level). Thus prices fall again, quotas become operative, involuntary stocks accumulate and so forth.

The decisive aspect of quota systems seems to be that generally neither operative quotas and involuntary stocks, nor inoperative quotas and increased price levels admit an equilibrium interpretation. Both situations long for adjustment processes, such that eventually one will induce the other. Prices then oscillate between high and low. Since this mechanism has not been present prior to stabilization, it tends to increase the price's variance and hence to counteract its potentially otherwise variance–decreasing effect.

As time goes by, such an extra oscillation of world market prices may have decreasing, constant, or increasing amplitude. I have already given a reasoning for increasing amplitude and it is easy to imagine cases of constant or decreasing amplitude. Yet while constant and increasing amplitude increases the "natural" variance of the price even asymptotically, decreasing amplitude does not. We thus have to recognize that the production–price–adjustment process initiated by a quota system may eventually converge to an equilibrium in which the production discouraging effect of pending quotas just outweighs the production incentive set forth by increased price levels. In this (in my eyes fairly rare) case a quota system might be able to live up to its objectives, provided the duration of the quota agreement is long enough.

There is a second possibility for a quota system to be successful: If all quotas were equal to the amount of *systematic* excess production, then quotas would simply set aside overflows of the crop in times of good harvests. These could be released when harvests are insufficient and would thus truely stabilize the price. Yet production would not be discouraged, since farmers expect to produce systematic production, which, after deducting consumption, would precisely fit the quota. If, additionally, the price function obeyed a special functional form (it might be linear, for instance), then the mean world market price would not be affected and might hence be neutral with respect to production.

This scenario depicts the ideal way a quota system should work. In fact, it very much resembles the mechanism of a buffer stock. However, given incomplete information, varying negotiating strength of participating countries, inevitable structural changes in domestic markets, etc., it deems very unlikely that a quota system can be setup this way other than by pure chance. Much more probable is the presumption that a quota system will give rise to the above described oscillations in production and prices, and it is also quite likely that these oscillations will not converge within the finite life of the agreement. For this reason the aptitude of quota systems for the objective of price stabilization seems highly questionable.

APPENDIX

REGRESSION DIAGNOSTICS

A1 Testing Procedures

All regressions in this study are of the form $y = X\beta + u$, where the regressor matrix X may include stochastic or endogenous regressors. Regressions have been run by either OLS or GLS. In both cases a couple of tests has routinely been applied to the regression residuals[196] in addition to the usual Durbin–Watson–, t–, and F–tests. They were designed to test for normality, serial independence, heteroskedasticity, non–linearities, and structural change. Here is a brief description of these tests:

A1.1 Testing for Normality

Normality of the regression residuals is a key assumption in many regression diagnostics, particularly in t– and F–tests. I have therefore checked the empirical distribution of the residuals by not less than four different tests for normality.

The Anderson–Darling test belongs to the class of empirical-distribution-function-tests (EDF–tests)[197]. The test statistics measures the goodness of fit for the empirical

---

[196]It is well known that GLS can be viewed as OLS applied to a transformed model (the original model premultiplied with the square root of the inverse of the covariance matrix). In the case of GLS the tests have been applied to the residuals of the transformed model.

[197]Other prominent EDF–tests are the Kolmogorov–Smirnov and the Cramér–von–Mises test. Power comparisons by Shapiro et al. (1968) and Stephens (1974) show these latter tests to be inferior to the Anderson–Darling statistic; hence I favored the Anderson–Darling test over the other two. But, using ingenious transformations due to Stephens (1974), there is almost no additional computational cost involved in determining all three of them rather than only one. Thus I routinely computed these three test statistics for the regressions run in this thesis. As was to be

distribution function of the regression residuals and the distribution function under the null hypothesis, i. e. the normal distribution function. (For a detailed exposition see Büning & Trenkler (1978)). Critical values are taken from Stephens (1974) and relate to the case where the first moment is known to be zero, while the variance is unknown and must be estimated from the data. (Table 1B from Stephens (1974)).

Two more tests for normality are the so–called moment tests, whose basic idea it is to compare estimates of the sample's standardized third or fourth moment with their expected values under the null of normality. The standardized third moment (known as $\sqrt{\beta_1}$) characterizes the skewness of the distribution, while the standardized fourth moment, β_2, characterizes its kurtosis. Under the null we have $\sqrt{\beta_1} = 0$ and $\beta_2 = 3$. Denoting the estimates of the sample analogues by $\sqrt{b_1}$ and b_2 two two–sided tests are constructed. The null is rejected whenever $\sqrt{b_1}$ or b_2 deviate too strongly from 0 or 3, respectively. Critical values for the test statistic $\sqrt{b_1}$ are taken from Pearson & Hartley (1966), critical values for b_2 can be found in d'Agostino & Tietjen (1971) (for a sample size of $n \leq 50$), in d'Agostino & Pearson (1973) ($60 \leq n \leq 200$) and in Pearson & Hartley (1966) ($200 \leq n \leq 5000$)[198].

There have also been attempts to combine $\sqrt{b_1}$ and b_2 to produce one final test statistic that is sensitive to departures from normality due to either skewness or kurtosis. Out of these I have selected the Bera–Jarque test (Jarque & Bera (1987)), which has explicitly been constructed for the use of regression residuals. Asymptotically, this test has optimum power properties and a chi–square distribution. The exact distribution is not known, but Jarque & Bera (1987) report a good finite sample performance.

None of these tests is exact, however. With the exception of the Bera–Jarque test all statistics require that actual disturbances (and not estimates thereof) be used, and for the Bera–Jarque test only the limiting distribution is known. Weisberg (1980) points out that estimated residuals as a linear combination of unobservable disturbances do always have a tendency to appear normal. On the other hand, Pierce &

---

expected, the Anderson–Darling test clearly outperforms the Kolmogorov–Smirnov and the Cramér–von Mises test: Almost always is the Anderson–Dar– ling statistic significant if any of the EDF–tests rejects the null at all. Therefore the "Tests for Normality"–tables suppress the results of the Kolmogorov–Smirnov and the Cramér–von–Mises test in order not to overload the tables with almost redundant test statistics.

[198] Pearson & Hartley (1966), Table 34 C, report a wrong critical value for the upper 1% level of b_2 and $n = 200$. The correct value should read 3.96, as Figure 2 in d'Agostino & Pearson (1973) shows.

Kopecky (1979) prove tests for normality to be asymptotically valid if computed from regression residuals[199]. Further, Pierce & Gray (1982) examine regression settings with small sample sizes ($n = 20$ and $n = 40$) and find the asymptotic approximation to be quite adequate.

Applying six different tests to the same sample does of course distort the level of the tests taken as a whole. This is a well–known problem and has recently been expressed in a formal model by Hillier (1991). However, except for very special circumstances, the joint distribution of the tests is unknown and properly defined critical regions do not exist. Yet the probability of at least one of the normality tests rejecting at the 5%–level, say, is undisputably larger than 5%, especially in small samples. See Pearson et al. (1977), who study the joint distribution of $\sqrt{b_1}$ and b_2. After experimenting with artificial data, I fixed the following decision rule, intended to ensure an approximate 5%–level for the above six tests:

In large samples (more than 50 observations) the null of normality will be rejected if either a single test is significant at the 1%–level or two tests (out of which at most one EDF–test) are significant at the 5%–level. In small samples (50 observations or less) the rule is very similar, the difference being (due to its asymptotic nature) strengthened standards for the Bera–Jarque test: In order to reject the null irrespective of any other statistic, this test is required to be significant at the 0.5%–level, while in combination with another test the Bera–Jarque statistic should be less likely than 0.01.

A1.2 Testing for Serial Independence

Serial correlation is often encountered in economic time series and the well–known Durbin–Watson test is the standard procedure to detect such departures from the classical assumptions. However, the Durbin–Watson test is merely a test for *first–order* autocorrelation of the regression residuals, but, especially when working with monthly data, serial dependence with much longer lags is conceivable.

Another procedure of testing for serial correlation is to apply a Kolmogorov–Smirnov test to the observations' cumulated periodogram, (see for instance Schlittgen & Streitberg (1989, pp. 274–281)). I call this test the Cumulated–Periodogram–test (CPT). Its null supposes normality and serial independence of the sample distribution.

---

[199]This, of course, enabled Jarque & Bera (1987) to construct their test for regression residuals.

I used this test in a regression subroutine, even though it is designed for true disturbances and not for regression residuals. In fact, Durbin (1969) provides a similar test explicitly for least squares residuals, but this test is slightly more complicated to handle (it involves an inconclusive region in the spirit of the Durbin–Watson test) and – just like the conventional Durbin–Watson test – it is not valid (not even asymptotically) in the case of lagged endogenous regressors (Durbin (1970)). Since most regressions in this study include lagged endogenous regressors, it is not clear whether Durbin's (1969) test would perform better than the CPT[200].

Only asymptotically is the periodogram of a time series an unbiased estimator of its spectrum. This makes it advisable to apply the CPT but to relatively large samples. I thus decided to reserve this test to samples of size 90 or larger[201].

A very popular test for serial dependencies is Box & Pierce's (1970) Q–statistic, based on the sum of squares of the regression residuals' first m estimated autocorrelations. If m is large enough, then the asymptotic distribution of the Q–statistic is chi–square with the degrees of freedom depending on m (and on the number of estimated parameters). However, a suitable choice of m is difficult to obtain. While in the proofs of the asymptotic properties m is a fixed constant and the sample size n grows larger and larger, the applications require the choice of an appropriate m for a typically fixed value of n. It is not difficult to see that the test becomes extremely conservative with a large m.

I experimented with various choices of m, particularly with choices such as $m \approx \sqrt{n}$, and I also used a modification of the test statistic suggested by Ljung & Box (1978). Still the results of the Q–statistic did not seem very reliable. The rate of convergence to the limiting distribution is apparently very slow, such that even in samples with more than 100 observations rejections of the null must be very cautiously received. Due to these problems I eventually decided to discard the Box–Pierce test altogether.

---

[200]Actually, I do not know whether the CPT is asymptotically valid if regression residuals are used in the place of true disturbances. Using consistent estimators for the residuals may be comforting, but does not replace a proof.

[201]Ninety is obviously an arbitrary value. In fact, I initially intended to set the limit equal to hundred, but it turned out that the applied work brought along many interesting regressions with 96 observations. In order to have the CPT available for them, I chose 90 observations as the minimum requirement for applying this test.

We are thus left with two tests for serial dependencies, the Durbin–Watson– and the Cumulative–Periodogram test[202]. They test the same null hypothesis (namely seria independence of the error terms) but specify different (yet intersecting) alternatives. Hence it is clear that the likelihood of *one* of the tests rejecting at its nominal 5%–level is again larger than 5%. As a slight correction of that I decided to reject the null whenever one of the tests is significant at the 5%–level, but to definitely accept it even if the Durbin–Watson statistic is actually inconclusive.

A1.3 Testing for Heteroskedasticity

Only one single test, the Goldfeld–Quandt test, is employed to check the assumption of a constant variance of the disturbances. My reason for not devoting more attention to this problem lies in the fact that only very rarely in Parts II and III does it deem appropriate to adjust estimation techniques for apparent heteroskedasticity. More precisely: With the exception of estimating the production functions (22) – (43), all regressions are run by OLS anyway in order to circumvene problems in testing for structural change or in the subsequent simulations. Hence for most regressions detection of heteroskedasticity does not entail any practical consequences; the test statistics are merely given for informative purposes. The production functions, however, *are* estimated by GLS whenever there is sufficient evidence for a non–constant variance of the error term. Since these functions display a truely exogenous regressor matrix and, in their overwhelming majority, normally distributed disturbances, an F–test such as the Goldfeld–Quandt test commends itself.

From Part I, we even have a model of the type of heteroskedasticity we may expect to encounter[203]: Stochastic production has been modeled as $(\Theta-1)$ times the expected value of the harvest. Hence, transformed to our present notation, we would suppose the variance of the error term to be positively correlated with $E[y] = X\beta$. Thus the setup of the test is as follows: Let $\hat{y} = X\hat{\beta}$ denote the estimated values of the endogenous variable. The sample is split into three equally large subsamples, where the first subsample contains the observations associated with the smallest $\hat{y}$–values and the third subsample contains the observations associated with the

[202]Numerous other tests for serial independence exist, but a comprehensive survey or discussion is clearly beyond the scope of this thesis. See Krämer & Sonnberger (1986) and Pagan & Hall (1983).

[203]This is why we do not need to employ a test for heteroskedasticity with a very general alternative such as White's (1980) test.

largest y–values. The test statistic is then the conventional F–statistic, i. e. the ratio of the estimated variances in the first and third subsample.

The Goldfeld–Quandt test does of course require normality of the disturbances. Whenever this hypothesis has to be rejected, the distribution of the Goldfeld–Quandt statistic and the corresponding P–values are simulated by bootstrap methods as outlined in Efron & Tibshirani (1986).

A1.4 Testing for Non–Linearities

The Reset test proposed by Ramsey (1969) and the so–called Rainbow test advanced by Utts (1982) are used to detect specification errors, particularly non-linear relationships. Both tests are parametric F–tests without any need to specify a particular alternative; a discussion can be found in Krämer & Sonnberger (1986).

In the use of Reset I follow a suggestion by Thursby & Schmidt (1977) to add squared, cubed, and fourth powers of the $\hat{y}$–values to the regressor matrix, while Rainbow is set up as recommended by Utts (1982), i. e. the sample is split into two equally large subsamples with reference to the magnitudes of the diagonal elements of the "hat matrix" $X(X'X)^{-1}X'$. In the case of non-normal error terms the test statistics are again bootstrapped in order to obtain estimates of the appropriate P–values.

A1.5 Testing for Structural Change

As structural change is extensively tested for in Part III, only one test is routinely applied to the regressions, namely the well–known Chow test. The alternative is specified such that the midpoint of the sample period is suspected to mark a unique structural shift. Since the Chow test is another parametric F–test, I do again resort to bootstrap procedures whenever the error distributions are significantly non-normal.

A2 Regression Statistics and P–Values

The following tables display the results of the above tests if applied to the regressions indicated in the first column of each table. I give P–values (or bootstrap estimates thereof) for the Bera–Jarque–, Goldfeld–Quandt–, Chow–, Rainbow–, and Reset test, while the actual test statistics are displayed for $\sqrt{b_1}$, b_2, the Anderson–Darling–, and the Durbin–Watson test. Bootstrap estimates always rely on 1000 independent drawings from the estimated distribution of the error term. Significance levels for the test statistics are indicated by stars.

Table A2.1

Tests for Normality

Null Hypothesis: Error Distribution is Gaussian

Equation #	Test Statistics			P-value	Null
	Anderson-Darling	$\sqrt{b_1}$	b_2	Bera-Jarque	
(22)	0.160	0.191	2.319	0.799	accepted
(23)	0.209	-0.181	2.187	0.662	accepted
(24)	0.462	-0.612	2.241	0.351	accepted
(25)	0.216	0.310	2.225	0.591	accepted
(26)	0.450	-0.233	3.517	0.812	accepted
(27)	0.320	-0.209	2.357	0.762	accepted
(28)	0.344	-0.426	2.275	0.486	accepted
(29)	0.308	0.182	2.639	0.922	accepted
(30)	0.688	-0.691	3.792	0.289	accepted
(31)	0.479	-0.831*	2.925	0.298	accepted
(32)	0.212	0.132	1.666*	0.444	accepted
(33)	0.622	-0.393	2.288	0.607	accepted
(34)	0.658	-0.937*	2.940	0.222	accepted
(35)	0.259	0.123	2.067	0.678	accepted
(36)	0.197	-0.241	2.228	0.660	accepted
(37)	0.488	-0.341	4.201*	0.413	accepted
(38)	0.312	-0.399	2.419	0.622	accepted
(39)	1.081	1.805**	6.672**	0.000**	rejected
(40)	0.540	-0.645	3.146	0.495	accepted
(41)	0.227	0.013	2.505	0.896	accepted
(42)	0.343	-0.525	3.064	0.616	accepted
(43)	0.892	-1.364**	4.870*	0.008**	rejected

Table A2.2

Specification Tests

Null Hypothesis: Absence of Serial Correlation, Heteroskedasticity, Structural Change, and Non–Linearities

Equa-tion #	Dependent Variable	Durbin-Watson Statistic	P-value			
			Goldfeld-Quandt	Chow	Rainbow	Reset
(22)	ARGPRO	1.54	0.488	0.783	0.328	0.878
(23)	AUSPRO	2.05	0.180	0.406	0.739	0.138
(24)	BRAPRO	1.71	0.306	0.029*	0.285	0.402
(25)	CANPRO	1.44	0.230	0.141	0.279	0.112
(26)	COLPRO	1.94	0.150	0.578	0.803	0.991
(27)	CUBPRO	1.92	0.300	0.378	0.285	0.487
(28)	DOMPRO	1.80	0.361	0.076	0.492	0.254
(29)	EECPRO	1.43	0.159	0.701	0.252	0.439
(30)	FIJPRO	2.59	0.248	0.319	0.100	0.870
(31)	GUYPRO	2.48 ?	0.405	0.995	0.994	0.999
(32)	INDPRO	1.50 ?	0.420	0.372	0.032*	0.438
(33)	JAPPRO	2.57	0.308	0.448	0.255	0.507
(34)	MAUPRO	2.15	0.387	0.973	0.938	0.988
(35)	MEXPRO	1.69	0.299	0.543	0.553	0.247
(36)	PHIPRO	1.51	0.287	0.596	0.705	0.857
(37)	SAFPRO	2.79 ?	0.337	0.322	0.052	0.977
(38)	SUPRO	1.47 ?	0.263	0.296	0.465	0.911
(39)	SWAPRO	1.50	0.065	0.104	0.016*	0.065
(40)	TAIPRO	2.70 ?	0.332	0.881	0.214	0.936
(41)	THAPRO	1.48	0.478	0.145	0.321	0.916
(42)	USAPRO	1.76	0.221	0.395	0.154	0.992
(43)	ROWPRO	1.63	0.339	0.253	0.571	0.213

* = significant at the 5%-level
** = significant at the 1%-level
? = inconclusive region of Durbin-Watson test

Table A2.3

Tests for Normality

Null Hypothesis: Error Distribution is Gaussian

Equation #	Test Statistics			P-value	Null
	Anderson-Darling	$\sqrt{b_1}$	b_2	Bera-Jarque	
(46)	0.627	0.309*	3.676*	0.020*	rejected
(49)	0.757	0.275*	3.570*	0.109	rejected
(51)	0.547	0.012	3.544	0.268	accepted

* = significant at the 5%-level
** = significant at the 1%-level

Table A2.4

Specification Tests

Null Hypothesis: Absence of Serial Correlation, Heteroskedasticity, Structural Change, and Non-Linearities

Equation #	Dependent Variable	# of observat.	P-value				
			CPT	Goldfeld-Quandt	Chow	Rainbow	Reset
(46)	ΔLNPR	238	0.850	0.382	0.251	0.001**	0.337
(49)	LNPR	238	0.562	0.141	0.774	0.071	0.082
(51)	WOREXC	213	0.236	0.112	0.183	0.157	0.603

* = significant at the 5%-level
** = significant at the 1%-level

Table A2.5

Tests for Normality

Null Hypothesis: Error Distribution is Gaussian

Equation #	Test Statistics			P-value	Null
	Anderson-Darling	$\sqrt{b_1}$	b_2	Bera-Jarque	
(57)	4.35**	0.25	7.87**	0.000**	rejected
(58)	5.74**	-0.28*	6.61**	0.000**	rejected
(59)	2.54*	0.65**	6.94**	0.000**	rejected
(60)	7.66**	-0.94**	7.91**	0.000**	rejected
(61)	2.23	-0.08	4.98**	0.000**	rejected
(62)	1.49	-0.66**	5.15**	0.000**	rejected
(63)	3.26*	-0.49**	5.97**	0.000**	rejected
(64)	2.87*	-0.36*	5.80**	0.000**	rejected
(65)	3.03*	-0.20	5.76**	0.000**	rejected
(66)	1.01	-0.57**	4.11**	0.000**	rejected
(67)	5.24**	0.37*	8.73**	0.000**	rejected
(68)	2.18	0.21	5.57**	0.000**	rejected
(69)	0.81	-0.20	4.39**	0.002**	rejected
(70)	4.11**	-0.36*	8.85**	0.000**	rejected
(71)	4.13**	-0.06	7.49**	0.000**	rejected
(72)	4.07**	0.06	5.59**	0.000**	rejected
(73)	7.24**	-0.22	8.96**	0.000**	rejected

* = significant at the 5%-level
** = significant at the 1%-level

Table A2.6

Specification Tests

Null Hypothesis: Absence of Serial Correlation, Heteroskedasticity, Structural Change, and Non–Linearities

Equation #	Durbin-Watson Statistic	P-value				
		Cumulat. Periodog.	Goldfeld-Quandt	Chow	Rainbow	Reset
(57)	1.889	0.194	0.400	0.307	0.012*	0.130
(58)	1.906	0.129	0.008**	0.219	0.362	0.429
(59)	1.987	0.999	0.373	0.293	0.102	0.091
(60)	1.852	0.321	0.489	0.231	0.000**	0.001**
(61)	1.993	0.999	0.062	0.255	0.004**	0.489
(62)	1.930	0.437	0.001**	0.080	0.440	0.095
(63)	2.034	0.999	0.054	0.403	0.001**	0.106
(64)	2.011	0.999	0.060	0.131	0.049*	0.004**
(65)	2.077	0.180	0.031*	0.603	0.001**	0.035*
(66)	2.053	0.973	0.003**	0.772	0.144	0.004**
(67)	1.869	0.408	0.131	0.333	0.000**	0.015*
(68)	1.997	0.929	0.027*	0.245	0.001**	0.219
(69)	2.154	0.321	0.000**	0.504	0.016*	0.502
(70)	2.048	0.462	0.024*	0.195	0.001**	0.079
(71)	2.003	0.999	0.118	0.341	0.000**	0.015*
(72)	1.876	0.309	0.009**	0.100	0.000**	0.014*
(73)	1.968	0.999	0.003**	0.441	0.001**	0.054

* = significant at the 5%-level
** = significant at the 1%-level
? = inconclusive region of Durbin-Watson test

Table A2.7

Tests for Normality

Null Hypothesis: Error Distribution is Gaussian

Equation #	Test Statistics			P-value	Null
	Anderson-Darling	$\sqrt{b_1}$	b_2	Bera-Jarque	
(76)	8.467**	-1.091**	8.553**	0.000**	rejected
(77)	2.762*	-0.533**	5.412**	0.000**	rejected
(78)	0.976	-0.712**	4.756**	0.000**	rejected
(79)	4.782**	0.640**	8.807**	0.000**	rejected
(80)	2.206	0.018	5.979**	0.000**	rejected
(81)	1.946	0.306*	6.671**	0.000**	rejected

Table A2.8

Specification Tests

Null Hypothesis: Absence of Serial Correlation, Heteroskedasticity, Structural Change, and Non-Linearities

Equation #	Durbin-Watson Statistic	P-value				
		Cumulat. Periodog.	Goldfeld-Quandt	Chow	Rainbow	Reset
(76)	2.021	0.951	0.369	0.220	0.000**	0.000**
(77)	1.992	0.999	0.247	0.351	0.070	0.004**
(78)	2.040	0.808	0.047*	0.066	0.299	0.022*
(79)	1.898	0.847	0.058	0.143	0.000**	0.037*
(80)	2.010	0.999	0.273	0.212	0.000**	0.269
(81)	1.856	0.557	0.056	0.129	0.002**	0.060

* = significant at the 5%-level
** = significant at the 1%-level
? = inconclusive region of Durbin-Watson test

Table A2.9

Tests for Normality

Null Hypothesis: Error Distribution is Gaussian

Equation #	Test Statistics			P-value	Null
	Anderson-Darling	$\sqrt{b_1}$	b_2	Bera-Jarque	
(82)	1.100	1.076**	4.344*	0.008**	rejected
(83)	0.373	0.374	3.611	0.280	accepted
(84)	1.994	-1.010**	4.121*	0.005**	rejected
(85)	0.650	-0.612*	3.707	0.119	accepted
(86)	0.892	0.981**	5.600**	0.000**	rejected
(87)	2.363*	-1.520**	12.897**	0.000**	rejected

Table A2.10

Specification Tests

Null Hypothesis: Absence of Serial Correlation, Heteroskedasticity, Structural Change, and Non–Linearities

Equation #	Durbin-Watson Statistic	P-value			
		Goldfeld-Quandt	Chow	Rainbow	Reset
(82)	1.942	0.042*	0.568	0.004**	0.404
(83)	1.587	0.022*	0.999	0.783	0.673
(84)	1.975	0.289	0.768	0.077	0.178
(85)	1.929	0.002**	0.697	0.176	0.794
(86)	1.911	0.485	0.506	0.064	0.105
(87)	1.932	0.102	0.227	0.032*	0.208

* = significant at the 5%-level
** = significant at the 1%-level
? = inconclusive region of Durbin-Watson test

Table A2.11

Tests for Normality

Null Hypothesis: Error Distribution is Gaussian

Equation #	Test Statistics			P-value	Null
	Anderson-Darling	$\sqrt{b_1}$	b_2	Bera-Jarque	
(88)	7.943**	-1.039**	8.270**	0.000**	rejected
(89)	1.245	-0.721**	4.981**	0.000**	rejected
(90)	3.014*	0.036	6.362**	0.000**	rejected
(91)	2.605*	-0.368*	7.023**	0.000**	rejected
(92)	2.663*	-0.589**	5.587**	0.000**	rejected
(93)	2.574*	-0.001	5.620**	0.000**	rejected
(94)	1.470	-0.787**	4.730**	0.000**	rejected
(95)	4.761**	0.632**	9.023**	0.000**	rejected
(96)	1.828	0.224	5.506**	0.000**	rejected
(97)	1.093	-0.513*	4.719**	0.000**	rejected
(98)	2.362*	-0.065	7.366**	0.000**	rejected
(99)	5.653**	-0.161	8.577**	0.000**	rejected

* = significant at the 5%-level
** = significant at the 1%-level

Table A2.12

Specification Tests

Null Hypothesis: Absence of Serial Correlation, Heteroskedasticity, Structural Change, and Non–Linearities

Equa-tion #	Durbin-Watson Statistic	P-value				
		Cumulat. Periodog.	Goldfeld-Quandt	Chow	Rainbow	Reset
(88)	1.953	0.999	0.363	0.183	0.000**	0.000**
(89)	2.093	0.912	0.483	0.176	0.528	0.182
(90)	2.003	0.759	0.241	0.612	0.016*	0.048*
(91)	2.065	0.863	0.078	0.568	0.001**	0.187
(92)	2.006	0.999	0.113	0.173	0.060	0.020*
(93)	2.062	0.313	0.015*	0.121	0.003**	0.015*
(94)	2.081	0.999	0.011*	0.444	0.052	0.020*
(95)	1.916	0.863	0.049*	0.351	0.000**	0.032*
(96)	1.998	0.999	0.062	0.150	0.000**	0.077
(97)	2.071	0.685	0.015*	0.087	0.005**	0.317
(98)	2.018	0.999	0.042*	0.277	0.000**	0.240
(99)	1.970	0.999	0.001**	0.241	0.000**	0.054

* = significant at the 5%-level
** = significant at the 1%-level
? = inconclusive region of Durbin-Watson test

Table A2.13

Tests for Normality

Null Hypothesis: Error Distribution is Gaussian

Equation #	Test Statistics			P-value	Null
	Anderson-Darling	$\sqrt{b_1}$	b_2	Bera-Jarque	
(100)	1.031	0.142	4.471*	0.176	accepted
(101)	0.781	-0.171	4.054*	0.158	accepted
(102)	1.086	-0.438	5.501**	0.000**	rejected
(103)	2.647*	-0.217	9.414**	0.000**	rejected
(104)	0.819	0.751**	4.127*	0.004**	rejected
(105)	2.125	-1.071**	5.149**	0.000**	rejected
(106)	1.441	-0.142	2.473	0.121	accepted
(107)	0.666	-0.535	3.904	0.169	accepted
(108)	0.774	-1.210**	6.382**	0.000**	rejected
(109)	0.142	0.101	2.197	0.710	accepted
(110)	2.998*	-0.469*	7.849**	0.000**	rejected
(111)	0.481	0.316	2.436	0.811	accepted

* = significant at the 5%-level
** = significant at the 1%-level

Table A2.14

Specification Tests

Null Hypothesis: Absence of Serial Correlation, Heteroskedasticity, Structural Change, and Non–Linearities

Equation #	Durbin-Watson Statistic	P–value				
		Cumulat. Periodog.	Goldfeld-Quandt	Chow	Rainbow	Reset
(100)	1.834	–	0.000**	0.148	0.005**	0.005**
(101)	1.703	–	0.032*	0.615	0.797	0.825
(102)	2.061	–	0.009**	0.153	0.381	0.495
(103)	1.686	–	0.265	0.072	0.026*	0.097
(104)	1.446 ?	–	0.433	0.088	0.259	0.290
(105)	1.983	–	0.192	0.406	0.094	0.083
(106)	2.158	–	0.111	0.577	0.216	0.108
(107)	1.906	–	0.002**	0.899	0.092	0.680
(108)	1.901	–	0.289	0.200	0.125	0.999
(109)	1.630	–	0.049*	0.154	0.006**	0.797
(110)	1.949	0.999	0.338	0.608	0.044*	0.017*
(111)	1.658	–	0.150	0.354	0.779	0.986

* = significant at the 5%-level
** = significant at the 1%-level
? = inconclusive region of Durbin-Watson test

Table A2.15

Tests for Normality

Null Hypothesis: Error Distribution is Gaussian

Equation #	Test Statistics			P-value	Null
	Anderson-Darling	$\sqrt{b_1}$	b_2	Bera-Jarque	
(112)	1.392	0.072	3.980*	0.028*	rejected
(113)	0.249	0.193	2.246	0.440	accepted
(118)	1.137	0.492**	3.452	0.004**	rejected
(119)	0.571	0.341*	3.234	0.320	accepted
(120)	0.887	-0.395	2.774	0.462	accepted

Table A2.16

Specification Tests

Null Hypothesis: Absence of Serial Correlation, Heteroskedasticity, Structural Change, and Non-Linearitles

Equation #	# of observat.	P-value				
		Cumulat. Periodog.	Goldfeld-Quandt	Chow	Rainbow	Reset
(112)	177	0.523	0.116	0.333	0.686	0.735
(113)	55	-	0.102	0.028*	0.551	0.956
(118)	190	0.732	0.492	0.121	0.087	0.540
(119)	190	0.623	0.116	0.671	0.137	0.102
(120)	48	-	0.072	0.875	0.061	0.308

* = significant at the 5%-level
** = significant at the 1%-level
? = inconclusive region of Durbin-Watson test

LIST OF ABBREVIATIONS

ACP	Africa, Caribbean, Pacific
ALG	Algeria
AD	Anderson–Darling
a. e.	almost everywhere
AR	autoregressive
ARG	Argentina
ARGINFDUM	Dummy for Argentinian hyperinflation
ARIMA	autoregressive integrated moving average
ARMA	autoregressive moving average
a. s.	almost surely
AUS	Australia
BET	basic export tonnages
BJ	Bera–Jarque
BML	(German) Federal Department of Agriculture (Bundesministerium für Landwirtschaft und Forsten)
BRA	Brazil
$\sqrt{b_1}$	Test for non–normal skewness
b_2	Test for non–normal kurtosis
CAN	Canada
CAP	Common Agricultural Policy
CEY	Ceylon, Sri Lanka
CHI	China
cif	Cost, insurance, freight
CMS	cumulated market share
COL	Colombia
CON	Consumption

CONASUPO	Compania Nacional de Subsistencia Populares (Mexico)
CPI	Consumer Price Index
CPT	Cumulated Periodogram Test
CSA	Commonwealth Sugar Agreement
CSE	Consumer Subsidy Equivalent
CUB	Cuba
CvM	Cramér–von–Mises
CZE	Czechoslovakia
Δ	Difference operator
DOM	Dominican Republic
DW	Durbin–Watson
E	Expectation operator
ECBRA	Residuals of cointegrating regression for LNBRASTO
ECMEX	Residuals of cointegrating regression for LNMEXSTO
ECWOR	Residuals of cointegrating regression for LNWORSTO
EDF	Empirical distribution function
EEC	European Economic Community (in the territorial definition of 1985)
EGY	Egypt
EXC	Excess production
FAO	Food and Agriculture Organisation
FIJ	Fiji
fob	free on board
FOC	first order condition
GDR	German Democratic Republic (East Germany)
GLS	Generalized least squares
GQ	Goldfeld–Quandt
GUY	Guyana
HFCS	high fructose corn syrup
IND	India
IAA	Instituto de Azúcar y Alcohól (Brazil)
IDS	Indonesia
i.i.d.	independent, identically distributed
IMF	International Monetary Fund
IPC	Integrated Program for Commodities
IRN	Iran
IRQ	Iraq

ISA	International Sugar Agreement
ISO	International Sugar Organisation
JAP	Japan
KOR	South–Korea
KS	Kolmogorov–Smirnov
L	Lag operator
LMC	Landell Mills Corporation
LN	natural logarithm
LNPR	natural logarithm of the real world market price of sugar
MA	moving average
MAL	Malaysia
MAU	Mauritius
MEX	Mexico
MOR	Morocco
NEX	net exports
NIG	Nigeria
OLS	Ordinary least squares
PAK	Pakistan
PHI	Philippines
POL	Poland
p., pp.	Page, pages
PR	real world market price of sugar
PREX3	rational expectation of PR, three months ahead
PREX9	rational expectation of PR, nine months ahead
PREX3D	PREX3, discounted to present value
PRWH	real world market price of wheat
PRO	Production
PSE	Producer Subsidy Equivalent
P–value	Probability–value; (null–based) probability of a test statistic being larger than the computed one
REE	rational expectations equilibrium
ROW	Rest of the world
SAF	South Africa (Republic of)
SQA	Sugar Quota Administration (Philippines)
STO	Stocks
SWA	Swaziland
SWI	Switzerland

SYS	systematic production
TAI	Taiwan (Republic of China)
THA	Thailand
TR	Trend
TRENDSQ	Quadratic trend term
TSC	Taiwan Sugar Corporation
UN	United Nations
UNCTAD	United Nations Conference on Trade and Development
US, USA	United States of America
USDA	US Department of Agriculture
WOR	World
WORM	World systematic excess supply
WORZ	World accidental excess production

References

Abbot, G. C. (1990): *Sugar*, London.

Abbot, P. C. (1979): *Modeling International Grain Trade with Government Controlled Markets*, American Journal of Agricultural Economics, 61, pp. 22–31.

Adams, F. G. (1978): *Implementation of Commodity Market Theory in Empirical Econometric Models*, Chapter 3 in Adams & Behrman (1978).

Adams, F. G. and Behrman, J. R. (1976): *Econometric Models of World Agricultural Commodity Markets*, Cambridge.

Adams, F. G. and Behrman, J. R. (1978): *Econometric Modeling of World Commodity Policy*, Lexington.

Adams, F. G. and Klein, S. A. (1978): *Stabilizing World Commodity Markets*, Lexington.

d'Agostino, R. B. and Pearson, E. S. (1973): *Tests for Departure from Normality. Empirical Results for the Distribution of b_2 and $\sqrt{b_1}$*, Biometrika, 60, pp. 613–622.

d'Agostino, R. B. and Tietjen, G. L. (1971): *Simulation Probability Points of b_2 for Small Samples*, Biometrika, 58, pp. 669–672.

Ahlfeld, H. (1970): *Die EWG und das Commonwealth Sugar Agreement*, F. O. Licht's Europäisches Zuckerjournal, No. 9, 12.3.70, Ratzeburg.

Ahlfeld, H. (1987): *Zuckervorräte, Preise und das generelle Mißtrauen gegenüber Vorratszahlen*, F. O. Licht's Europäisches Zuckerjournal, No. 13, 8.5.87, Ratzeburg.

Akiyama, T. and Varangis, P. (1988): *Impact of the International Coffee Agreement's Export Quota System on the World Coffee Market*, Paper presented at the XXVth International Conference on International Commodity Market Modeling, World Bank, Washington D. C.

Ansley, C. F. and Newbold, P. (1979): *On the Finite Sample Distribution of Residual Autocorrelations in Autoregressive Moving Average Models*, Biometrika, 66, pp. 547–553.

Bale, M. D. and Lutz, E. (1981): *Price Distortions in Agriculture and their Effects: An International Comparison*, American Journal of Agricultural Economics, 63, pp. 8–22.

Bartens, A. and Mosolff, H. (1988): *Zuckerwirtschaftliches Taschenbuch 1987/88*, Berlin.

Behrman, J. R. (1979): *International Commodity Agreements: An Evaluation of the UNCTAD Integrated Commodity Program*, in: Cline, W. R.: *Policy Alternatives for a New International Economic Order*, New York.

Bigman, D. (1982): *Coping with Hunger: Towards a System of Food Security and Price Stabilization*, Cambridge, Mass..

BML (1989): *Agrarbericht*, Bundesministerium für Landwirtschaft und Forsten, Bonn.

Box, G. E. P. and Jenkins, G. M. (1970): *Time Series Analysis, Forecasting and Control*, San Francisco.

Box, G. E. P. and Pierce, D. A. (1970): *Distribution of Residual Autocorrelations in Autoregressive Integrated Moving Average Time Series Models*, Journal of the American Statistical Association, 65, pp. 1502–1526.

Büning, H. and Trenkler, G. (1978): *Nichtparametrische Statistische Methoden*, Berlin.

Chu, K. and Morrison, T. K. (1984): *The 1981–82 Recession and Non–Oil Primary Commodity Prices*, IMF Staff Papers, pp. 93–140.

Chu, K. and Morrison, T. K. (1986): *World Non–Oil Primary Commodity Markets*, IMF Staff Papers, pp. 139–184.

Davies, N. and Newbold, P. (1979): *Some Power Studies of a Portmanteau Test of Time Series Model Specification*, Biometrika, 66, pp. 153–155.

Dickey, D. A., Bell, W. R., and R. B. Miller (1986): *Unit Roots in Time Series Models: Tests and Implications*, American Statistician, 40, pp. 12–26.

Dickey, D. A. and Fuller, W. A. (1981): *Likelihood Ratio Statistics for Autoregressive Time Series with a Unit Root*, Econometrica, 49, pp. 1057–1072.

Dufour, J. M. (1982): *Recursive Stability Analysis of Linear Regression Relationships*, Journal of Econometrics, 19, pp. 31–76.

Durbin, J. (1969): *Tests for Serial Correlation in Regression Analysis Based on the Periodogram of Least–Squares Residuals*, Biometrika, 56, pp. 1–15.

Durbin, J. (1970): *An Alternative to the Bounds Test for Testing Serial Correlation in Least–Squares Regression*, Econometrica, 38, pp. 422–429.

Efron, B. and Tibshirani, R. (1986): *Bootstrap Methods for Standard Errors, Confidence Intervals, and Other Measures of Statistical Accuracy*, Statistical Science, 1, pp. 54–77.

Engle, R. F. (1982): *Autoregressive Conditional Heteroscedasticity with Estimates of the Variance of the United Kingdom Inflation*, Econometrica, 50, pp. 987–1007.

Engle, R. F. and Granger, C. W. J. (1987): *Co–Integration and Error Correction: Representation, Estimation, and Testing*, Econometrica, 55, pp. 251–276.

Engle, R. F. and Yoo, B. S. (1987): *Forecasting and Testing in Cointegrated Systems*, Journal of Econometrics, 35, pp. 143–159.

Ezekiel, M. (1938): *The Cobweb Theorem*, Quarterly Journal of Economics, 52, pp. 255–280.

FAO: *Production Yearbook*, Rome.

FAO (1977): *The Fourth World Food Survey*, Rome.

FAO (1985): *Sugar: Major Trade and Stabilization Issues in the Eighties*, Rome.

Friedman, M. (1957): *A Theory of the Consumption Function*, Princeton.

Frohn, J. (1984): *An Econometric Model for the World Market Price of Sugar*, Frankfurt a. M.

Fuller, W. A. (1976): *Introduction to Statistical Time Series*, New York.

Ghosh, S., Gilbert, C. L., and Hughes Hallet, A. J. (1987): *Stabilizing Speculative Commodity Markets*, Oxford.

Gilbert, C. L. (1986): *Commodity Price Stabilization: The Massell Model and Multiplicative Disturbances*, Quarterly Journal of Economics, 100, pp. 635–640.

Girvan, N. P. (1987): *Transnational Corporations and Non–fuel Primary Commodities in Developing Countries*, World Development, 15, pp. 713–740.

Gordon–Ashworth, F. (1984): *International Commodity control, A Contemporary History and Appraisal*, London.

Granger, C. W. J. (1964): *Spectral Analysis of Economic Time Series*, Princeton

Granger, C. W. J. (1969): *Investigating Causal Relations by Econometric Models and Cross–Spectral Methods*, Econometrica, 37, pp. 424–438.

Granger, C. W. J. (1981): *Some Properties of Time Series Data and Their Use in Econometric Model Specification*, Journal of Econometrics, 16, pp. 121–130.

Granger, C. W. J. and Newbold, P. (1974): *Spurious Regressions in Econometrics*, Journal of Econometrics, 2, pp. 111–120.

Green, J. R. and Majumdar, M. (1975): *The Nature of Stochastic Equilibria*, Econometrica, 43, pp. 647–660.

Grissa, A. (1976): *Structure of the International Sugar Market and its Impact on Developing Countries*, Development Center of the OECD, Paris.

Hagelberg, G. B. (1978): *Weltzuckerpreise: Eine Zeitreihenanalyse*, F. O. Licht's Europäisches Zuckerjournal, No. 8, 3.3.78, Ratzeburg.

Hagelberg, G. B. and Harris, S. A. (1976): *Pluralism and Uncertainty in the World Sugar Economy*, Food Policy, August 1976.

Hall, R. E. (1978): *Stochastic Implications of the Life Cycle Permanent Income Hypothesis: Theory and Evidence*, Journal of Political Economy, 86, pp. 971–988.

Hannah, A. C. (1987): *Der Zuckerzyklus, strukturelle Veränderungen und Internationale Zuckerabkommen*, in: F. O. Licht's Europäisches Zuckerjournal, No. 14, 21.5.87, Ratzeburg.

Herrmann, R. (1988): *Internationale Agrarmarktabkommen: Analyse ihrer Wirkungen auf den Märkten für Kaffee und Kakao*, Tübingen.

Hildenbrand, W. and Radner, R. (1979): *Stochastic Stability of Market Adjustment in Disequilibrium*, in: Green, J. and Scheinkman, J. A. (eds.): *General Equilibrium, Growth and Trade*, New York.

Hillier, G. H. (1991): *On Multiple Diagnostic Procedures for the Linear Model*, Journal of Econometrics, 47, pp. 47–66.

Hoff, F. L. and Lawrence, M. (1985): *Implications of World Sugar Markets, Policies and Production Costs for US Sugar*, USDA Agricultural Economic Report No. 543, Washington D. C.

Huber, P. J. (1981): *Robust Statistics*, New York.

Hwa, E. C. (1979): *Price Determination in Several International Primary Commodity Markets: A Structural Analysis*, IMF Staff Papers, pp. 157–188.

Hwa, E. C. (1985): *A Model of Price and Quantity Adjustments in Primary Commodity Markets*, Journal of Policy Modeling, 7, pp. 305–338.

ISO (1988): *Sugar Year Book*, London.

ISO (1987): *Statistical Bulletin*, International Sugar Organisation, London.

Jaenicke, B. (1985): *Die Internationalen Zucker–Übereinkommen von 1977 und 1984*, Saarbrücken.

Jarque, C.M. and Bera, A. K. (1987): *A Test for Normality of Observations and Regression Residuals*, International Statistical Review, 55, pp. 163–172.

Johansen, S. (1988): *Statistical Analysis of Cointegration Vectors, Journal of Economic Dynamics and Control*, 12, pp. 231–254.

Kaldor, N. (1939): *Speculation and Economic Stability*, Review of Economic Studies, 7, pp. 1–27.

Kaldor, N. (1964): *Stabilizing the Terms of Trade of Underdeveloped Countries*, in: Essays on Economic Policy, Volume II, London.

Kanbur, S. M. R. (1984): *How to Analyse Commodity Price Stabilization? A Review Article*, Oxford Economic Papers, 36, pp. 336–358.

Keynes, J. M. (1938): *The Policy of Government Storage of Foodstuffs and Raw Materials*, Economic Journal, 48, pp. 449–460.

Kirchgässner, G. (1981): *Einige neuere statistische Verfahren zur Erfassung kausaler Beziehungen zwischen Zeitreihen*, Göttingen.

Koester, U. (1985): *Agricultural Market Intervention and International Trade*, European Review of Agricultural Economics, 12, pp. 87–99.

Kohn, M. (1978): *Competitive Speculation*, Econometrica, 46, pp. 1061–1076.

Kohne, W. (1981): *Robustifizierte statistische Verfahren unter Abhängigkeitsannahmen*, Dissertation, Siegen.

König, H. und Wolters, J. (1972): *Einführung in die Spektralanalyse ökonomischer Zeitreihen*, Meisenheim am Glan.

Kottmann, T. (1989): *A New Approach to Rational Expectations: Selection and Learning*, University of Bonn, Discussion Paper No. B–120.

Krämer, W. (1980): *Eine Rehabilitation der gewöhnlichen Kleinst–Quadrate Methode als Schätzverfahren in der Ökonometrie*, Frankfurt.

Krämer, W. (1985): *Trend in ökonometrischen Modellen*, Königstein/Taunus.

Krämer, W., Ploberger, W., and Alt, R. (1988): *Testing for Structural Change in Dynamic Models*, Econometrica, 56, pp. 1355–1369.

Krämer, W., Ploberger, W., and Kontrus, K. (1989): *A Comparison of Two Significance Tests for Structural Stability in the Linear Regression Model*, Chapter 10 in: Raj, B. (editor): *Advances in Econometrics and Modelling*, Dordrecht.

Krämer, W. and Sonnberger, H. (1986): *The Linear Regression Model under Test*, Wien.

Krueger, A. O. (1983): *Protectionism, Exchange Rate Distortions, and Agricultural Trading Patterns*, American Journal of Agricultural Economics, 65, pp. 864–871.

Labys, W. C. (1978): *Bibliography of Commodity Models*, Chapter 8 in Adams & Behrman (1978).

Labys, W. C. (1980): *Commodity Price Stabilization Models: A Review and Appraisal*, Journal of Policy Modeling, 2, pp. 121–136.

Li, G. (1982): *Robust Regression*, Chapter 8 in: Hoaglin, D. C., Mosteller, F. and Tukey, J. W.: *Exploring Data Tables, Trends, and Shapes*, New York.

Licht, F. O. (1972): *Europäisches Zuckerjournal*, No. 40, 3.11.72, Ratzeburg.

Licht, F. O. (1981): *Europäisches Zuckerjournal*, No. 42, 11.11.81, Ratzeburg.

Licht, F. O. (1984): *Erste Anzeichen einer Beendigung des Vorratsaufbaus*, Europäisches Zuckerjournal, No. 28, 1.10.84, Ratzeburg.

Licht, F. O. (1986): *Europäisches Zuckerjournal*, No. 30 , 28.10.86, pp. 603–606, Ratzeburg.

Lilliefors, H. W. (1967): *On the Kolmogorov–Smirnov Test for Normality with Mean and Variance Unknown*, Journal of the American Statistical Association, 62, pp. 399–402.

Ljung, G. M. and Box, G. E. P. (1978): *On a Measure of Lack in Fit in Time Series Models*, Biometrika, 65, pp. 297–303.

LMC (1983): *A World Survey of Sugar and HFCS Production Costs*, Landell Mills Commodity Studies, 1983 Update, London.

Lucas, R. E. (1976): *Econometric Policy Evaluation: A Critique*, in: Brunner, K. and Meltzer, A. H.: *The Phillips Curve and Labor Markets*, Amsterdam.

Macbean, A. and Nguyen, D. T. (1987): *International Commodity Agreements: Shadow and Substance*, World Development, 15, pp. 575–590.

Manegold, D. and Sommer, U. (1986): *The EC Sugar Policy in a World Context – A Review of Long Term Developments*, F. O. Licht's International Sugar Report, Ratzeburg.

Massell; B. F. (1969): *Price Stabilization and Welfare*, Quarterly Journal of Economics, 83, pp. 284–298.

McCabe, B. P. M. (1989): *Misspecification Tests in Econometrics Based on Ranks*, Journal of Econometrics, 40, pp. 261–278.

McGregor, A. (1978): *The Lomé convention and the ACP Sugar Exporters: The Political Economy of Conflicting Policies*, Ph.–D.–thesis, Cornell University.

McNicol, D. L. (1978): *Commodity Agreements and Price Stabilization*, Lexington.

Monke, E. A., Cory, D. C., and Heckerman, D. G. (1987): *Surplus Disposal in World Markets: An Application to Egyptian Cotton*, American Journal of Agricultural Economics, 69, pp. 570–579.

Monke E. A. and Taylor, L. D. (1985): *International Trade Constraints and Commodity Market Models: An Application to the Cotton Market*, Review of Economics and Statistics, 67,pp. 98–107.

Muth, J. F. (1961): *Rational Expectations and the Theory of Price Movements*, Econometrica, 29, pp. 315–335.

Nerlove, M. (1958): *The Dynamics of Supply: Estimation of Farmers' Response to Price*, Baltimore.

Newbery, D. and Stiglitz, J. E. (1981): *The Theory of Commodity Price Stabilization*, Oxford.

OECD (1987): *National Policies and Agricultural Trade*, Paris.

OECD (1988): *Agricultural Policies, Markets, and Trade; Monitoring and Outlook*, Paris.

Oi, W. Y. (1961): *The Desirability of Price Instability under Perfect Competition*, Econometrica, 29, pp. 451–476.

Ouliaris, S, Park, J. Y., and Phillips, P. C. B. (1989): *Testing for a Unit Root in the Presence of a Maintained Trend*, Chapter 1 in: Raj, B. (editor): *Advances in Econometrics and Modelling*, Dordrecht.

Pagan, A. R. and Hall, A. D. (1983): *Diagnostic Tests as Residual Analysis*, Econometric Reviews, 2, pp. 159–218.

Palm, F. C. and Vogelwang, E. (1986): *A Short–Run Econometric Analysis of the International Coffee Market*, European Review of Agricultural Economics, 13, pp. 451–476.

Palm, F. C. and Vogelwang, E. (1988): *Policy Simulations Using a Quarterly Rational Expectations Model for the International Coffee Market*, Discussion Paper, University of Limburg.

Park, J. Y. and Phillips, P. C. B. (1988): *Statistical Inference in regressions with Integrated Processes, Part I*, Econometric Theory, 4, pp. 468–497.

Park, J. Y. and Phillips, P. C. B. (1989): *Statistical Inference in regressions with Integrated Processes, Part II*, Econometric Theory, 5, pp. 95–131.

Pearson, E. S., d'Agostino, R. B. and Bowman, K. O. (1977): *Tests for Departure from Normality: Comparison of Powers*, Biometrika, 64, pp. 231–246.

Pearson, E. S. and Hartley, H. O. (1966): *Biometrika Tables for Statisticians*, Volume I, Cambridge.

Perron, P. (1988): *Trends and Random Walks in Macroeconomic Time Series, Further Evidence from a New Approach*, Journal of Economic Dynamics and Control, 12, pp. 297–332.

Perron, P. (1989): *The Great Crash, the Oil Price Shock, and the Unit Root Hypothesis*, Econometrica, 57, pp. 1361–1401.

Phillips, P. C. B. (1987a): *Time Series Regression with Unit Roots*, Econometrica, 55, pp. 277–302.

Phillips, P. C. B. and Ouliaris, S. (1988a): *Asymptotic Properties of Residual Based Tests for Cointegration*, Cowles Foundation Discussion Paper No. 847, Yale University, New Haven.

Phillips, P. C. B. and Ouliaris, S. (1988b): *Testing for Cointegration Using Principal Components Methods*, Journal of Economic Dynamics and Control, 12, pp. 205–230.

Phillips, P. C. B. and Perron, P. (1988): *Testing for a Unit Root in Time Series Regression*, Biometrika, 75, pp. 335–346.

Pierce, D. A. and Gray, R. J. (1982): *Testing Normality of Errors in Regression Models*, Biometrika, 69, pp. 233–236.

Pierce, D. A. and Kopecky, K. J. (1979): *Testing Goodness of Fit for the Distribution of Errors in Regression Models*, Biometrika, 66, pp. 1–5.

Pindyck, R. S. and Rubinfeld, D. L. (1976): *Econometric Models and Economic Forecasts*, New York.

Ploberger, W., Krämer, W. and Kontrus, K. (1989): *A New Test for Structural Stability in the Linear Regression Model*, Journal of Econometrics, 40, pp. 307–318.

Pollock, D. S. G. (1979): *The Algebra of Econometrics*, Chichester.

Ramsey, J. B. (1969): *Tests for Specification Error in Classical Linear Least Squares Regression Analysis*, Journal of the Royal Statistical Society, 31, pp. 350–371.

Rieder, P. and Egger, U. (1983): *Agrarmärkte*, Zürich.

Robinson, P. M. (1987): *Asymptotically Efficient Estimation in the Presence of Heteroskedasticity of Unknown Form*, Econometrica, 55, pp. 875–891.

Rose, H. (1980): *Zuckerrohranbau in Brasilien*, in: Bericht über die Studienreise ..., Verband Süddeutscher Zuckerrübenanbauer e. V., Worms.

Said, S. E. and Dickey, D. A. (1984): *Testing for Unit Roots in Autoregressive Moving Average Models of Unknown Order*, Biometrika, 71, pp.599–607.

Samuelson, P. A. (1972): *The Consumer Does Benefit from Feasible Price Stability*, Quarterly Journal of Economics, 86, pp. 476–493.

Sargent, T. J. and Wallace, N. (1975): *"Rational" Expectations, the Optimal Monetary Instrument, and the Optimal Money Supply Rule*, Journal of Political Economy, 83, pp. 215–228.

Schlittgen, R. and Streitberg, B. H. J. (1989): *Zeitreihenanalyse*, 3rd edition, Munich.

Schmidt, E. (1978): *Das Internationale Zuckerabkommen von 1977 – eine formelle und materielle Analyse*, Braunschweig.

Schmidt, E. (1981): *Einige theoretische und praktische Versuche zur kurzfristigen Vorhersage des Zuckerangebots und der Zuckernachfrage in der Welt*, in: F. O. Licht's Europäisches Zuckerjournal, No. 11, 20.3.81, pp. 185–211.

Schröder, J. (1991): *Maßnahmen zur Verbesserung der Effizienz der EG–Zuckermarktpolitik*, unpublished Ph.–D–thesis, Bonn, forthcoming.

Schwert, G. W. (1989): *Tests for Unit Roots: A Monte Carlo Investigation*, Journal of Business and Economic Statistics, 7, pp. 147–159.

Scott, P. (1981): *Australian Agriculture, Resource Development and Spatial Organisation*, Budapest.

Serfling, R. J. (1968): *The Wilcoxon Two–Sample Statistic on Strongly Mixing Processes*, Annals of Mathematical Statistics, 39, pp. 1202–1209.

Shapiro, S. S., Wilk, M. B. and Chen, H. J. (1968): *A Comparative Study of Various Tests for Normality*, Journal of the American Statistical Association, 63, pp. 1343–1372.

Sims, C. A. (1988): *Bayesian Skepticism on Unit Root Econometrics*, Journal of Economic Dynamics and Control, 12, pp. 463–474.

Sims, C. A., Stock, J. H., and Watson, M. W. (1990): *Inference in Linear Time Series Models with Some Unit Roots*, Econometrica, 58, pp. 113–144.

Statistisches Bundesamt: *Länderberichte*, Wiesbaden.

Stephens, M. A. (1974): *EDF–Statistics for Goodness of Fit and Some Comparisons*, Journal of the American Statistical Association, 69, pp. 730–737.

Stock, J. H. (1987): *Asymptotic Properties of Least Squares Estimators of Cointegrating Vectors*, Econometrica, 55, pp. 1035–1056.

Stock, J. H. and Watson, M. W. (1988): *Variable Trends in Economic Time Series*, Journal of Economic Perspectives, 2, pp. 147–174.

Strangmann, U. (1981): *Lieferabkommen für Agrarprodukte; Darstellung und Beurteilung aus der Sicht ausgewählter Entwicklungsländer am Beispiel des AKP–Zuckerprotokolls*, Frankfurt.

Sturgiss, R., Wong, G. and Borrell, B. (1987): *Policy Intervention, Price Variability, and the International Sugar Agreement*, Discussion Paper 87.1, Bureau of Agricultural Economics, Canberra.

Takayama, A. (1985): *Mathematical Economics*, Cambridge.

Tewes, T. (1988): *Auswirkungen der Internationalen Zuckerabkommen*, in: Hoffmeyer, M.: *Internationale Rohstoffabkommen: Ziele, Ansatzpunkte, Wirkungen*, Kiel.

Thursby, J. G. and Schmidt, P. (1977): *Some Properties of Tests for Specification Error in a Linear Regression Model*, Journal of the American Statistical Association, 72, pp. 635–641.

Turnovsky, S. J. (1976): *The Distribution of Welfare Gains from Price Stabilization: The Case of Multiplicative Disturbances*, International Economic Review, 17, pp. 133–148.

Turnovsky, S. J. (1978): *Stabilization Rules and the Benefits from Price Stabilization*, Journal of Public Economics, 9, pp. 37–57.

UNCTAD (1974): *An Integrated Program for Commodities*, UN doc. TD/B/C.1/166, Geneva.

UNCTAD (1976): *Integrated Program for Commodities*, UN doc. ID/RES/93(IV), Geneva.

Utts, J. M. (1982): *The Rainbow Test for Lack of Fit in Regression*, Communications in Statistics – Theory and Methods, 11, pp. 1801–1815.

Waugh, F. V. (1944): *Does the Consumer Benefit from Price Instability?*, Quarterly Journal of Economics, 58, pp. 602–614.

Weisberg, S. (1980): *Applied Linear Regression*, New York.

West, K. D. (1988): *Asymptotic Normality, When Regressors Have a Unit Root*, Econometrica, 56, pp. 1397–1417.

Wolffram, R. and Beckers, K. (1989): *Das AKP–Zuckerabkommen: Beurteilung aus entwicklungs– und finanzpolitischer Sicht; Fallstudie Mauritius*, Frankfurt a. M.

Working, H. (1949): *The Theory of Price of Storage*, American Economic Review, 39, pp. 1254–1262.

Wymer, C. R. (1975): *Estimation of Continuous Time Models with an Application to the World Sugar Market*, in: Labys, W. C.: *Quantitative Models of Commodity Markets*, Cambridge.

Zeller, F. (1988): *Konkurrenzsituation auf dem Weltzuckermarkt*, Kiel.

Vol. 307: T.K. Dijkstra (Ed.), On Model Uncertainty and its Statistical Implications. VII, 138 pages. 1988.

Vol. 308: J.R. Daduna, A. Wren (Eds.), Computer-Aided Transit Scheduling. VIII, 339 pages. 1988.

Vol. 309: G. Ricci, K. Velupillai (Eds.), Growth Cycles and Multisectoral Economics: the Goodwin Tradition. III, 126 pages. 1988.

Vol. 310: J. Kacprzyk, M. Fedrizzi (Eds.), Combining Fuzzy Imprecision with Probabilistic Uncertainty in Decision Making. IX, 399 pages. 1988.

Vol. 311: R. Färe, Fundamentals of Production Theory. IX, 163 pages. 1988.

Vol. 312: J. Krishnakumar, Estimation of Simultaneous Equation Models with Error Components Structure. X, 357 pages. 1988.

Vol. 313: W. Jammernegg, Sequential Binary Investment Decisions. VI, 156 pages. 1988.

Vol. 314: R. Tietz, W. Albers, R. Selten (Eds.), Bounded Rational Behavior in Experimental Games and Markets. VI, 368 pages. 1988.

Vol. 315: I. Orishimo, G.J.D. Hewings, P. Nijkamp (Eds), Information Technology: Social and Spatial Perspectives. Proceedings 1986. VI, 268 pages. 1988.

Vol. 316: R.L. Basmann, D.J. Slottje, K. Hayes, J.D. Johnson, D.J. Molina, The Generalized Fechner-Thurstone Direct Utility Function and Some of its Uses. VIII, 159 pages. 1988.

Vol. 317: L. Bianco, A. La Bella (Eds.), Freight Transport Planning and Logistics. Proceedings, 1987. X, 568 pages. 1988.

Vol. 318: T. Doup, Simplicial Algorithms on the Simplotope. VIII, 262 pages. 1988.

Vol. 319: D.T. Luc, Theory of Vector Optimization. VIII, 173 pages. 1989.

Vol. 320: D. van der Wijst, Financial Structure in Small Business. VII, 181 pages. 1989.

Vol. 321: M. Di Matteo, R.M. Goodwin, A. Vercelli (Eds.), Technological and Social Factors in Long Term Fluctuations. Proceedings. IX, 442 pages. 1989.

Vol. 322: T. Kollintzas (Ed.), The Rational Expectations Equilibrium Inventory Model. XI, 269 pages. 1989.

Vol. 323: M.B.M. de Koster, Capacity Oriented Analysis and Design of Production Systems. XII, 245 pages. 1989.

Vol. 324: I.M. Bomze, B.M. Pötscher, Game Theoretical Foundations of Evolutionary Stability. VI, 145 pages. 1989.

Vol. 325: P. Ferri, E. Greenberg, The Labor Market and Business Cycle Theories. X, 183 pages. 1989.

Vol. 326: Ch. Sauer, Alternative Theories of Output, Unemployment, and Inflation in Germany: 1960–1985. XIII, 206 pages. 1989.

Vol. 327: M. Tawada, Production Structure and International Trade. V, 132 pages. 1989.

Vol. 328: W. Güth, B. Kalkofen, Unique Solutions for Strategic Games. VII, 200 pages. 1989.

Vol. 329: G. Tillmann, Equity, Incentives, and Taxation. VI, 132 pages. 1989.

Vol. 330: P.M. Kort, Optimal Dynamic Investment Policies of a Value Maximizing Firm. VII, 185 pages. 1989.

Vol. 331: A. Lewandowski, A.P. Wierzbicki (Eds.), Aspiration Based Decision Support Systems. X, 400 pages. 1989.

Vol. 332: T.R. Gulledge, Jr., L.A. Litteral (Eds.), Cost Analysis Applications of Economics and Operations Research. Proceedings. VII, 422 pages. 1989.

Vol. 333: N. Dellaert, Production to Order. VII, 158 pages. 1989.

Vol. 334: H.-W. Lorenz, Nonlinear Dynamical Economics and Chaotic Motion. XI, 248 pages. 1989.

Vol. 335: A.G. Lockett, G. Islei (Eds.), Improving Decision Making in Organisations. Proceedings. IX, 606 pages. 1989.

Vol. 336: T. Puu, Nonlinear Economic Dynamics. VII, 119 pages. 1989.

Vol. 337: A. Lewandowski, I. Stanchev (Eds.), Methodology and Software for Interactive Decision Support. VIII, 309 pages. 1989.

Vol. 338: J.K. Ho, R.P. Sundarraj, DECOMP: an Implementation of Dantzig-Wolfe Decomposition for Linear Programming. VI, 206 pages.

Vol. 339: J. Terceiro Lomba, Estimation of Dynamic Econometric Models with Errors in Variables. VIII, 116 pages. 1990.

Vol. 340: T. Vasko, R. Ayres, L. Fontvieille (Eds.), Life Cycles and Long Waves. XIV, 293 pages. 1990.

Vol. 341: G.R. Uhlich, Descriptive Theories of Bargaining. IX, 165 pages. 1990.

Vol. 342: K. Okuguchi, F. Szidarovszky, The Theory of Oligopoly with Multi-Product Firms. V, 167 pages. 1990.

Vol. 343: C. Chiarella, The Elements of a Nonlinear Theory of Economic Dynamics. IX, 149 pages. 1990.

Vol. 344: K. Neumann, Stochastic Project Networks. XI, 237 pages. 1990.

Vol. 345: A. Cambini, E. Castagnoli, L. Martein, P Mazzoleni, S. Schaible (Eds.), Generalized Convexity and Fractional Programming with Economic Applications. Proceedings, 1988. VII, 361 pages. 1990.

Vol. 346: R. von Randow (Ed.), Integer Programming and Related Areas. A Classified Bibliography 1984–1987. XIII, 514 pages. 1990.

Vol. 347: D. Ríos Insua, Sensitivity Analysis in Multi-objective Decision Making. XI, 193 pages. 1990.

Vol. 348: H. Störmer, Binary Functions and their Applications. VIII, 151 pages. 1990.

Vol. 349: G.A. Pfann, Dynamic Modelling of Stochastic Demand for Manufacturing Employment. VI, 158 pages. 1990.

Vol. 350: W.-B. Zhang, Economic Dynamics. X, 232 pages. 1990.

Vol. 351: A. Lewandowski, V. Volkovich (Eds.), Multiobjective Problems of Mathematical Programming. Proceedings, 1988. VII, 315 pages. 1991.

Vol. 352: O. van Hilten, Optimal Firm Behaviour in the Context of Technological Progress and a Business Cycle. XII, 229 pages. 1991.

Vol. 353: G. Ricci (Ed.), Decision Processes in Economics. Proceedings, 1989. III, 209 pages 1991.

Vol. 354: M. Ivaldi, A Structural Analysis of Expectation Formation. XII, 230 pages. 1991.

Vol. 355: M. Salomon. Deterministic Lotsizing Models for Production Planning. VII, 158 pages. 1991.

Vol. 356: P. Korhonen, A. Lewandowski, J . Wallenius (Eds.), Multiple Criteria Decision Support. Proceedings, 1989. XII, 393 pages. 1991.

Vol. 357: P. Zörnig, Degeneracy Graphs and Simplex Cycling. XV, 194 pages. 1991.

Vol. 358: P. Knottnerus, Linear Models with Correlated Disturbances. VIII, 196 pages. 1991.

Vol. 359: E. de Jong, Exchange Rate Determination and Optimal Economic Policy Under Various Exchange Rate Regimes. VII, 270 pages. 1991.

Vol. 360: P. Stalder, Regime Translations, Spillovers and Buffer Stocks. VI, 193 pages . 1991.

Vol. 361: C. F. Daganzo, Logistics Systems Analysis. X, 321 pages. 1991.

Vol. 362: F. Gehrels, Essays In Macroeconomics of an Open Economy. VII, 183 pages. 1991.

Vol. 363: C. Puppe, Distorted Probabilities and Choice under Risk. VIII, 100 pages . 1991

Vol. 364: B. Horvath, Are Policy Variables Exogenous? XII, 162 pages. 1991.

Vol. 365: G. A. Heuer, U. Leopold-Wildburger. Balanced Silverman Games on General Discrete Sets. V, 140 pages. 1991.

Vol. 366: J. Gruber (Ed.), Econometric Decision Models. Proceedings, 1989. VIII, 636 pages. 1991.

Vol. 367: M. Grauer, D. B. Pressmar (Eds.), Parallel Computing and Mathematical Optimization. Proceedings. V, 208 pages. 1991.

Vol. 368: M. Fedrizzi, J. Kacprzyk, M. Roubens (Eds.), Interactive Fuzzy Optimization. VII, 216 pages. 1991.

Vol. 369: R. Koblo, The Visible Hand. VIII, 131 pages.1991.

Vol. 370: M. J. Beckmann, M. N. Gopalan, R. Subramanian (Eds.), Stochastic Processes and their Applications. Proceedings, 1990. XLI, 292 pages. 1991.

Vol. 371: A. Schmutzler, Flexibility and Adjustment to Information in Sequential Decision Problems. VIII, 198 pages. 1991.

Vol. 372: J. Esteban, The Social Viability of Money. X, 202 pages. 1991.

Vol. 373: A. Billot, Economic Theory of Fuzzy Equilibria. XIII, 164 pages. 1992.

Vol. 374: G. Pflug, U. Dieter (Eds.), Simulation and Optimization. Proceedings, 1990. X, 162 pages. 1992.

Vol. 375: S.-J. Chen, Ch.-L. Hwang, Fuzzy Multiple Attribute Decision Making. XII, 536 pages. 1992.

Vol. 376: K.-H. Jöckel, G. Rothe, W. Sendler (Eds.), Bootstrapping and Related Techniques. Proceedings, 1990. VIII, 247 pages. 1992.

Vol. 377: A. Villar, Operator Theorems with Applications to Distributive Problems and Equilibrium Models. XVI, 160 pages. 1992.

Vol. 378: W. Krabs, J. Zowe (Eds.), Modern Methods of Optimization. Proceedings, 1990. VIII, 348 pages. 1992.

Vol. 379: K. Marti (Ed.), Stochastic Optimization. Proceedings, 1990. VII, 182 pages. 1992.

Vol. 380: J. Odelstad, Invariance and Structural Dependence. XII, 245 pages. 1992.

Vol. 381: C. Giannini, Topics in Structural VAR Econometrics. XI, 131 pages. 1992.

Vol. 382: W. Oettli, D. Pallaschke (Eds.), Advances in Optimization. Proceedings, 1991. X, 527 pages. 1992.

Vol. 383: J. Vartiainen, Capital Accumulation in a Corporatist Economy. VII, 177 pages. 1992.

Vol. 384: A. Martina, Lectures on the Economic Theory of Taxation. XII, 313 pages. 1992.

Vol. 385: J. Gardeazabal, M. Regúlez, The Monetary Model of Exchange Rates and Cointegration. X, 194 pages. 1992.

Vol. 386: M. Desrochers, J.-M. Rousseau (Eds.), Computer-Aided Transit Scheduling. Proceedings, 1990. XIII, 432 pages. 1992.

Vol. 387: W. Gaertner, M. Klemisch-Ahlert, Social Choice and Bargaining Perspectives on Distributive Justice. VIII, 131 pages. 1992.

Vol. 388: D. Bartmann, M. J. Beckmann, Inventory Control. XV, 252 pages. 1992.

Vol. 389: B. Dutta, D. Mookherjee, T. Parthasarathy, T. Raghavan, D. Ray, S. Tijs (Eds.), Game Theory and Economic Applications. Proceedings, 1990. ??, ?? pages. 1992.

Vol. 390: G. Sorger, Minimum Impatience Theorem for Recursive Economic Models. X, 162 pages. 1992.

Vol. 391: C. Keser, Experimental Duopoly Markets with Demand Inertia. X, 150 pages. 1992.

Vol. 392: K. Frauendorfer, Stochastic Two-Stage Programming. VIII, 228 pages. 1992.

Vol. 393: B. Lucke, Price Stabilization on World Agricultural Markets. XI, 274 pages. 1992.